[QUINTILIAN]

THE MAJOR DECLAMATIONS

II

LCL 548

[QUINTILIAN]

THE MAJOR DECLAMATIONS

VOLUME II

EDITED BY

ANTONIO STRAMAGLIA

TRANSLATED BY

MICHAEL WINTERBOTTOM

WITH NOTES BY
BIAGIO SANTORELLI AND
MICHAEL WINTERBOTTOM

HARVARD UNIVERSITY PRESS
CAMBRIDGE, MASSACHUSETTS
LONDON, ENGLAND
2021

First published 2021

LOEB CLASSICAL LIBRARY® is a registered trademark
of the President and Fellows of Harvard College

Library of Congress Control Number 2021932924
CIP data available from the Library of Congress

ISBN 978-0-674-99741-7

*Composed in ZephGreek and ZephText by
Technologies 'N Typography, Merrimac, Massachusetts.
Printed on acid-free paper and bound by
Maple Press, York, Pennsylvania*

DECLAMATION 6

INTRODUCTION

A man is captured by pirates while traveling at sea and sends home a letter, asking his family to ransom him. The news throws his wife into despair; she loses her sight by weeping. Despite the woman's opposition, their son sets sail and rescues Father by taking his place. When the young man dies in chains, his body is cast into the sea and washes ashore near his city. Father tries to bury him, but Mother appeals to a law forbidding burial for those who have abandoned their parents in distress.

The narrative framework of this case exploits the traditional motifs of the fictional world of declamation: the hostile actions of pirates[1] lead to a family crisis, resulting in a woman's blindness due to excessive weeping;[2] Son attempts to solve the crisis by offering himself as a substitute,[3] but in doing so he breaks the law that requires chil-

---

[1] Abductions by pirates feature in *DM* 5; Sen. *Controv.* 1.2, 1.6, 1.7, 7.4 (very close to this theme); [Quint.] *Decl. min.* 257, 342, 373; Calp. Fl. 52; Petron. 1.3 mocks the abuse of this motif in school declamations. See further n. 5, and in general van Mal-Maeder (2007, 10–14).

[2] Cf. *DM* 16; Sen. *Controv.* 7.4; Calp. Fl. 10. See Stramaglia (1999b, 134–36n118); Zinsmaier (2009, 157n3, 174n78); Schneider (2013, 145–46n128).

[3] *Manus vicariae*: cf. *DM* 9 and 16; *Decl. min.* 257.11 and esp. 342 (in other cases featuring pirates); Calp. Fl. 26. See Santorelli (2014b, 181nn22–23) for further bibliography.

CONTENTS

dren to assist their parents.[4] This same theme is reported
and discussed by some later Greek sources,[5] but our declamation yields the only preserved development—inter-
estingly, with some Roman coloring. Father claims his
rights as a Roman citizen—not as a generic member of
Sophistopolis—to better highlight the harshness he had to
suffer at the pirates' hands (17.6); and among his *exempla*
we find mentions of Cicero and Verres (9.2–4).[6]

Pleading against Mother for the burial of Son, Father
tries to win the judges' sympathy by giving a tragic account
of the sufferings he himself endured while in chains; by
denouncing the cruelty of his wife, who is treating their
late son as a stepmother rather than a mother; and, most
of all, by stressing the piety of Son, who aimed at assisting
both his parents and rescued Father in order to bring him
back to Mother at the price of his own life (2.4–3.6).

In narrating the events leading to Son's death, the
speaker "colors" some points that would have put Father
in an unfavorable light: he was traveling with the sole purpose of earning more wealth to leave to his Son (3.7); when
he was kidnapped and wrote home, the family had money
sufficient to pay the ransom, yet pious Son decided to
leave it all behind with his handicapped Mother (5.1–2);

[4] On this "law" in general, see Introduction to *DM* 5, n. 2;
denial of burial as its provision for offenders is attested only in
relation to this theme (in its various forms, see n. 5): cf. Zinsmaier
(2009, 33–43).

[5] Schol. Hermog. *RG* IV.267.9–16 Walz; Sopat. *RG* V.107.26–
108.10 W.; Syrian. II.196.23–197.10 Rabe; Lib. *Decl.* 46 is also
similar. See Calboli Montefusco (1984, 173–74).

[6] Additionally, a Roman color could be detected in the reference to ownership trough possession (*usucapio*) in 6.1. Cf. General Introduction, §4.

Father was unwilling to let the exchange take place, but Son insisted on him making it (6.1–9).

The disposition of arguments is meant to reflect Father's hurry to reach a verdict (after all, Son is waiting for a burial as they speak: 3.2): he tries to win the case by moving Mother and the judges with prayers (8.9–10.3) and arguments supporting the duty of burial for any mortal (10.4–11.7); then he considers the law, discussing the *scriptum* and *voluntas* of the phrase "abandon his parents" and its applicability to this case (11.8–14.5). Comparison of the sufferings that both Father and Mother were enduring is used to prove that all the Son did was to choose to assist the parent in greater misfortune (14.6–18.6), who was also the only one who *could* be relieved (19.1–20.1). Praise of Son's piety and heroism (20.2–22.8) leads to a somber finale: Father promises to join Son on the funerary pyre (23.4) if he wins the case; to shroud him with his own body, or else to resort to other people or to the sea itself to grant Son some sort of burial (24.3–5), if he loses.

The structure may be analyzed thus:[7]

> PROEM 1.1–3.6
> NARRATION 3.7–8.8
> ARGUMENTATION
>   *Confirmatio* (as prayers to Mother) 8.9–11.7
>   *Refutatio* 11.8–21.8
> EPILOGUE 22.1–24.5

This speech is particularly close to *DM* 9 in language, rhythm, and content. The "milder" interpretation of the *patria potestas* seen in both pieces seems coherent with

---

[7] Zinsmaier (2009, 60–61; cf. also 65 and n. 202).

DECLAMATION 6

the culture of the Hadrianic age; combined with linguistic arguments, this suggests dating *DM* 6 to the early second century AD.[8] Part of the manuscript tradition has handed down to us an alternative title, *Manus caecae* (The Blind Woman's Hands), which should be regarded as a later addition.[9] A reply to our speech is included in the collection of *Antilogiae* by Patarol.[10]

[8] See General Introduction, §4.
[9] Stramaglia (2018a).
[10] (1743, 203–28).

6

Corpus proiectum[1]

QUI IN CALAMITATE PARENTES DESERUERIT, INSEPUL-
TUS ABICIATUR. Qui habebat uxorem et filium, captus a
piratis scripsit domum de redemptione. Uxor flendo oculos amisit. Filius retinente matre profectus vicariis manibus redemit patrem. Idem in vinculis decessit. Abiectus in
mare et appulsus ad litus patrium est eiectus. Vult illum
sepelire pater, mater prohibet.

1. Etiamsi, iudices, in hac asperrima condicione fragilitatis
humanae, in qua nemo prope mortalium impune vivit,
haec omnibus natura est, ut sua cuique calamitas praecipue misera atque intoleranda videatur, inter omnes tamen
hoc constet necesse est, infelicitatem meam tantum ceteras supergressam, ut prorsus haec sit, quae fleri debeat
usque ad caecitatem. Quid enim passus sum tam leve, ut
non comparatio mei felices aliorum etiam miserias faciat?
2 Grave est a piratis alligari; magis dicat hoc, qui sciat quam

---

[1] -pus -tum *Str.*[14] (*q.v.*): INCIPIT CORPORIS PROIECTI IPSA EST
MANVS CAECAE B V Φ* *in praescript.*

6

The body cast up by the sea

A SON WHO ABANDONS HIS PARENTS IN MISFORTUNE IS TO BE CAST OUT UNBURIED. A man who had a wife and son was captured by pirates, and wrote home about a ransom. His wife lost her sight by weeping. Though his mother tried to stop him, the son set off, and redeemed his father by taking his place. He died in captivity. Thrown into the sea and carried on to the shore of his homeland, he was cast up there. His father wishes to bury him, his mother forbids it.

(Speech of the father)

1. Although, judges, in the exceedingly harsh circumstances to which human vulnerability is subject, that leave almost no mortal life unscathed, it is natural for each to think his own calamity especially pitiable and beyond bearing, yet all must agree that my ill luck has gone so far beyond that of others that it is *this* that ought to be wept for to the point of blindness. Have I suffered anything so trivial that comparison with me does not make even the misfortunes of others into strokes of luck? (2) It is hard to be put in chains by pirates—that may be said the more

cito capti moriantur. Alligatus sum, sed tamen miser magis
3 queror quod solutus sum. Indigna est impietas in suos:
quae quanta versetur in hoc iudicio, videtis. Sed mihi hoc
quoque querendum est, quod me et uxor nimium dilexit
4 et filius. Quid ego putarem in rerum natura posse reperiri,
quod orbitate acerbius videretur? Non contingit mihi,
5 quod ceteris miserrimum est, filium efferre. Parum est
quod iuveni singularis exempli causa mortis fui, et, tam
pretiosa redemptus anima, senex ominosus morte filii mei
vivo; parum est quod mihi luctum meum fluctus nuntia-
runt, et aliud agenti patri subito ad litus orbitas appulsa
est, quod miserum iuvenem toto iactatum mari, etiam si
nemo interpellasset, sero sepelirem: adhuc supremo pro-
hibeor officio, et, ne quid solacii contingat, perdo etiam
6 maris misericordiam. Inicit errantem corpori manum mulier et piratis et tempestate crudelior, atque, ut accedat
dolori meo cumulus, quae hoc facit, uxor mea est! 2. Ne
quis tamen erret ignotus: non est filii mei noverca, sed
mater.² O facinus, o cladibus nostris mutata natura! Mater
ignem ultimum filio negat, et mulier, quae maritum sua

---

² *dist. vulg.*: sed mater *cum seqq. iungit* Helm¹ 343

---

¹ Because the body had meanwhile been shattered by the
harshness Son had to suffer (cf. 6.8.8) and, after his death, by the
sea (6.23.1).

² Which was kind enough to cast up a body he is unable to
bury.

³ The blind woman cannot properly direct her hand. The
phrase revives the half-dead legal metaphor of the laying on of
hands (to drag a debtor to court).

⁴ Cf. 6.20.7. One aim of the speaker is to temper criticism of
Wife by reminding his audience of her former virtues.

readily by someone who knows how quickly prisoners die; yes, I was put in chains, but, in my sorry state, I have to complain rather of my release. (3) Lack of dutiful affection toward one's kin is a dreadful thing; and how great a part that plays in this case you all see. But *I* also have to complain that I was loved to excess both by my wife and by my son. (4) What could I imagine on earth more bitter than to be bereaved? Yet *I* am not having the chance to bear my son to his grave, something that every other father counts the saddest thing of all. (5) It is not enough that I caused the death of a model son, and that after being ransomed at the cost of so precious a life, I owe my continued existence—as an old man under an ill omen—to my son's death. It is not enough that the news of my sorrow was brought to me by the waves, so that a father engaged with other business suddenly found his bereavement cast up on the beach, not enough that, even if no one had interfered, I should be too late[1] to bury a pitiable youth after he had been tossed around over all the sea. No, I am still being barred from carrying out my last duty—and, to take away any crumb of comfort, I am wasting even the pity of the sea.[2] (6) More cruel than both pirates and storms, a woman lays her uncertain[3] hand on the body; and, to crown my pain, it is my own wife who is doing this! 2. But let no one who is unaware of the circumstances be under any illusion: she is my son's mother, not his stepmother. The outrageousness of it! How her nature has been changed[4] by our catastrophes! It is his mother who denies her son fire at the last, and a woman who misses her husband even

9

quoque[3] debilitate[4] desiderat[5] (quis hoc de ista credat?),
filium non flet, funditus eversa fulmen hoc clademque[6]
non sentit. Comparet dolorem: quanto minore causa ex-
caecata est!

2   Huius, iudices, poenae ab ipsa morte repetitae[7] crimen
ego sum:[8] ego et ablegavi[9] filium meum et infamavi, et, ne
non accedat gravissimi doloris comes paenitentia, in illum
mortiferum carcerem mersi. Quo fato parentes miser sor-
titus est, ut illi vitam pater, sepulturam mater auferret?

3 Nam ut pietatem filii mei semel indicem: patrem redemit.
Si, quod ego redierim, uxor irascitur, reddat rationem cur
acceptis litteris meis fleverit.

4   Atquin miserrimus iuvenis quomodo magis temperare
potuit officia? Lex parentibus in calamitate ferre opem
iubebat;[10] uterque parens erat calamitate devinctus, unus
autem succurrere utrique non poterat. Invenit <iter>[11] tamen ingeniosa pietas et utrique subvenit dispendio sui:
ipse venit ad patrem, me remisit ad matrem.

    3. Hoc si defendendum est, agnosco partis meas: cau-
sam planctibus agam; flere enim certe per legem licet.

---

3 sua q. *Wint.*[7] *143* (q. sua *Watt*[3] *48*): suum q. V: q. suum B Φ:
usque ad *Zins.*

    4 -tate V E P: -tato A: -tata (-ta`ta´ B) *cett.*: -tatem *Zins.*

    5 -ravit *Sch., sed vd. Wint.*[7] *143*

    6 clademque *Obr.*: gladiumque *codd.*

    7 -tae *agn. Plas.* 7: -te *codd.*

    8 *h.l. dist. Reitz.*[2] 7 (*firm. Håk.*[2] *53–54*): *post* crimen *vulg.*

    9 ableg- *Sh. B.*[2] *195–96*: allig- *codd.*

    10 -beat γ β: -bet C[2]

    11 <iter> tamen *Wal.*[2] *6–7* (*cf. 1.12.4*): tamen <viam> *Leh.*:
invenit *absolute poni frustra contend. Helm*[1] *343 et dub. Håk.*

at the cost of her own disablement (who would believe it of the woman you see before you?) is not weeping for her son: she is so profoundly overturned that she cannot feel this thunderbolt of disaster. Let her compare the pain in the two cases: how much less good a reason she had[5] to lose her sight!

(2) Judges, *I* am to blame for this penalty that has been claimed from death itself. It was I who sent my son off,[6] I who brought him into disgrace,[7] and, to ensure that remorse should accompany my harrowing grief, I who plunged him into that deadly prison. What fate allotted the poor boy such parents—a father to rob him of life, a mother to rob him of burial? (3) For to prove his affection a single phrase is enough: he redeemed his father. If my wife resents my coming home, let her explain why she wept when she got my letter.

(4) Yet how could this most unfortunate of youths have managed both his obligations better? The law bade him help his parents in distress: both parents were in the grip[8] of distress, but one person could not help both. All the same, his inventive sense of duty found <a way>: he came to the aid of both by sacrificing himself. *He* went to his father, *he* sent me back to his mother.

3. If this requires justification, I see my role plainly: I shall plead with laments, for at least the law permits tears.[9]

---

[5] Then (when her husband was imprisoned, but still alive), as opposed to now (when her son is dead).   [6] By writing about a ransom.   [7] By urging him to rescue me, *I* caused him to be thought neglectful of his mother.   [8] *devinctus* applies literally to Father, metaphorically to Mother.

[9] I.e., I can shed them in court if not at the funeral.

11

Alioquin diu laudare non expedit, diligenter defendere
contrarium est actioni nostrae: ut impetremus funus, mo-
2 ramur. Dum nos litigamus, dum circa cadaver nostrum
orbi rixamur, dum agitur causa defuncti, dum sepulcro
lege praescribitur, dum dantur legitima dicentibus tempora, putrescit interim corpus; nec tutum[12] in sicco iacet:
cadaver ab incursu avium ferarumque tantum miseran-
3 tium corona custodit. Convenerunt etiam alieni parentes,
totus in spectaculum populus effusus est, et ignoto quoque
corpori publica humanitas quasi quasdam fecit exequias.
Deflent omnes homines, dolent; plurimorum tamen illa
vox est: "Iuvenis insepultus iacet miser,[13] nec patrem ha-
4 bet fortasse nec matrem." Iam hominis figuram vetustas
paene consumpsit, iam lenta tabes in terram defluxit, iam
soluta cute ossa nudantur. Quamlibet duraveris animo,
non ferres tamen ista, si videres.
5　Sed audire certe potes. Ille est filius noster, cuius
spes ipsas amavimus, quem apud omnia templa et surdos
votis deos superstitem precati sumus, a quo sepeliri op-
tavimus, ille amabilis infans, ille blandus puer, ille iuvenis
etiam ante hoc crimen piissimus, ille, dum par fortuna
6 parentium fuit, propensus in amorem tui. Mentior, nisi,

[12] tut- *Helm[1] 343*: tot- *codd.*
[13] *dist. Håk.: post* iacet *vulg.*

---

[10] I am trying to win burial, but all I am doing is delaying while
the body rots.
[11] I.e., while it is being discussed if burial should be enforced
by law.
[12] Cf. 15.4.5.
[13] Cf. 5.9.2.

For the rest, extensive praise is not helpful, and to mount a careful defense damages our case: to obtain a burial, we—delay.[10] (2) While we are at law, while we, the bereaved, dispute about our corpse, while we plead the cause of the dead man, while burial is being laid down by law,[11] while the speakers are being allotted their legal time-limits: all this time the body is rotting away. Nor is it lying safe even though it is on dry land: only a ring of mourners guards it from the assault of birds and beasts. (3) The parents of other youths too have gathered there, the whole population has poured out to view the sight, and the sympathy of the public has given a sort of funeral even to the body of an unknown. Every one is weeping and wailing; but what most people are saying is: "Here lies unburied a pitiable young man; perhaps he has no father and no mother." (4) Already the form of a human being has been almost effaced by the passing hours, already the flesh has drained slowly away into the earth,[12] already the skin has dissolved and the bones are being laid bare.[13] However hard of heart you may have become, you could not bear the sight of these things, if you could see.

(5) But at least you can *hear*. That is our son there, whose very promise we so loved, the son for whom we prayed in every temple—to gods who did not listen to our vows—that he would outlive us, the son by whom we hoped to be buried: that delightful child, that engaging boy, that youth who was entirely dutiful even before he committed this "crime,"[14] the son who while his parents' luck remained equal was inclined rather to love *you*. (6) I

---

[14] I.e., the abandoning of his mother.

cum peregrinatio mea nos diduceret,[14] maluit esse cum matre.

7　　Me per omnia maria volitantem, ut plus filio relinquerem, circumvenit saevius ipso mari latrocinium. 4. Describam nunc ego pendentem fluctibus carcerem et catenas macie mea laxatas et detritam lateribus meis consciam malorum carinam et obrutam perennibus tenebris feralis loci cruentam caecitatem? Ista vero, si quid pudoris ha-

2　beo, tacenda sunt. Alioquin quis mihi ignoscet, quod vica-

3　rium accepi? Etiam scripsisse paenitet. O litterae fletibus tremulae, o parum alligatae manus, o dolenda[15] uxoris oculis epistola! Cur indicavi, cur scripsi quod uxor ac filius ultimum legerent, ut incertum sit utrum me carius redi-

4　mant an lugeant? Cognita clade, rarissimi uxor exempli et prorsus talis filii mater totos efflevit oculos, fontemque illum perennium lacrimarum tantum caecitas clusit; si non tenuisset filium, vicerat.

5　　Continuus inde planctus, incredibilis maestitia, assidua lamentatio fregit[16] iuvenem nescio in me magis an in te futurum impium, si non redemisset quem tu sic desiderabas. Ergo profectionem apparat, ut, quoniam reddere

---

[14] did- P: ded- *cett.*　　　[15] del- π ACD δ P
[16] fregit *Sh. B.*[3]: fuit *codd.*

---

[15] *Mentior, nisi . . .* amounts to *Mentior, nisi verum est quod dico: . . .* ; cf. 6.19.4.

[16] The speaker takes Son's initial decision not to set off with his father as a sign of his greater affection for his mother.

[17] Cf. 5.16.5, 9.4.3, 16.8.7.　　　[18] I.e., loosely enough to be able to write the letter that now I regret.

[19] The letter contained the last words read both by Wife, who later lost her sight, and by Son, who set off and subsequently died.

should be hiding the truth, were I not to say that,[15] when my journey overseas was parting us, he was happier to be with his mother.[16]

(7) As I hurried across every sea in order to bequeath more to my son, I was beset by a pack of pirates crueler than the sea itself. 4. Shall I now describe the prison poised on the wave crests, the chains hanging loose on my shrunken frame,[17] the hold of the ship, scene of my woes, worn away by the pressure of my sides, the cruel blackness of that deathly place plunged in never-ending dark? No, these things I must suppress, if I have any sense of shame. (2) Otherwise who will forgive me for agreeing to a substitute? I am ashamed even to have written. (3) O the handwriting that wavered as I wept, O the hands too loosely bound,[18] O the letter that it caused my wife's eyes such pain to read! Why did I give them the news, why did I write the words, the last thing my wife and son would read,[19] so that it is a moot point whether ransoming me or mourning me costs them more? (4) Hearing of the disaster, my wife, a paragon of her sex and in every way fit to be the mother of such a son, wept her eyes completely away: only blindness closed that fount of perpetual tears.[20] If she had not tried to keep her son back, she would have surpassed him.[21]

(5) After that, continuous wails, incredible grief, constant lament broke the young man down:[22] I don't know if he would have been more undutiful to me or to you, if he had failed to ransom one you so sorely missed. So he arranged his departure: as he could not give his mother her

---

[20] Cf. 1.17.6 and n. 104. [21] In piety.

[22] At first, Son was hesitant to set off, as he feared that Mother would not survive if left alone: cf. 6.4.8.

matri non poterat oculos, redderet virum oculis cariorem.
6 Sed videlicet est quaedam ultima calamitatium rabies, et
novissime in furorem vota ipsa vertuntur. Retinuit iuve-
7 nem et epistolis meis legem opposuit. O vanae figuratio-
nes et pectora hominum alto errore confusa! Nemo illam
8 non putabat timere de filio. Itaque iuvenis, quod ad solacium pertinere credidit, commendavit amicis custodiam
matris, substituit vici curae[17] suae propinquos—neque
enim aliter usque ad reditum meum caeca vixisset. Quic-
9 quid humana[18] ratio valet, contulit. Si potuisset redimere
oculos matris, qua pietate fuit, vicarios suos dedisset. Ipse
profectus est solo comitatus animo, nec se putavit ire sine
pretio, quamvis ad piratas ferret inanis manus. 5. Dicat
aliquis: "Adeo domi nihil reliqueras, adeo longa aetate sic
vixeras, ut ne pretium quidem tui paraveris?" Si hoc ita
esset, testor deos, de redemptione litteras non misissem.
2 Fuit unde redimi possem, iudices, fuit: sed illud totum
filius matri reliquit.
3   Navigat ergo per horridos fluctus et gementia litora et
spumantes scopulos et quacumque miser relatus[19] est
inauspicatum metiens iter, prorsus ominose retentus, per-
versis etiam votis, qui optaret alligari a piratis, quos vi-
4 tare[20] quoque miserum est. Quaerit haec omnia impius ille

---

[17] *vel* vici *vel* curae *del. Bur.*
[18] -narum B V, *sed cf. 13.15.6*   [19] de- *Sch., sed cf. Bur.*
[20] visit- M E (*def. Zins.*), *sed vd. ad Angl. vers.*

---

[23] A rhetorical commonplace: cf., e.g., Sen. *Controv.* 1.7.17.
[24] In fact, she was fearful for herself: cf. 6.20.4.
[25] Keeping out of the way of pirates is a grievous business; all
the more grievous must have been to head in their direction in
order to be imprisoned. Cf. 9.20.2; *Decl. min.* 343.14.

eyes back, he would give her back a husband more dear to her than her eyes. (6) But catastrophe evidently leads in the end to a loss of reason, and our prayers themselves ultimately turn into madness.[23] She kept the young man back, and called in the law to counter my letter. (7) O vain fantasies, O men's hearts deeply confounded in error! Everyone thought she was afraid for her son.[24] (8) So the young man, believing that this conduced to her comfort, entrusted the charge of his mother to friends, and appointed relatives to take his place in looking after her—in no other way could she, in her blindness, have survived until my return. He contributed whatever was humanly possible. (9) If he could have redeemed his mother's eyes, he would have given his own as substitutes, such was his sense of duty. He set off himself, with only his courage for company: he did not think he was going without taking a ransom price with him, even though the hands he brought to the pirates were empty. 5. Someone may say: "Had you then left nothing at home? Had you then lived so long without even making enough money to ransom yourself?" If that were so, I swear before the gods, I should not have written about a ransom. (2) There *was* enough to ransom me, judges, yes, there was: but my son left it all behind for his mother.

(3) Off he sails, then, steering an inauspicious course through rough waves and moaning shores and foaming rocks, wherever he was carried, poor man. It was indeed no good omen that he had been held back, and his own prayers were topsy-turvy, for he wished to be put in chains by pirates whom it is grievous even to avoid.[25] (4) All this he sought out, that undutiful child, for his parents' sake:

17

filius propter parentes, quod non praestitisset frater fratri,
non uxor viro, (quid differimus ultra?) non pater filio.

5   Dii immortales, caeli, maris, inferorum praesides, uni
mihi adhuc omnes male experti, vos tamen solos habeo
testes, quam invitus redemptus sim; miserum me: perît
6 qui sciebat! Nam ut primum pervenit iuvenis ad piratas
adferens redemptionis meae se pretium, e ferali navicula
avidus exiluit vicarias oblaturus manus; stravit se ad genua
singulorum, et, ut cupiditas fecerat blandum, obsecravit
omnibus precibus, miserabili planctu et lacrimis paene
7 maternis. Nemo umquam sic, ut solveretur, rogavit. Nec
sane difficile fuit impetrare a piratis captivitatem; maior
illi pugna mecum fuit. 6. Non dignum illud spectaculum
latronibus erat, cum pater filiusque de vinculis conten-
derent, et sibi quisque carcerem vindicaret: ego iam usu
defendebam meum et in his annis iam maturam mortem
2 asserebam; at ille contra: "Ego te in calamitate deseram?
Ego alligatum relinquam? Et quomodo ad matrem redibo,
quae misera desiderio tui dies noctesque fletibus iungit,
3 quae vivere sine te non potest?" Non dicebat tamen
omnia, et, cum adsiduos planctus et inrequietas diceret
lacrimas, adiciebat: "Iam paene caeca est. Fortasse, si
4 redieris, videbit. In summa: non recedo; fas est mihi
etiam invitis parentibus pie facere. Non recedo; si perse-
veras, demus piratis lucrum: aut vicarius ero, aut comes."

---

26 Cf. 6.24.4.   27 Cf. 9.8.9, 16.9.2–3.

28 A probable allusion to the Roman principle of usucapion,
i.e., acquisition of ownership of something through prolonged
possession.

29 Recalling the same law that Mother later would invoke
against Son.

brother would not have done so much for brother, wife for husband, even—why put off saying this any further?—father for son.

(5) Immortal gods, who preside over sky, sea and underworld, from *all* of you I alone till now have experienced ill; yet I have no other witnesses to my reluctance to be ransomed. Ah me, the one who did know has perished! (6) Now, as soon as the young man reached the pirates, bringing himself as my ransom money, he leaped from the fatal ship eager to offer the hands that would substitute for mine. He fell at their knees in turn.[26] His eagerness made him persuasive; he besought them with every kind of prayer, pitiable lament, tears almost like his mother's. No one has ever begged like that—to be released.[27] (7) Of course, it was easy enough to get the pirates to imprison him; he had more trouble with *me*. 6. That was a show which robbers did not deserve to watch, when father and son were in competition to be chained, each claiming prison for himself. On my side I pleaded that it was mine by prolonged use,[28] and at my age the death I requested was overdue; but in reply he said: (2) "Shall I abandon you in your great trouble?[29] Shall I leave you in chains? And how shall I go back to my mother, who—poor woman—weeps without cease night and day for lack of you, who cannot live without you?" (3) He was not telling the whole story, though; and when he went on to speak of her constant laments and unremitting tears, he added: "Now she is all but blind. Perhaps, if you return she will see. (4) In short, I am not going back; it is my sacred duty to act the dutiful son even though my parents do not wish me to. I am not going back; if you do not weaken, let us give the pirates a bonus: I shall be either your substitute or your

19

[QUINTILIAN]

5 Quantum inter haec flevit, quamdiu cecidit oculos suos!
6 Si perseverassem, duos excaecaveram. Obstupuerunt pietate tanta etiam latrones, et per immobiles ante vultus
fletus cucurrit. Non tenuissent fortasse iuvenem, nisi re-
7 dempturos parentes talem filium credidissent. Ipse in se
transtulit ferreos nexus, et hilarior alligatus est filius quam
8 solutus est[21] pater. Supremum tamen et—nefas!—in ae-
ternum me iam catenatis manibus amplexus, postquam
mei cura discesserat,[22] "Matrem" inquit "tibi per haec
merita commendo: tu illam tuere, defende, ama, ne re-
9 linque. Sic paria faciemus: illic tu eris vicarius meus.[23] Si
haec feceris, non irascetur mihi fortasse mater quod ab illa
recessi." 7. Sic in navim filii mei male permutatus vector
imponor, et, qua visum oculi dederunt, ad piratas e puppe
prospecto. Curva litora et emensum[24] sideribus fretum et
turritos rupium[25] scopulos retro lego. Miserum me, quam-
2 diu a piratis etiam navigatur! Mandata tamen tua, fili,
perago: assideo,[26] sustento—immo mehercules tu assides,
fili, tu sustines, propter quem mihi etiam huius propensior
cura est: dum recedere ab uxore nolo, filium non redemi.
3 At illum interim cotidie situs carceris strangulat, in-
sidunt ossibus catenae; exemplum saeculi in myoparone

---

[21] del. Wint.[3]   [22] dec- Bur., sed vd. Zins.
[23] sic—meus dist. Reitz.[2] 44   [24] em- Sch.: imm- codd.
[25] rupium Håk.: urbium codd.
[26] -deo π γ (cf. mox assides): -do cett.

---

[30] Cf. 16.9.7–8.
[31] Since Son knew that Father would be safe, after release.
[32] Father was reluctant to abandon his son: so sailing *away* from the pirate ship—normally a reason for joyous speed—was

companion." (5) How much he wept amid all this, how long did he keep striking his own eyes! If I had not given way, I should have blinded the *two* of them. (6) Even the pirates were astounded at such a show of affection, and tears ran down faces till then unmoved. Perhaps they would not have kept the young man, had they not believed that a son like this would certainly be ransomed by his parents. (7) He personally transferred the iron fetters to his own hands, and the son was happier to be bound than the father to be freed.[30] (8) For the last time and—horrors!—for ever he embraced me with his hands already in chains. Now that his worries over *me* had departed,[31] "In the name of what I have done for you," he said, "I commend my mother to you: look after her, guard her, love her, do not leave her. (9) In that way we shall be quits: you will substitute for me there. If you do this, perhaps my mother will not be angry that I left her." 7. So, by an ill exchange, I was embarked to sail on my son's ship, and as long as my eyes could see I gazed toward the pirates from the stern. I retraced the curving coastline, the sea I had crossed with the help of the stars, the towering rocks of the cliffs. Ah me, what a long time it takes even to sail away from pirates![32] (2) Anyway, my son, I am now doing what you told me to: I sit by her, I support her—or rather *you* sit by her, *you* support her: for it is for your sake that *my* care for her is more attentive. It was just because I did not want to abandon my wife that I failed to ransom my son.

(3) But he, meanwhile, is being stifled every day by the moldering prison. His chains are biting into his bones.

as slow and painful to him as Son's journey *to* the pirates had been (6.5.3) (AS).

moritur. Mater, iam satis est: habes poenas super legem.
4 Sepelissent talem virum etiam ipsi piratae, nisi eos conscientia scelerum metusque poenarum ab omni litore ar-
ceret. Quod unum poterant, secundis proiecere ventis.
5 Excepit mitior matre tempestas, et, si qua dici potest calamitatium felicitas, prospero cursu cadaver tantum quod
non ad ipsa maiorum sepulcra depositum est. Narretur res
saeculo nostro diversa et nescio utra parte mirabilior: filii
6 corpus matri maria rettulerunt, mater mari. Magnam quidem partem agnosco culpae meae: ego uxorem adduxi, et,
ne miseram matrem dolore fraudarem, ipse meis umeris
adversariam meam usque ad litora tuli. Et sane [adver-
sus][27] prima verba orbitatis animo aestimantem fefelle-
7 runt. Quis autem non dolentis adfectum putasset, cum
diceret defuncto filio mater: "Quid enim navigasti? Quid
8 maria ingressus es? Quid piratas petisti?" Nam illa quidem
vulgatissima orbitatis vox est: "Fili, cur[28] me reliquisti?"
Etiam cum tota supra corpus incubuit, amplexam putavi,
etiam cum iniecit tollentibus manum, "Et hoc" inquam
"solent facere matres, ut funus morentur." 8. At ista legem
recitat et in cadaver fili perorat.

[27] *del. Wint.*[9] *utpote e super.* adversariam *ortum:* adfectūs *Sch.*
(*quo tamen displiceat mox sing.* adfectum)
[28] cur *Ꞩ*: cui *codd.*

---

[33] Cf. 9.20.3.
[34] Cf. 10.4.3.
[35] Completing the scene on the beach. Her deceptive words
in fact lead on to a denunciation of her son (there, not in court).

This example for a whole age is dying in a pirate's galley. Mother, enough is enough! Your punishment has gone beyond the requirements of the law. (4) Such a man even the pirates would have buried, were it not that guilty conscience and fear of punishment barred them from every coast. They did the one thing they could: they threw him overboard when the winds were in the right direction. (5) A gale that was kinder than his mother took him over, and, if one can speak of good fortune amid calamity, the body had a prosperous journey, and was brought to rest at almost the very spot where his ancestors lie buried. Let a tale be told which goes quite against our age,[33] and I don't know which half of it makes it more remarkable: the sea gave back to a mother the body of her son, she gave it back to the sea. (6) Mine, I recognize, is the greater part of the guilt: *I* took my wife; so that the wretched mother should not be deprived of her agony, I set my adversary on my shoulders and brought her to the beach. And admittedly her first words in her bereavement deceived me when I weighed them up. (7) But who would not have thought it a sign of grief when the mother said to her dead son: "Why did you sail? Why did you go to sea? Why did you seek out the pirates?" (8) That, of course, is the most common thing for the bereaved to say: "My son, why did you leave me?" Even when she flung herself full length on top of the body, I thought it an embrace. Even when she laid hands on the men lifting the body, I said to myself: "This too is what mothers often do, to delay the funeral."[34] 8. But then the woman starts reciting the law and inveighing against the body of her son.[35]

2
3   Tace, tace, misera! Ita tu istud optasti? Sola scilicet
calamitatibus nostris adhuc defuit culpa, ut, cum saevitia
nimiae quoque felicitatis turpis sit, procedat inauditum
antea monstrum: misera crudelis ⟨quae⟩,[29] si quid irati dii
reliquerunt, si quid infelicitas oblita est, suis manibus per-
4   dere cupiat. Detracta est fortunae invidia, quando suo
quoque iudicio mater post amissum filium parum misera
est. Lacrimas ipsas novissime perdo: inanis domi libitina
5   plangitur, derisus dissignator redit, refertur rogus. Inter
haec omnia non gemitus ullus matris, non lacrimae, non
questus. Putes adpulsum ad litus aliquem esse piratam.
6   Unde hunc illi animum? Si mala sua ideo non sentit, quia
non videt, et hoc boni caecitas habet, eruat aliquis oculos
meos. Sed[30] tenebrae corporis affectibus non obstant.[31]
7   Estne haec uxor mea, estne ille filius noster? Liceat dubi-
8   tare, si fieri potest.[32] Et sane vix iam dinoscendam speciem
vetustas reliquit: sed adtritae manus et tumida vestigia
vinculorum et testis longae captivitatis macies, infelicia
argumenta, consentiunt. Miserum me, certus luctus est:
filium agnosco; uxorem non agnosco.
9   Ergo quoniam de iure longior pugna, et[33] nobis festi-
nandum est, sint primae precum partes. Adeste, universi
utriusque sexus parentes, dum matrem in exequias filii

---

[29] -ra cru- *sine dist. Bur.,* ⟨quae⟩ *Sch.*   [30] si B V
[31] *gravius dist. Gr.-Mer.*   [32] *gravius distinxi*
[33] et *Håk.*[2] 57.28: est *codd.*

---

[36] An indignant reaction on the part of Mother is implied. Cf.
also 6.21.5.   [37] Cf., e.g., 2.9.1–2.
[38] If it is possible that this woman does not have feelings for
this unfortunate youth, may I be allowed to doubt that she is actually my wife, and he is actually our son.

(2) Silence, silence, wretched woman![36] Is that what you wanted? (3) All that was lacking to our calamities, it seems, was guilt; repellent as is the savagery caused by an excess of good luck, there comes before us a prodigy previously unheard of: a woman at once wretched and cruel, <who> desires to destroy with her own hands anything left behind by the angry gods, anything that has been overlooked by unhappiness. (4) No need now to reproach fortune, when a mother is by her own judgment not wretched enough after the loss of her son. On this last occasion I shed even tears in vain: an empty bier is lamented indoors, the undertaker goes home mocked, the pyre is removed. (5) Amid all this no groan from the mother, no tears, no complaint. You might think some *pirate* had been washed up. (6) Why is she in this frame of mind? If she doesn't feel her ills because she cannot see them, and this is one advantage of blindness,[37] then may someone tear out *my* eyes!—But physical darkness does *not* get in the way of emotion. (7) Is this my wife, is that our son? May it be possible to have doubts, if that can be![38] (8) And indeed, it is true that the passage of time has left him scarcely recognizable; but the chafed hands, the weals left behind by chains, the emaciation that bears witness to a long imprisonment—these unlucky signs are in accord. Ah me, my grief is beyond doubt: I recognize my son; my *wife* I do not recognize.

(9) So, as the legal wrangle is becoming too long, and I must hurry on, let prayers come first.[39] Assemble here, all parents of both sexes, while I beg a mother to bury her

[39] Metarhetoric: see Stramaglia (2016, 33). For the hurry, cf. 6.3.1–2.

10   rogo. Per matrimonium te vetus et per mutuam caritatem,
quae utrique nostrum magno constat, adice,[34] per commune pignus, per annos pariter actos et beneficio filii
plures, per meum in te obsequium, iam mei miserere,
11   cuius soles. Crede mihi: hoc, quod patior, carcere peius
12   est, captivitate crudelius. Mea ista poena est. Quid tibi
tantum mali feci, quid offendi? Certe ego te non reliqui.

     9. Iam si totum adfectum in hunc consumpsisti virum,
et omnis per oculos misericordia effluxit, tulerit sane filius
2   noster merito poenas, dederit spiritum supplicio. Nihil de
praeteritis loquamur; quod postulavit Cicero etiam ab illo
3   crudelissimo Siciliae tyranno: mors sit extremum.[35] [Quod
quidem cum permissum non esset, pernoctabant ante
ostium carceris pretio redimentes sepeliendi potestatem
[[Quid tandem hic[36] Marcus Tullius?]] patres matresque
4   miserae.][37] Tu vende saltem, quod sub Verre crudelissi-
mum fuit. Certe ego filium redimam, nec mihi pretium
diu quaerendum est: habeo manus.

---

[34] -ce *Reitz.*[2] *6.3*: -ci B V γ δ: -cio β
[35] -mum *Hamm.*[2] *522 e Cic.* Verr. *II.5.119*: -mam B V: -ma
malorum Φ   [36] hic *Helm*[1] *345*: hoc *codd.*
[37] quod—miserae *interpolationem esse,* quid—Tullius *adno-
tationem e margine illuc irreptam, ostendit Helm*[1] *344–45*

---

[40] The wife wept herself blind when she heard of the husband's kidnapping; the speaker is trying to prove her "customary"
affection from this single case.
[41] I.e., Verres. What follows is a quotation from Cic. *Verr.*
II.5.119, *verum tamen mors sit extremum*: Verres' infamous executioner, Sextius, used to require payment from the parents of
convicts sentenced to death, to let them bury the bodies of their
children rather than have them thrown to beasts.

son. (10) I beg you by our long-standing marriage and the affection we feel for each other, which is costing us both so dear, yes, and by the common pledge of our union, by the years we spent together, prolonged thanks to our son, and by my devotion to you: pity me now, as you are accustomed to do.[40] (11) Believe me: what I am suffering now is worse than prison, more cruel than captivity. It is *me* you are punishing. (12) What have I done to you that is so bad, what is my offense? At least *I* did not leave you.

9. If you have by now used up all your feelings on me, your husband, and all your compassion has drained away through your eyes, let us suppose that our son has been punished as he deserved, and has paid with his life. (2) Let us not speak of the past; as Cicero too asked of that most cruel tyrant of Sicily:[41] let death be the end. (3) [Though when this was not granted, they spent the night in front of the jail door paying money for license to bury the body, [[What ever is Marcus Tullius doing here?]] the fathers and pitiable mothers.][42] (4) At least do what under Verres was the cruelest option: put the body up for sale.[43] I shall pay for my son, no doubt of it, and I do not need to look far for the price: I have hands.[44]

---

[42] 6.9.3 must have originally been a note in the margin, providing the context for the preceding Ciceronian quotation (cf. Cic. *Verr.* II.5.118); the *marginale* then intruded into the text, bringing within itself a further note, which expressed a reader's surprise at finding a reference to Cicero.   [43] To be buried by the highest bidder.   [44] I.e., "substitute hands" (*manus vicariae*): Father will pay the price for Son's burial by committing suicide—his own corpse being offered in exchange for Son's body and thrown into the sea, while Son will be buried; cf. 6.24.1 (AS).

5   Nihil moveris nunc, et debilitatem tuam iactas. Singulare feminis exemplum ostendi narrarique desideras:
6 sepulturam filii maritus a te impetrare non potuit. Vade
hercule, si libet, et corpus in fluctum[38] repelle, aut, si
parum celebri loco videtur abiectum, inice manum et,
ne minus te satiet alienum ministerium, ipsa potissimum trahe:[39] alteram manum cadaveri impone, alteram
‹duci›.[40] Duc, qua frequentissimum rotis iter est et nigra
limo via; proterat miserum onustum vehiculum et sanctis-
7 simum pectus ungulae rumpant. Ipsa, quoniam deficeris[41]
oculis, elisum caput et oppressa ponderibus praecordia
manibus tuis pertracta; si quidem istis audeas, etiam den-
8 tibus lacera. Litigamus, consistimus,[42] in diversum abi-
mus; nempe, cum viceris, omnia paria habebimus praeter
9 animum. Non sepelies? Vide, quaeso, vide ne, dum litigas,
harenam fluctus aggeret, iniciat humum misericors populus. Obsta,[43] si cuius clementia tumulum fecerit, effode,
et, cum talis sis mater, aude indignari et exclama: "Magis
amavit patrem."
10   Cruces succiduntur, percussos sepeliri carnifex non vetat, ipsi piratae nihil amplius quam proiciunt. 10. Mater

---

[38] -us V Φ, *sed cf. Håk.*² 57   [39] -hes B V δ: -hens *Håk.*³ 127
[40] -ram ‹duci›; duc *Håk.*³ 127–28: -ra duc *codd.*
[41] -fic- ⟨ *(def. Reitz.*² 10.8)*: -fec- *codd.*
[42] *comma vulg.*: *colon Håk.*   [43] -ta π: -tas *cett.*

---

[45] Contrast 6.9.1.
[46] Cf. n. 2.
[47] I.e., under heavy loads dropping off vehicles on to pass-
ersby, as in Juv. 3.257–61, or, perhaps, under heavily laden wag-
ons, crushing the body under their weight.

(5) You are unmoved still: in fact, you are only making a display of your affliction.[45] Evidently you want to be shown, your story told, as a remarkable example for women: your husband could not win burial for your son from you. (6) Go if you like, by heaven, and push the body back into the surf; or, if you think it was cast up at too secluded a spot, make your claim on it,[46] and, for fear another's services might reduce your satisfaction, drag it yourself rather: put one hand on the corpse, one ⟨on your guide⟩. Take it to where the road is crowded with wheeled traffic and the way is black with mud; let a laden cart crush the wretched boy, and hooves smash that revered breast. (7) As for you, since you cannot see, pass your hands over the head shattered, the chest crushed under heavy loads.[47] If you have the effrontery to use your teeth, tear him with them, to add to it all. (8) We are at law, we are before the court, we are going in opposite directions; but certainly, when you have won, we shall be quits—except for our states of mind.[48] (9) Will you refuse to bury him? Take care, please, take care that, while you litigate, the surf doesn't pile the sand over him, that the people in their pity don't cast earth upon him.[49] If anyone is merciful enough to make a funeral mound, get in the way, dig the body out. Since that is the sort of mother you are, lose your temper, if you dare, and cry: "He loved his father more."

(10) Crosses are taken down,[50] the executioner does not forbid the burial of the beheaded, even pirates do no more than throw a body over the side. 10. If the mother

---

[48] They will be quits, as both have lost their only son; yet only Father will *feel* his bereavement (see also 6.10.1, 6.15.2).

[49] Cf. 5.6.8, 6.11.3.   [50] I.e., after the victims die.

—quamquam hoc nomen profanari nefas est—si perse-
verat esse filii sui noverca, ut hac crudelitate videatur
digna quae orbitatem suam intellegat, si ultra hostium
adfectum, qui caesos acie saepe tumularunt, ultra tyran-
nos, ultra latrones parum habet non sepelire, nisi aliorum
quoque officia praeciderit, et tantum quod non petita ex
fluctibus aqua restinguit ignem, si adeo non genuit filium
sed effudit, et illo infelici partu ingratum uteri pondus
exposuit, licet imputet nobis, ut volet, quod tueri[44] non
potest, singulare mariti desiderium, dicam tamen quod
2   sentio: excusatius odisset virum quam filium. Quamquam
in hoc mutuae caritatis affectu[45] paria fecimus: illa oculos
propter matrimonium neglexit, ego filium; vicem caecita-
3   tis orbitate persolvi. Tamen, quod[46] inter haec quoque
mala privatim doleam necesse est, omnem illam, quam
contraxerat, perdit[47] opinionem: iam inimici triumphant,
iam passim locuntur: "Illa exempli[48] mulier, illa saeculi
decus, virum redimi noluit nec filium sepeliri."
4   Equidem, iudices, ut sentio, neminem non mortalium
favere hominis sepulturae convenit, quia haec una res est,
cuius exemplum ad omnes pertineat, ideoque non nisi ab

---

[44] *fort.* teneri (*si quod* ut *pronomen capiatur,* ad *desiderium
proleptice spectans*): quod—potest *secl. Zins.*   [45] eff- B
[46] quod π: quae E: quo *cett.*   [47] -didit *Wint.*[7] 143
[48] -lum *Watt*[2] 23, *sed. vd. Zins.*

---

[51] Which she has not (yet) felt so far, as her behavior toward
her son's body proves (AS).
[52] Same point as in 6.9.5: your love for your husband is no
support for your case.
[53] Whose journey set the whole tragedy going.

(though it is abominable for that word to be desecrated) persists in being a stepmother to her own son, so that for this cruelty she seems to deserve to *feel* her bereavement at last;[51] if, outdoing the heartlessness of enemies, who have often buried those slain in battle, outdoing tyrants, outdoing bandits, she thinks it not enough to refuse burial unless she also cuts short the efforts of others to perform that duty, and all but puts out the funeral fire with water from the waves of the sea; if in fact she did not give birth to her son but ejected him, bringing by those unlucky pangs into the light a burden her womb found unwelcome; though she may, if she likes, ask us to count in her favor something that cannot actually provide any defense—her unparalleled longing for her husband:[52] I shall for all that say what I feel: she would have better reason to hate her husband[53] than to hate her son. (2) On the other hand, in this reciprocal feeling of affection we are quits: she neglected her eyes for the sake of her husband, I neglected my son; I have balanced her blindness with my loss. (3) Yet—and this is something that I especially have to grieve for even amid these ills—she is losing all the reputation she had won: by now her enemies are triumphant, by now everyone is saying: "That exemplar of a woman, that glory of her age, did not want either the ransoming of her husband or the burial of her son."

(4) Indeed, judges, in my opinion every mortal ought properly to favor a man's burial, because this is the one thing that sets a precedent for everyone; and hence it is only from the most horrible parricide that a penalty is

5 ultimo parricidio exigitur poena trans hominem. Etiam si
qua sunt iura quae obstent, si tamen angustus saltem detur
accessus, per quem intrare humanitas possit, vera clementia occasione contenta est. 11. Sive omnis in defunctis
sensus perit, et ad operiendam foeditatem subtrahendam-
que dolori materiam mortui viventium causa sepeliuntur,
seu, cum ad infernas sedes anima migravit, unus hic luce
viduis honos, et suprema face, ut vates ferunt, petitam
ulterioris ripae stationem[49] contingunt—quae vera esse et
2 credo miser et opto, cito iturus ad filium—, certe rerum
natura, ut in generandis alendisque hominibus quae necessaria erant ex se ipsa prospexit, ita, cum rursus opus
suum resolvit, corpora nostra quam primum reducere ad
principia festinat; ut desertis etiam locis circa cadaver
tracta imbribus terra concrescit, adgerunt pulverem venti,
et liquefacta multa die membra paulatim humus bibit,
etiamsi nullus operit, ita[50] ipsa longo tempore in terram
3 ossa desidunt. Nobis vero adversus exanimes genuit non
solum miserationem, quae cogitationi nostrae subit, sed
etiam religionem. Inde ignotis quoque corporibus transe-
untium viatorum conlaticia sepultura, inde iniecta ab alie-
4 nis humus. Facinus indignum! Cum haec ita sint, sepultus
esset filius meus, nisi incidisset in matrem.

---

[49] -ita . . . -ne (contingunt quae *eqs.*) B V δ
[50] ita *Wint.*[7] *143*: ad B: at V Φ

---

[54] Cf., e.g., *Decl. min.* 299.th., "PARRICIDES ARE TO BE CAST
AWAY UNBURIED"; and 2.14.4, on the Roman practice of punishment by sack (*poena cullei*) for parricides.   [55] The law in the
theme.   [56] Cf. 10.16.8.

[57] The torch used to light the funeral pyre. Cf. Prop. 3.13.17,
mortifero iacta est fax ultima lecto.

exacted which goes beyond the living person.[54] (5) There are, maybe, legal rules that stand in the way;[55] but if even a narrow window is available through which human kindness may enter, true mercy is happy to take the opportunity. 11. It may be that the defunct lose all sensation, and the dead are buried for the sake of the living, to draw a veil over a foul sight and remove the source of grief.[56] Or, perhaps, when a soul has gone to the world below, this one honor is accorded those bereft of the light, and, as the poets say, with the last torch[57] they attain the place on the further bank that they longed for[58]—things which, in my wretchedness, I believe and wish to be true, for soon I shall go to join my son. (2) In either case, just as nature, in producing and nourishing men, saw to it that what they needed should be available from herself, so, when she comes in turn to dissolve her own product, she hastens to reduce our bodies to their elements as soon as possible. Hence even in unfrequented places the earth brought there by the rain hardens around the body, the wind piles up dust, and the earth gradually drinks down limbs turned to liquid over many days, even if no one covers them; and similarly, after a long time, even the bones sink into the ground. (3) Indeed nature has produced in us not only the pity which comes into our minds with regard to the dead, but also a religious awe. This is why even unknown bodies receive burial from the contributions of passing travelers, why strangers throw earth on graves.[59] (4) What an outrage! This being the case, my son would have been buried—if he hadn't fallen into the hands of his mother.

[58] The bank of the Acheron river: cf., e.g., Verg. *Aen.* 6.314; Stat. *Theb.* 1.297; and the parody of the motif in Juv. 2.149–52.

[59] Cf. 6.9.9 and n. 49.

5   Et haec, iudices, non ideo ego dico, ut adfectu iura
corrumpam, neque vobis praecipio, sed adversariae ex-
probro. Legem quidem istam quidni[51] horream, cum id
unum miserrimo iuveni sit obiectum, quod in calamitate
6 non deseruerit patrem? Sed quatenus luctus nostri in ius
vocantur, et flenti disputandum est, et orbitati suae mater
7 irascitur, superemus quam exorare non possumus. Ecquando[52] duorum hominum miseriora vota vidistis, iudices?[53] Pater, si vicerit, filium suum efferet;[54] mater, si
vicerit, abiciet.[55]

8   Quae tamen lex est? QUI PARENTES IN CALAMITATE
DESERUERIT, INSEPULTUS ABICIATUR. Omnis nobis in
hac prorsus[56] causa, iudices, de scripto et intellectu legis
contentio est, utrum verborum ambiguitate an voluntatis
fide standum[57] sit. 12. Pars enim diversa id nititur,[58] parentem fuisse in calamitate eam, quae deserta sit; cuius rei
poena est abici insepultum. Quid tum fuerit in causa, quid
sit postea consecutum, quomodo legem intellegere conveniat, subterfugit dicere, neque a vestigio scripti recedit,
2 sed nuda recitatione contenta est. Nos neque omnibus
personis neque omnibus causis[59] scriptam esse legem, et

---

[51] quid mihi *Sch.* (*corrob. Reitz.*² 65.5)   [52] ecq- ⊊ (*def.*
*Håk.*⁴ 153): et q- *codd.*   [53] iudices *Sh. B.*⁴ 196 (*ad fin. sen-*
tentiae, velut 9.8.8, 9.19.4, 9.20.3): ut deis B V: ut de his Φ
[54] -ret *Sh. B.*⁴ 196: -rat B Φ: afferat V   [55] -iet *Sh. B.*⁴ 196:
-iat *codd.*   [56] *scripsi* (*cf. ad mendi orig. Cappelli 291, ad*
sensum ThlL X.2.2160.24ss.): prius *codd., damn. Håk. propter*
omnis   [57] fide standum ⊊ (*def. Bur.*): fide statutum B Φ:
fides tantum V   [58] id ni- B V Φ* (*vd. ad constr. Prop. 1.3.8,*
2.29.40): inni- M, *unde* <hoc> inni- *Wint.*⁷ 144: *fort.* ibi ni-, *cf.*
Cic. Verr. II.2.155 Ubi nitere?
[59] causis *Håk.*: caecis *codd.* (*def. Helm*¹ 381)

(5) And I do not, judges, say this to try to undermine the laws by rousing emotion: I am not giving you orders, but reproaching my opponent. As to this law, why should I not shudder at it,[60] when the only thing brought against my most unfortunate son is that he did *not* abandon his father in misfortune? (6) But since our laments are summoned to the courtroom, and I have to argue amid my tears, and the mother is angry with her own dead child, let us defeat her if we cannot win her over. (7) Judges, have you ever seen two human beings with more pitiable aims? If he wins, the father will bury his son; if she wins, the mother will cast him out.

(8) But what does the law say?[61] A SON WHO ABAN-DONS HIS PARENTS IN MISFORTUNE IS TO BE CAST OUT UNBURIED. Certainly all that is in dispute between us in this case, judges, concerns the letter and the meaning of the law: are we to take our stand on its ambiguous phrasing or on our confidence in its intention? 12. Now the other side relies on the plea that *she* was the parent who was abandoned in misfortune, something for which the penalty is to be cast out unburied. What was in question at the time, what happened later, how it is proper to understand the law, she dodges mentioning; she does not depart from the written provision, and is happy with a bare recital.[62] (2) *Our* contention is that the law was not framed for all persons or all cases; that the young man had sound and

---

[60] Ironic.

[61] What follows is a metarhetorical discussion: see Stramaglia (2016, 30–31).

[62] A commonplace: cf. *Rhet. Her.* 2.14.

iuveni iustas ac necessarias recedendi causas, et, cui rei
semper ius satis plenum est, bonum animum fuisse, post-
remo non hoc esse deserere contendimus, atque eo causam demittimus,[60] ut non sit absolvendus adulescens nisi
3 etiam laudandus. Qui[61] autem dubitat an scripti voluntatem sequi conveniat, is mihi videtur quaestionem temptare in certis.[62]

4 Qua de re ideo pauciora adiciam, quod nobis quoque,
si ita pergitis, adferet quandam cavillationem ista ser-
monis ambiguitas, ac videri potuerit[63] omnem actionem
partis adversae prima statim recitatione[64] subvertere.
5 Nam lex cum dicit: QUI PARENTES IN CALAMITATE DESE-
RUERIT, ⟨eum significat, qui duos deseruerit;⟩[65] rursus-
que cum dicit: INSEPULTUS ABICIATUR, non utique id
significat, ut non liceat eum sepeliri, postquam proiectus
6 est. Quare aut mihi quoque permittite sic agere, quomodo volo, aut—quod magis vestram religionem decet—
indignam sanctissimis auribus verborum captionem ex
utraque parte praecidite, et, cum filium singularis exempli
probavero, fortiter sentite nullam umquam a maioribus
nostris poenam scriptam esse pietati.

13. Atque[66] in eo quod primum proposueram, non ad
hanc rem pertinere legem, non diu versabor, neque[67]

---

[60] dem- *Reitz.*[2] 64: dim- *codd.*

[61] quis B V δ, *unde* quisquis *Håk.*

[62] in certis (*vel* iam certus) *Håk.*, *mox dist.* ⟨: incertus *codd.*

[63] -terit Φ   [64] retractatione B (*def. Reitz.*[2] 65.4)

[65] *cetera suppl. Reitz.*[2] 65, duos *scripsi* (et patrem *Reitz.*[2]) *coll.*
6.14.6, 6.15.1   [66] at AE δ β

[67] ne, quae dubitationem [quam] non habent, adferant moram *Reitz.*[2] 69 (*vd. seqq. adnn.*)

compelling reasons to leave; that his intentions were good (something to which the full weight of the law always attaches); and finally that this is not a case of deserting. In fact, the nub of our case is that the youth is not just to be acquitted, but positively applauded. (3) As for anyone who has doubts whether it is proper to follow the intention or the written word, he seems to me to be raising queries in matters that are beyond dispute.

(4) On this point I shall only add a little for the very reason that, if you[63] pursue this line, the ambiguity of phrasing will allow *us* too some scope for casuistry, and may be seen to overturn the contention of the other side at the very first recital. (5) When the law says WHO ABANDONS HIS PARENTS IN MISFORTUNE, ‹it means someone who abandoned *both*›; on the other hand, when it says IS TO BE CAST OUT UNBURIED, it certainly does not mean that it is not allowed for him to be buried after he is cast up by the sea. (6) Therefore you[64] must either let me too conduct the case as I wish, or else—as better befits your sense of religious duty—you must deny to both parties a captiousness that is unworthy of your sacred ears, and, when I have proved him to be a son of unique quality, take the strong line that no penalty has ever been laid down by our ancestors for dutiful sons.

13. Now as to my first contention,[65] that the law is not applicable to this case, I shall not dwell on it for long, or

---

63 Mother and her advocate.

64 Judges. Cf. what follows and 1.5.4.

65 Cf. 6.12.2. The *argumentatio* is not laid out very clearly.

2 dubitatione,[68] quam non habet,[69] adferam moram. Neque
enim puto, si aetas impediet infantem, valetudo aegrum,
res legatum, dux militem, nihilominus obstricta crudelitas
non accipiet rationem necessitatis,[70] et, cum semel ap-
paruerit patere in eiusmodi causis defensionem, potero
plane esse securus, nec timebo ne teneri videatur filius
meus, si non potuit omnibus succurrere, dum in ipsa lege
3 occupatus est. Pater alligatus [est],[71] mater caeca est; unus
utrique filius; magna locorum distantia; habet lex in medio
debitorem. Duc ad utrum mavis; ad utrumque non potes,
nisi hanc condicionem misero imponimus, ut, quicquid
fecerit, proiciendus sit: si exierit, mater sepeliri vetabit, si
remanserit, pater.

4   Non puto[72] fore dubium quin ius in hac lege fuerit et
mihi, nisi forte, ut omnia inique iniusteque conquiritis, hic
quoque unius occasione verbi aliud putatis iuvare parentes, aliud non deserere, id est, de hoc dubitare vultis,
utrum parentibus ubique ferri oporteat auxilia, ut ego aestimo, an vero non mereatur adiutorium nisi qui praesente
5 filio miser est. Nam si deserere in calamitate nil aliud
putamus esse quam a misero discedere, duo simul scelera
permittimus: primum illud, ut etiam qui aderit possit im-

---

[68] -em B V S   [69] -et M ψ: -ent *cett.*
[70] neque—necessitatis *anacoluthon auctoris (vd. Zins.)*
[71] *delevi, et om.* B
[72] puto *Sh. B.*² *196*: dubito *codd. (sc. ex inseq.* dubium)

---

[66] Cf. 6.12.3.   [67] Cf. 16.5.7. Such exceptions were recommended by Quintilian (cf. 5.10.97).
[68] The "enforced cruelty" is Son's unavoidable act of unkind-
ness in leaving Mother to save Father.

cause delay by raising doubts the law does not leave room for.[66] (2) Indeed, if an infant is to be prevented by his age, a sick man by his state of health, an ambassador by his mandate, a soldier by his general,[67] no less—I think—will enforced cruelty admit the plea of necessity:[68] and once it becomes evident that a clear defense is available in cases of this kind, I shall be free of all anxiety, and shall not be afraid my son may be found liable if he was not able to help everyone, being in the grip of the law itself.[69] (3) His father is in chains, his mother is blind; both have the one son; a long distance separates the two of them; in between them is the person bound by the law. Take him to which-ever you prefer; you cannot take him to both, unless we impose on the wretched youth terms by which he will be cast out unburied whatever he does: if he goes, his mother will forbid him burial, if he stays, his father will.

(4) I don't think there will be any doubt that, this being the law, I too[70] had a just case, unless perhaps, ready as you are to rake up all the unfair and unjust points you can muster, here too, relying on a single word, you think "help-ing" parents is one thing, "not deserting" them another: that is, you want to raise a question as to whether—as I think—help has to be given to parents under all circum-stances wherever they are, or whether the only parent who deserves aid is one who is wretched while the son is pres-ent. (5) For if we think "abandoning in calamity" consists only in going away from one of them when in distress, we are allowing two simultaneous wrongs: first, that even a

[69] Explained in what follows (6.13.3). See also 16.1.2.
[70] As well as Mother.

39

pune nihil praestare, siquidem absolutus est hac lege qui
secundum miserum stetit—quo quidem modo non adiu-
tores calamitosis parentibus filios damus, sed spectatores.
14. Accedit[73] illud vel gravius, quod, cum rerum necessitas
cotidie nos dividat, si quaedam fortuna parentes nos
deprehenderit, quamvis exiguo divisus[74] spatio impune
opem non feret, non succurret, ut hac saltem se calumnia
defendat: "Non reliqui, si[75] non accessi:[76] neque pede,
2   quod aiunt, uno a parente discessi." Solutus erit omni
auxiliandi necessitate, quando vestra interpretatione ab-
sentia impietatis occasio est.
3   Hoc voluisse legum latorem putamus, ut natus ex no-
bismet ipsis, in rebus adversis praesidium[77] parenti, labore
atque praestantia[78] solveret lucis usuram ubicumque—
4   nisi forte non sumus parentes nisi palam. Quid est ergo
non deserere? Opem ferre, non deesse. Omnia haec enim
5   eo spectant, ut auxilio liberorum tuti sint parentes. Quod
cum ita sit, tam ad me lex ista pertinuit quam ad matrem.
6   Duo unum vocabamus; videamus quo ire debuerit.
Poteram quidem fortiter dicere: "Pater iussi.[79] Hoc nomen omni lege maius est: tribunos deducimus,[80] candida-

---

73 -ced- *Dess.*[2]: -cid- B V: dehinc -cid- Φ

74 -sos *Bur.*   75 si *Sh. B.*[2] *196 (firm. Str. ap. Zins.)*: (reliquis)set B: sed V: *om.* Φ   76 absc- Φ*   77 praeditum B V
δ, *sed vd. Håk.*[2] *59*   78 -sen- J, *sed vd. Luc. 73*

79 iussi Φ: eius si B: ius si V: eius sum M: ei iussi *Klotz*[1]
80 didici- B V *unde* decidi- *Watt*[2] *23, sed vd. Zins.*

---

71 Without doing anything to help.
72 I.e., "If I did not go to him, that does not mean that I abandoned him" (Shackleton Bailey [1976b, 196]).

son who is present can fail to provide assistance without being penalized, granted that the son who was in the presence of a parent in distress[71] is not guilty under this law—indeed, in this manner we make sons not helpers of parents in misfortune, but lookers-on. 14. Then comes a further, even more important point: every day, necessity separates us from each other. If some mischance overtakes us parents, a son who is even a tiny distance away will go unpunished if he fails to bring help, fails to succor, for he can at least defend himself by the sophistry: "I did not abandon my parent, though I did not go to him or her:[72] I did not, as they say, go one foot away from him or her." (2) He will be absolved of any need to help, for on your interpretation absence is grounds for neglecting filial duty.

(3) *Our* opinion, rather, is that the intention of the legislator was this: that a child born of our very own flesh and blood should, as payment for the gift of life, help his parent in adversity by his effort and his services absolutely everywhere—unless we are only parents when we are in sight. (4) What then is "not to abandon"? It is to give aid, not to be lacking. For the aim of all this is that parents should be kept safe by the help of their children. (5) This being so, this law applied to me as much as to his mother.

(6) The two of us were calling on the services of a single son; let us see where he had to go. For sure, I might have taken a strong line:[73] "I, his father, ordered him. The name 'father' out-trumps every law: we can[74] drag tri-

---

[73] Father might have asserted in court that he, in his supreme power, ordered Son to go and that the latter had no alternative.

[74] Sc., if they are our sons.

tos ferimus, ius nobis vitae necisque concessum est. Si non
fecerit quod iubeo, non deferam illum ad sepulturam.
7 Necesse habuit parere: non deseruit, sed abductus est.
Crede, non contemptu tui venit in carcerem."[81] 15. Sint
sane iura paria, sedeatque medius inter duos filius iudex:
non comparabo personas, quamvis apud omnes gentes
plus iuris habeat pater. Sit sane natura communis: non
imputabo quod nomen dedi, quod familiam, quod impensas, quod, dum illi adquiro, captus sum. Non indulgentiae
2 discrimen excutiam, de qua iam lite concessum est. Fue-
rint quidem ista facienda, sed ego ius meum reprimo.
Inter duos parentes aecus[82] adfectus est; exorabit qui prior
3 rogaverit. Tempore certe vinco: ante miser esse coepi. Tu
adhuc integra es, ego iam alligatus sum; tu sana in domo,
ego iam paene defunctus in carcere; tibi adhuc non opus
4 est filio, ego iam rogo. Nempe calamitas tua nata est post
epistolam meam. Nisi te flentem consolari filius voluisset,
ante caecitatem tuam exisset. Noli mirari, si te gratia
vinco: ante exoravi filium, quam tu rogares.

[81] *verba personata hic finit Wint.*[9] (*vd. ad Angl. vers.*): *post
sepulturam* (*§6*) *Håk.*
[82] aecus *Håk.*[3] *128 ex* aequus E: caecus *cett.*

---

[75] Despite their *sacrosanctitas*. Cf. Cic. *Inv. rhet.* 2.52; also
[Quint.] *Decl. min.* 286.2.   [76] Cf. (Gabriella Moretti, *per
litteras*) Quint. 6.3.25, *dicebatur . . . consul (Isauricus) a patre
flagris aliquando caesus*, where it may well be left implied—for
the sake of brevity, this being an incidental remark—that this man
was flogged when still a *candidate* for the consulship.
[77] All these words (6.14.6–7) portray an imaginary scenario:
Father did *not* order Son at the time, merely wrote "about a
ransom."   [78] While disclaiming his full rights under *patria
potestas*, Father now gives other reasons why he had a better

bunes away,[75] have candidates for office flogged;[76] we are granted power of life and death. If he does not do what I order, I shall not allow him burial. (7) He *had* to obey; he did not abandon you: he was taken away from you by force. Believe me, he did not allow himself to be imprisoned out of any lack of respect for you."[77] 15. Suppose our rights to be equal,[78] suppose our son is sitting as judge between us: I will not compare the roles involved,[79] though in all peoples the father has more rights. Let us grant that our son is by *nature* common to us both: I will not take credit for giving him name, patrimony, money, for my being taken prisoner when I was off making money for *him*. Nor will I go into the difference between your affection and mine: that has already been conceded by the bringing of this case.[80] (2) To be sure, one ought to have made all these points; but I restrict my own just claims. Between two parents a son's feelings are equal: the parent who asks first will be the one whose plea is heard.[81] (3) *I* undoubtedly win on timing: my misfortune preceded yours. You are still hale and hearty, I am now in chains; you are in good health at home, I am all but dead in prison; you don't yet need your son, I am already begging him. (4) In fact, your calamity came about *after* you got my letter. If my son had not wanted to comfort you in your distress, he would have left before you became blind. Don't be surprised if I am favored above you: my son answered my request before you made yours.

claim than the mother.   [79] I.e., father and mother. A meta-rhetorical hint: cf. 1.13.1–2.   [80] The fact that he has brought the case to stop Mother's veto on burial shows that he is the kinder (DAR).   [81] Father renounces his stronger claim (cf. 6.14.6) and proceeds to take the "weaker" line: he asked first.

5   Se[83] quisquam figuratione quadam in hac malorum condicione[84] iudicem ponat (fortuna quaeso absit): cuius tanta calamitas fuit?[85] Abstulerat quidem tibi oculos nimius adfectus:[86] [et] de quinque rerum sensibus pars una cessabat, et tenebras, etiam salvis luminibus alternas,[87] continua nox duxerat.[88] 16. Maius est tamen malum, quod sic fletur. Nam ut merito queri possis ablatas videndi voluptates, impeditos rerum actus, tamen, si non iniqui iudices sumus nec ambitiose miseri, sunt quae[89] his mederi possint; referam[90] non solum quia vincenda mihi, sed ma-

2 gis etiam quia consolanda es. Nam quando omne tormentum corporis abest, dolorque membrorum, qui totam cogitationem in se rapit, feliciter cessat, superest ut cruciet nimium otium et assidua quies, res, si non sint necessitate,

3 iocundae.[91] Nam visus damnum sarciunt reliquae voluptates: odor, gustus, tactus, auditus. Quibus tamenetsi deesse summam fatendum est, non est tamen maximae

4 calamitatis loco numeranda parum plena felicitas. Domus certe propria lectusque genialis, conventus propinquorum, sermo amicorum, ipsa (quod raro contingit) honesta calamitas et in quacumque fortuna beata libertas: tot vo-

5 luptates obruere possunt unum dolorem. Nam lucis desiderium, si malis meis compares, etiam delicatum est.

83 se *Gron.*: si *codd.*: si ‹se› *Sh. B.*[2] *196*
84 contenti- *Watt*[3] *49–50, sed vd. Str.*[7] *308–9*
85 fortuna—fuit *sic fere dist. Ed. Oxon.* (*vd. Str.*[7] *308*)
86 *dist. atque* et *del. Wint.*[7] *144*
87 -as V (*def. Wint.*[7] *144*): -ans B Φ   88 iunx- *Bur.*
89 quae *Sch.* (*et vd. Dess.*[1] *97*): qui *codd.*
90 ‹quae› re- *Sch.*
91 nam quando—iocundae *deleverit Zins., sed vd. Str. ap. Zins.*

(5) Let one imagine oneself as having (heaven forbid!) to make a judgment in this choice of ills: whose was the really great misfortune? True, excess of emotion had deprived you of your eyes: one of your five senses was wanting, for an unbroken night had brought you the darkness that alternates with light even when the eyes are undamaged. 16. But it is a greater evil[82] that is wept for like that. Though you would be justified in complaining of the loss of the pleasures of sight and the hindrance to your activities, yet, if we judge impartially and do not make a display of our misery, there are ways of remedying these things. I shall mention them not only because I have to defeat you, but still more because I have to comfort you. (2) When all physical agony is absent, and pain in the limbs, which demands one's complete attention, happily ceases, there remain to torture one excessive leisure and constant tranquility: things that are agreeable, if they are not forced upon one. (3) For loss of one's sight is made up for by the other pleasures—smell, taste, touch, hearing. And although the full tally is admittedly lacking, one cannot count incomplete happiness as the greatest of misfortunes. (4) Surely one's own house and matrimonial bed, the company of relatives, conversation with friends, even—a rare event—even a calamity incurred for honorable reasons, and the blessedness of freedom whatever one's fortune:[83] all these pleasures can blot out a single grief. (5) Indeed regret for the loss of sight, if compared

---

[82] I.e., than blindness itself. As Father goes on to say, there are ways of mitigating blindness: so blindness is not as bad as what in this case caused it.   [83] This list of consolations ends in allusions to Mother's "honorable calamity" (6.16.6) and her freedom, which the pirate's prisoner lacked (cf. 6.17.5).

Num[92] enim aliquid rerum natura genitura est spectaculo
nostro novum, ac[93] non, quicquid speciosissimum pulcher-
rimumque visuri sumus, vidimus? [tenebrae][94] Nempe
cotidie nox oritur, et aequam temporum portionem involvit obscuritas, et ex parte sui ipsa quodammodo caeca
6   natura est. Cui alienis oculis uti licet, audire, imperare,
cuius ministeriis officia non desunt (non enim defuerunt),
nisi se erigit et fortunae suae rationem reddit, et praesertim in tam bona caecitatis conscientia, animi vitio miser
est. 17. Non debet dolere quispiam,[95] qui potest gloriari.
2   Quamquam cuilibet[96] [et][97] quacumque causa hunc
incursum passo ‹leve›,[98] levius est tamen malum feminae:
non enim navigatis, non legationem obitis, non frequenti
peregrinatione variatis aspectus, non militaris vos, non
forensis ratio deducit. Alioquin semper estis intra domum,
3   uno plurimum loco levibus officiis adfixae. Tuum quidem
adfectum si bene novi, nulla magis causa caecitatem
doluisti, quam quod ad redimendum maritum ire non
posses.
4   Haec tua calamitas erat; aestimemus meam. Nulli quidem gravior visa est quam tibi, audi tamen quam multa in
5   illis epistolis non scripserim. O fili, in quibus te malis reliqui! Iam illa principalis ac maxima[99] dono deum concessa
libertas, nec hominum solum sed ferarum volucrumque

---

92 num *Håk.*: non *codd.*   93 an *Bur.*
94 *del. Håk., et om.* Φ   95 quipp- Φ
96 cuil- *Bur.*: cuiusl- *codd.*   97 *secl. Russ.*[2] *144*
98 -so ‹leve› *Wint.*[7] *144*: -sa B V: -sae Φ   99 -mo *Helm*[1] *368*

---

84 Cf. 16.11.3.
85 Women are normally tied to the home, but *you*—in your

with *my* problems, can even be self-indulgent. Is nature ever going to produce anything new for us to gaze at? Have we not seen all the fairest and most beautiful things we are ever going to see? Every day night comes on, and half of our life is wrapped in obscurity: nature is in a way herself in part blind. (6) When someone is able to employ the eyes of others, to hear, to give orders, when there is no shortage of slaves to give their services (and there never has been),[84] then if he fails to get to his feet and count his blessings—especially if he is aware that his blindness came about for such a good reason—his feeling ill-done by is a fault of character. 17. No one should grieve if he can boast.

(2) This affliction is, to be sure, a ⟨light⟩ burden for anyone who has suffered its onset for any reason at all; but it is lighter for a woman. You women do not go to sea, you do not act as envoys, you do not see different sights on repeated travels, you have no military or forensic business to take you out of the house. In fact you are always within four walls, generally tied to one spot attending to trivial duties. (3) Yet if I know your feelings, you grieve for your lost sight especially because you were not able to go to ransom your husband.[85]

(4) This was your misfortune; let us now assess mine. No one, true, thought it more serious than you did; but let me tell you all the things I did *not* write in that letter. (5) My son, what evils I left you in! The first thing I was stripped of was liberty, the foremost and greatest gift from the gods, something rooted and innate in the conscious-

extraordinary devotion—regret your loss of sight because it prevented you from coming to rescue me (which otherwise you would have done).

6 sensibus fixa et ingenita, primum spolium fuit. Me ipse perdidi, teneor venale mancipium: et civis Romanus merces fio, et libertatem senex dedisco, et natus ingenuus

7 venire opto. Minimum est ‹quod›[100] habitamus in fluctibus, hiberni nos ferunt venti: non statio, non sedes, non quies; et,[101] quod malorum meorum maxima portio est,

8 tam miseri sunt etiam domini mei. Cito praetereunda est memoria propter me uxori gravis,[102] mihi propter filium. 18. Transeo hirsutos hostium vultus et immanium barbarorum feros fremitus, tantumque mihi cotidie esse metuendum quantum pati captus, audere pirata potuisset.

2 Nihil est desiderio suorum gravius; timui ne quem ex meis viderem. Nihil tempestate minacius; cotidie naufragium optavi. Nam mortem, confiteor, senili inertia una causa

3 minus cupiebam: ne defunctum nemo sepeliret. Quam vestem relictam captivo putas, nisi quae praeda non erat? Quales epulas cibosque praebent, qui ipsi rapto vivunt?

4 Nam illa quidem satis digne[103] quis dixerit, udum carcerem et inundata sentina vincula et impositum nuda trabe inrequietum latus, revinctas pone tergum[104] manus, alligatos, tamquam esset qua fugeremus, pedes? Solae in car-

---

[100] *add. Sch.*   [101] et *Sch.*: sed *codd.*

[102] -is ς: -ius *codd.*: -is, ‹gravior› *Håk.[4] 154*

[103] -ne β: -na *cett.*   [104] pone tergum π: pone tergo (*ex* -net e-) B: pene tergo V: post tergum Φ: pone terga *Dess.[1] 71–72*

---

[86] And not a generic citizen of Sophistopolis: see Introduction to the present declamation.

[87] As a slave: even this would be preferable to being held by pirates.   [88] Because I and then my son suffered like that.

[89] It prevented him from seeing its squalor. What for Mother

ness not of men only but of wild animals and birds. (6) I have lost my identity, I am held as a slave for sale; I am a Roman citizen,[86] yet I am becoming an article of merchandise. In my old age I am coming to unlearn the ways of liberty: free by birth, I long to be sold.[87] (7) The least of it is <that> we live on the ocean wave, that we are driven about by winter storms: no home port, no base, no peace and quiet; and—this is what makes the greatest part of my troubles—my masters are as unhappy as I. (8) I must pass quickly over these memories, that are a burden to my wife because of me, and to me because of my son.[88] 18. I will say nothing of the enemy's bearded faces, of the bestial grunts of the uncouth barbarians, of the way I had every day to fear all a prisoner could have suffered, all a pirate could have dared to inflict. (2) Nothing is worse than to miss one's own family; yet I was afraid I might see one of my kin. Nothing is more to be dreaded than a storm; yet every day I prayed for shipwreck. As for killing myself—I confess—, being but a powerless old man I had a single reason not to long for it: the fear that no one might bury me if I died. (3) What clothes, do you imagine, were left to the captive except ones not worth stripping him of? What sort of banquets and food are on offer from people who themselves live on what they steal from others? (4) Then again, who could adequately describe all that: the dank prison, chains awash in the bilge, the lack of rest for one lying on a bare plank, hands bound behind the back, feet chained as if there was some way of escape for me. Only the darkness was a consolation in the prison.[89]

was the only loss—i.e., inability to see—for Father was the only consolation.

49

5   cere tenebrae iuvabant. Saepe de auribus questus sum,
quae sonum flagellorum gemitumque caesorum quamvis
impexis[105] obrutae comis acciperent, dira[106] metus sui
6   exempla. Miserum me, fili: nempe morbo peristi. Com-
para terram mari, domum navi, lectulum carceri, libertatem servituti, desiderium oculorum totius corporis
damno—quo nos longius ducit calamitatium nostrarum
misera contentio? Caeci etiam litigare possunt, captivi nec
vivere.

      19. Verum haec etiamsi in aequo ponerentur, multum
tamen in alteram partem debuisset[107] habere momenti
quod plus mihi poterat[108] prodesse quam tibi. Eo[109] labo-
ris[110] oportet incumbere, ubi effectus promittitur; stulta
2   cura est, quae spem non habet. Ego redimi poteram, tu
sanari non poteras. Qualiscumque ista calamitas, inemen-
dabilis cecidit: non remedium accipere, non vicarium po-
3   test. Adsedisset scilicet lectulo inefficax sedulitas et acceptis epistolis meis iuvenis filius nihil aliud quam cum matre
flevisset? Quia profectus est, alterius saltem[111] parentis
calamitas emendata est. Si remansisset, et matrem caecam
4   haberet et patrem captivum. Adice eo[112] quod tibi non
necessaria filii praesentia fuit: adsidere enim, cibos minis-

---

105 impexis M² E P: -it S: implexis (am- V) *cett.*
106 dira *Bur.*: dura *codd.*   107 -et D: -ent *cett.*
108 -at *Obr.* (*firm. Reitz.² 52.13*): -ant *codd.*
109 eo B V: et E: ei *cett.*   110 -ris *Russ.¹ 44*: -re V P: -ri *cett.*
111 saltem *Str.⁷ 309*: tamen *codd.*   112 adicio Φ

---

90 As opposed to my eyes.
91 Overstated: in fact Son did *not* die of a normal illness, but
wasted away as a result of his brutal imprisonment.

(5) Often I had to complain of my *ears*[90]—even though they were buried in unkempt masses of hair—for allowing me to hear the crack of whips and the groans of the flogged, dreadful instances of what each had to fear for himself. Ah, my son: you, I have no doubt, died of *disease*![91] (6) Compare land to sea, home to ship, couch to prison, liberty to slavery, blindness to impairment of the entire body—how much further is our miserable competition in misfortunes to lead us? The blind can even go to law, captives cannot even live.

19. But even if these things were equally balanced,[92] it should all the same have weighed heavily on one side that he could be of more use to me than to you.[93] One should concentrate on the part of a task where there is promise of success; it is foolish to take trouble where there is no hope on offer. (2) I could be ransomed; you could not be healed. However we assess that misfortune,[94] it came upon you with no prospect of cure: it cannot be remedied, it cannot find a substitute. (3) Should he have sat by the bedside, a sedulous but ineffectual carer, and once he had received my letter should my young son have done no more than join his mother in weeping? Because he set out, at least the misfortune of one parent was relieved. If he had stayed at home, he would have ended up with both a blind mother and a captive father. (4) What is more, our son's presence was not imperative for you. Anyone was

---

[92] I.e., even if our sufferings were equal (as 6.18.6 shows, they were not).

[93] Cf. 16.1.3.

[94] And the speaker has earlier downplayed it.

trare, manum porrigere quilibet poterat; mentior, nisi factum est.[113] Me ab illis captum tam dura condicione venalem, quod utique in confessione est, nemo alius redemisset quam filius meus.

5   Et ego sic ago, tamquam hoc tantum[114] filius propter me fecerit. Quamquam in hoc litigatu[115] quodammodo tibi ipsa excidisti, et—tamquam[116] id agas, ut merita tua iniuria vincas—novum induisti rigorem, non prohibeo tamen testimonium: ad redemptionem meam filium ipsa misisti, cum sic plangeres, cum mortem precareris, cum te omni viduatam voluptate clamares, cum saepius gemeres capti-
6   vitatem meam quam caecitatem tuam. Non erat illi ferreum pectus nec cor silice concretum, ut haec pati posset aequo animo. Tu filium prima docuisti sibi non parcere. Potius quam plus fleres, potius quam ipsam rescinderes[117] caecitatem, 20. profectus est, maritum tibi reddidit. O crimen grave! Si hoc ante fecisset, videres.

2   At retinere non potuisti. Non dicam tibi: habet pietas impetum suum, nec ullum dominum novit adfectus; nec
3   ille te potuit[118] retinere, ne fleres. Audi quod est verius:

[113] poterat—est *dist. Obr.*

[114] tantum *post* me *transp. Wint.*[7] *145*

[115] hoc litigatu Φ* (*hapax, ut vid.; similia ap. Str.*[4] *159.210*): hac (hoc V) -gato B V: hac lite tu *Wint.*[7] *145*

[116] tam- *Wiles 69*: quam- *codd.*

[117] fleres . . . rescinderes (*et comma post* caecitatem) *Bur.*: -re . . . -re *codd.*

[118] te po- V ψ δ S (*def. Reitz.*[2] *70.2*): po- te *cett.*

---

[95] See n. 15.

[96] Son's action helped Mother as well as Father (cf. 6.20.1).

capable of sitting with you, giving you food, lending you his hand—which I think I am right to say *did* happen.[95] I, the prisoner of those men, and for sale on such hard terms, could only have been ransomed by my son: that all will agree.

(5) And I am arguing as if my son did this only for me.[96] Although in this suit you have in a way been untrue to yourself, and—as though it were your aim to surpass your good deeds by causing injury—have put on a new sternness, I do not reject your testimony:[97] it was you who sent our son to ransom me, by lamenting like that, by praying for death, by shrieking that you had been widowed of every pleasure, by bewailing my captivity more often than your blindness. (6) His breast was not clad in iron, his heart was not hard as flint,[98] that he could bear this with equanimity. You were the first to teach your son not to spare himself.[99] Rather than have you weep more, rather than have you tear out your sightless eyes, 20. he set forth, and gave you back your husband. A serious crime, indeed! If he had done this earlier, you would be able to see.

(2) But you[100] were not able to stop him going. I shall not say to you: "A sense of duty has its own impulses, and strong feelings know no master: he could not stop *you*— weeping."[101] (3) Let me tell you something closer to the

[97] I.e., I accept your account of what happened—and turn it against you.

[98] Cf. 10.2.8, 12.26.3.

[99] By crying the fate of your husband without sparing your eyes.

[100] So you claim.

[101] Just as you were not able to prevent him from going.

aliud putavit. Non erat credibile obstare te redemptioni
4 meae. Interpretatus est maternum metum, et maris domui
nostrae male experti periculum credidit timeri. Nisi[119] tibi
5 non paruisset, nemo non vos putasset colludere. Ceterum
me poterat non redimere, cum tu clamares: "Caeca sum,
oculos desiderio viri perdidi, solitudinem ferre non possum"? Ita ille ad redemptionem meam excusatius profectus esset, si me minus desiderasses? Dubitabitur an tua
6 causa fecerit? Et filium et virum habere non poteras; reddidit tibi quem magis amabas. Siste iam lacrimas, maritum
7 reducem, incolumem accipe. Quid irasceris, quae tanta
mutatio est? Quis hoc crederet? Quereris discessisse
quem odisti, cum eum nolis redisse quem diligis.

8 Atquin si—ut supra probavimus—is parentes in calamitate deserit, qui opem non fert, et—ut nunc ostende-
mus—optimus filius corpore suo adiutoria matri redemit,[120] profecto opem tulit, id est, non deseruit. Nam
si—ut[121] ante dixi—ne[122] vestigio quidem abisse a miseris
licet, ne ipsorum quidem causa, qui adiuvantur, discedere
fas erit, nec cibos saltem petere aut alia usibus necessaria

---

[119] -eri. nisi *Helm[1]* 382: -ens ne si B V Φ*, *at vd. Håk.*: -ens ne
nisi *Dess.[2]*

[120] ‹me› red- *Sh. B.[4]* 197, *sed vd. Str. ap. Zins.*

[121] nam sicut *Reitz.[2]* 43

[122] sine B V, *unde* si ne *Reitz.[2]* 43

---

[102] For this idiomatic meaning of *aliud putare*, see Sen. *Ben.*
4.38.1; Håkanson (2014b, 26).

[103] An addition to the theme.

[104] Cf. 6.19.5.

[105] Cf. 6.2.1.

truth: he was under a wrong impression.[102] It was not credible that you were standing in the way of my being ransomed. (4) He took it as being a mother's dread, and thought the danger she feared was the sea, of which our family had had bad experiences.[103] Had he not disobeyed you, everyone would have thought the two of you were in collusion. (5) But could he fail to go to ransom me when you cried: "I am blind, I have lost my eyes because I pine for my husband, I cannot bear being alone"? Would it have been more excusable for him to go to ransom me if you had longed for me less? Will anyone doubt that he did it for *your* sake?[104] (6) You could not have both son and husband; he gave you back the person you loved more. Now stop crying, welcome your husband home, returned to you safe and sound. (7) Why are you getting angry, what is this great change?[105] Who would have credited it?—you complain of the departure of one you hate,[106] while you would rather the one you love had not come back.

(8) But if, as I proved earlier,[107] to fail to give one's parents aid in misfortune is to abandon them, and if, as I shall now show, this excellent son bought help for his mother at the expense of his own body, surely he did give her aid, that is, he did not abandon her. For if, as I said before, it is not permitted even to be an inch[108] away from the unfortunate, it will be wrong to go away even for the sake of those who are being helped, and there will be no chance even to go in search of food or other necessities of

[106] The son, her hatred for whom is deduced from her present behavior.
[107] Esp. 6.14.4.
[108] Cf. 6.14.1.

9   parare continget. Si vero, dum adiuvatur parens, nihil refert ubi sit ille qui adiuvat, quia praesens cura exhibetur,
quidquid tibi ego praestiti [filio][123] ad auctorem muneris,
id est, ad redemptorem meum, transferendum est. Non
assedi, non consolatus sum, non ministravi, non ‹opem›[124]
tuli, non denique totus tibi redivi? 21. Verum fatendum
est: si desertam te putas, mea culpa est.

2   Sed iam tempus est ista, quae non excusanda[125] debent
videri, verum pulchra atque magnifica, animo maiore defendere et, cum iudicium agatur exempli, tandem causam
suam intellegere. Hoc saltem habebis, miserrime fili,
quod honoratis contingere funeribus solet: defunctus lau-
3 daberis. Omnia licet huc revocemus praeterita, et ad ca-
nendas unius laudes universorum vatum scriptorumque
ora consentiant, vincet tamen res ista mille linguas, ip-
samque—si sit aliqua corpore uno—Facundiam materia
superabit, etiamsi nihil dixero, nisi quod obiectum est.
4 Lucem libertatemque patri filius reddidit, et, quod ante
inauditum est, magis me amavit quam vellem. Ingressus
est maria, in quibus iam minimum periculi tempestas
habet, et, quod inter ista difficillimum est, amore mei vicit

---

[123] *om.* Φ (*cf. ad 6.16.5*), *edd.*: filio B (*gloss. videl. ad illud* ad
auctorem—meum): filii V: ‹pro› filio *Reitz.*[2] 43

[124] *h.l. add. Reitz.*[2] 43: opem non E: *om. cett.*

[125] -anda *Sch.*: -ata *codd.*

---

[109] Son, though far away, made it possible for Father to give
help on the spot (*praesens*) to Mother.

[110] All these things I was able to do only because Son made
them possible. So (cf. below), if you call all that being "abandoned," then it is I who have "abandoned" you.

life. (9) But if, when a parent is being helped, it makes no difference where the helper is, because care is being provided on the spot, all I did for you is to be credited to the person who made my service possible, that is, to my ransomer.[109] Did I not sit by you, did I not wait on you, did I not bring you ⟨help⟩—in a word, did I not return to you in one piece?[110] 21. The truth must be told: if you think you were abandoned, the fault is mine.

(2) But it is time now to defend with more spirit deeds that are not to be reckoned merely excusable, but glorious and splendid, and, since it is a paragon who is being judged, finally to comprehend the real nature of his case.[111] At least, my most unfortunate son, you will receive what customarily attends the funerals of the honored dead: after your death, you will be praised. (3) Summon though we may hither all the feats of the past, and supposing that the mouths of all poets and prose writers sing the praises of a single man in unison, yet this deed will be too much even for a thousand tongues:[112] indeed the topic will surpass Eloquence herself—assuming she were housed in a single body—even if I say no more than what my son is accused of. (4) My son restored light and liberty to his father, and, what is without precedent, he loved me more than I should have wished. He entered upon the high seas, where a storm is the least of dangers, and—something that is hardest in these circumstances—he surpassed even his

[111] I.e., the whole scope of Son's actions and the reasons why he is worthy of being considered an *exemplum*.

[112] I.e., Son's sacrifice exceeds all past acts of heroism and is too great for any encomiast to praise it.

5   etiam matrem suam. Tace, nefaria lingua; ergo tu ista lau-
6   das? Tu melius, uxor, quae facturum retinebas?[126] Obtulit
se captivitati: quia sciebat grave esse alligari, malis patris
successit. Subît libens poenam pietas etiam sceleribus gra-
7   vem. Comparate nunc, si quis patrem per hostes solus
tulit, qui, cum venientia in patrem tela excepisset, simplici
tamen morte defunctus est. Unum legimus, qui vicarias
pro patre non quidem piratis aut mari manus obtulerit, sed
8   ubi redimi posset. Me miserum! Dicendum est quod hoc
ipso admoneor exemplo: in honorem pietatis etiam damn-
ati sepeliuntur.

    22. Haec alii laudant,[127] ego queror. Te quidem, iuve-
nis, omnia saecula loquentur, et admirabile exemplum
tenaci memoriae traditum in ipsa astra sublimem[128] pin-
2   nata Virtus feret; sed mihi ista laus tua caro constat. Non
erat satius lectulo matris incumbere et in huius ministeriis
deditum secura otia impendere? Soli tibi contigerat ut
3   posses patrem excusate non redimere. Me interim, ut coe-

---

126 tu melius—retinebas *huc transp. Håk.[4] 154 ex §6 (post*
gravem), *interrog. dist. Wint.[9]*
127 -dent *vel* -dabunt *Wint.[7] 145*
128 -me *Sch., sed vd. Bur.*

---

113 Cf. 6.8.2 and n. 36.
114 Antilochus, killed by Memnon while covering the escape
of his father, Nestor, who had been surrounded by the enemy
(Pind. *Pyth.* 6.28–42; Auson. *Epitaph.* 7.4).
115 Unlike the wretched son, whose death was painful and
whose corpse was left to rot.
116 Cimon: when his father, Miltiades, was imprisoned for being too poor to pay a fine and died in jail, Cimon offered himself

mother in his love for me. (5) Silence, wicked tongue:[113] will *you* then praise these deeds? Will *you* laud them better, wife, you who held him back when he proposed to do them? (6) He offered himself to captivity: because he knew it was a grave hardship to be put in chains, he took over his father's misfortunes. Dutifulness willingly took upon itself a punishment that would have been harsh even for a criminal. (7) Compare now the man[114] who single-handed carried his father through the ranks of the foe: though he took on his own body the weapons aimed at his father, for all that *he* died a straightforward[115] death. We do read of one son[116] who offered himself as substitute for his father: not, indeed, to pirates or the sea, but in circumstances where he could be ransomed. (8) Ah me! I cannot help but remark what this example itself suggests to me: in honor of dutifulness, even the condemned are buried.[117]

22. Others praise these deeds; *I* lament them. Of you certainly, young man, all ages will speak, and as a wonderful example, entrusted to memory for safe keeping, you will be borne on high to the very stars on the wings of Virtue; but from me your glorious reputation demands a heavy price. (2) Would it not have been better to stay by your mother's bed, and to live a quiet, carefree life devoted to looking after her? You alone had the chance of being able *not* to ransom your father with a good excuse. (3)

as a substitute so that his father could be buried (cf. Val. Max. 5.3.ext.3, 5.4.ext.2; Sen. *Controv.* 9.1; [Quint.] *Decl. min.* 302.5; Lib. *Decl.* 11; Penella [2020, 117–19]).

117 Miltiades had been sentenced to prison and yet was granted burial; Son is still unburied, despite being an example of *pietas*.

perat, tabes lenta consumeret, me, quae debebat sola, senem mors redemisset, et, cum exanime corpus in fluctus
esset abiectum, si contigisset similis tempestas, quod ae-
4 quius erat, tu me, fili, sepelisses. Fefellit te ingenitus honestis animis gloriae amor, spes[129] tibi perpetuae laudis
imposuit. Ubi virtus, ubi pietas? Peristi, miser, et male
5 audis. Non morienti pater adsedi, non aegri caput molliori
sede composui, non fatigatum latus mutavi, non spiritum
excepi. Absens ⟨es⟩ exstinctus; reversus[130] mortem tuam
6 inveni. Nemo aegro vincla laxavit, nemo manus ferro sor-
didas ad accipiendos remisit cibos. Tantum catenarum
7 causa solutus es.[131] Neglectus, despectus—quidni, vilis
senis vicarius—, inter[132] tot ardentissima febrium desideria non habuisti quem posceres. Quomodo te vincula
composuerant, iacuisti. Matrem, patrem, propinquos tan-
8 tum cogitasti. Numquid indulgeo mihi, quod te puto ex-
spirasse[133] in carcere meo?
9   Nondum matri satisfactum est. Quoniam poenas a cadaveribus exigis, audi sequentia tempora. 23. Mors ipsa
filii tui naufragium fecit: per tot fluctus volutatum corpus

---

[129] -es ς: -em *codd.*   [130] ⟨es⟩ exstinctus; rev- *scripsit et*
absens—mortem *dist.* Best 194: exstinctus ev- *codd.*
[131] es ς: est *codd.*   [132] solutus—inter *dist.* Russ.[3]
[133] exsp- E: sp- V: insp- *cett.*

---

[118] The pirates removed the chains from Son's body before
throwing him off-board, not out of human compassion, but only
to reuse them: an addition to the theme.

[119] And this caused more pain, due to the weight of chains on
the suffering limbs. Cf. 5.17.1.

[120] Sc., rather than having been thrown into the sea while still

Meanwhile I should have been consumed by a slow wasting—as I had begun to be—, I should have been freed by death—the only proper ransomer—as an old man; and, after my dead body had been cast into the waves, if a like storm had happened to come up, *you*, my son, would have buried *me*—the fairer outcome. (4) You were misled by the love of glory that is inborn in noble hearts, the hope of eternal fame deceived you. Where now is virtue, where dutifulness? You died, poor boy—and are ill spoken of. (5) I, your father, did not sit by you when you were dying; when you lay ill I did not move your head into a more comfortable position, I did not turn you over when you were tired of lying on one side; I did not receive your last breath. I was not there when ‹you› died; when I returned, I found you dead. (6) No one loosened the bonds on your sick body, no one undid your rust-stained hands to enable you to take food. You were freed only for the sake of the chains.[118] (7) Neglected and looked down upon—of course you were, as the deputy of a worthless old man—you had no one to ask for, amid so many and so heated cravings of fever you had no one to summon to your side. You lay in the posture in which you had been chained.[119] Mother, father, relations you could do no more than imagine. (8) Am I being too kind to myself if I suppose you drew your last breath in my prison?[120]

(9) The mother is not yet satisfied. Since you demand punishment from corpses, listen to what happened next. 23. Death itself shipwrecked your son: his corpse swelled

alive (cf. 5.20.3): a hypothesis aired for the sake of pathos, though contrary to the theme. "My" prison, because I should have died in it myself.

intumuit, tot inlisum scopulis, tam spatiosis tractum hare-
nis; numquam tamen infelicius, quam cum venit in ter-
2 ram. O quam grave est mori! Quanto gravius, quod ego
vivo![134] Superstes filii mei vivo omnibus diis hominibus-
que, sed ante omnis mihi, et invisus et infestus, et, ut[135]
uxoris quoque pietatem perderem,[136] in funere filii divor-
3 tium fecit. Video haec rerum naturae bona, quae filio abs-
tuli. Omnis me aetas mei admonet luctus: senectus, ad
quam non pervenit miser;[137] pueritia, quam nunc[138] transi-
4 vit; adulescentia, in qua periit. Supersum ut, si felicissime
cesserit, rogum meum videam et edaces circa corpus filii
mei flammas; si hoc non contigerit, nigrum cadaver et
deforme etiam ignotis spectaculum. Inter haec mala cre-
detis, puto, si dixero: vellem oculos non habere!
5 Quid nunc amplius[139] ad te, uxor, preces convertam
inritas, male temptatas? Tu vero perge et bono tuo utere.
Felicem te, quod in hac fortuna irasceris! 24. Ad hos[140]
confugiendum est: per communes casus, per calamitatem
meam, humanae calamitatis exemplar, ita vos coniuges
vestrae sic ament, non sic desiderent, ita hoc orbitatis
meae ultimum exemplum sit, ita vobis habere tam pios
filios non necesse sit, miseremini! Si vicarium accipitis,

---

134 *dist. Håk.*[4] *154*
135 et ut *Dess.*[2]: ut V: et B Φ
136 -em V: -e B Φ
137 -er *Reitz.*[2] *63*: -era *codd.*
138 nunc Φ (*cf. OLD*[2] *§4*): non B V: modo *Reitz.*[2] *63*
139 *signum interrog. posuit vulg., amovit Håk.*
140 hos ⟨ς⟩: hoc *codd.*

---

121 A further addition to the theme.

up, tossed on so many waves, dashed against so many rocks, swept across all those stretches of sand; but it was never more unlucky than when it came to land. O how hard it is to die! (2) Yet how much harder for me to *live*! I survive my own son, hated and abhorred by all gods and men, but above all by myself; and, so that I might lose my wife's affection too, she divorced me at my son's funeral.[121] (3) I see around me here all the good things of the world of which I robbed my son. Every stage of life prompts me to grieve: old age, which the poor boy did not attain; childhood, which he just now traversed; youth, in which he died. (4) It remains, at the very best, for me to see my[122] funeral pyre, and the flames circling hungrily around my son's body; or, if this does not come to pass, to see the blackened corpse—a sight loathsome even to strangers. Amid these woes, you will, I think, believe me if I say: I should rather not have eyes!

(5) Why should I now, wife, go on[123] directing my prayers to you any longer, unavailing as they are in their vain attempts? Go on, exploit your advantage. Happy you are indeed, to feel anger in circumstances like these! 24. I must take refuge with these judges here. By our shared experience of human adversity, by my misfortune, a paradigm of human misfortune, pity me: so may your wives love you like this, but not miss you like this, so may this be the last example of a bereavement like mine, so may it not be necessary for you to have sons so dutiful. If you can

---

[122] Father is suggesting that he will build a pyre for Son and himself if he wins the case; if he loses, he himself will lie unburied along with Son (cf. 6.24.3) (AS).

[123] After the vain prayers of 6.8.9–9.4.

2   me proicite! Non invidiosae preces sunt, nihil ominosum
peto.[141] Non laeta sententiam vestram sequetur gratulatio,
non ad templa deducar, sed ad sepulcra. Etiam cum vi-
3   cero, flendum est. Si vero vincimur, ibo in litus miser,
planctibus aves abigam aut me feris obiciam,[142] me corpori
filii mei velut tumulus imponam; iacebimus duo insepulta
4   cadavera. Aut circa singulorum domos, ad[143] genua prae-
tereuntium ibo, et recepto tamen[144] miseris more supplex
non cibos petam, non stipem; mendicabo terram et con-
latas miserantium manu glebas, aut—quod certe licet—
5   filium in mare proiciam: "Iam, crudeles aquae et venti
male secundi, reddo vobis vestrum beneficium; ferte quo
libet, licet ad barbaros, licet ad hostes, licet ad piratas.
Fortasse aliquis iubebit sepeliri; certe, quod sciam, nemo
prohibebit."[145]

[141] nihil ominosum (*vel* -si) *conieci*, peto *Reitz.*[2] 84: nihil hominis impero O: nihilominus impero (-rio D H[ac] S) *cett.*

[142] me—obiciam *huc transp. Håk.*[2] *60 ex §4 (ante* aut circa)

[143] ac *Sch.*

[144] tamen *Håk.*[2] 60: tam *codd.*: iam ς

[145] iam—prohibebit *sermocin. esse (cf. 6.14.6–7) significavi*

accept a substitute, cast *me* out. (2) My prayers are not such as to arouse odium, I ask for nothing of ill omen. No cheerful rejoicing will follow your verdict, I shall be escorted not to temples[124] but to tombs. Even after I win, I must weep. (3) But if we are defeated, I shall go in my wretchedness to the shore; I shall frighten off the birds of prey with my wails, or throw myself in the path of the wild animals. I shall place myself over my son's body like a funeral mound. We shall lie there, two unburied corpses. (4) Or I shall go around the homes of individuals, I shall fall at the knees of passers by.[125] And yet I shall not ask for food or money, as the unhappy usually do: I shall beg for earth and clods brought by the hand of those who pity me, or—and this is surely allowed—I shall cast my son into the sea: (5) "Now, cruel waters and winds fair but foul, I give you back your present;[126] carry it where you will, be it to barbarians, be it to enemies, be it to pirates. Perhaps someone will order burial; at any rate, so far as I know, no one will forbid it."

---

[124] Traditional place to show gratitude for a victory: cf. 4.5.3.
[125] Cf. 6.5.6, 9.23.3.
[126] Cf. 6.7.5.

DECLAMATION 7

INTRODUCTION

This speech is given during a trial for murder.[1] A young man has been killed at night, while he was on his way home; the only witness of the crime was his father, Poor Man, who asserts that the murderer is his long-standing enemy, Rich Man. In the absence of any other witness, Poor Man demands to be subjected to interrogation by torture, so as to corroborate his statement; Rich Man opposes, appealing to the law that prohibits the use of torture on freeborn individuals.

The background for this case is the enmity between Rich Man and Poor Man: in accordance with a tradition going back to the Second Sophistic, Rich Man is a violent character, who enjoys inflicting suffering on his innocent victim and does not refrain from involving his enemy's son in this feud.[2]

DM 7 gives Poor Man's speech. It is based on the assumption that torture is a suitable means of collecting evidence and that a statement extracted by torture is absolutely reliable: the pain inflicted by the torturer, in fact, is regarded as able to overcome any strength of mind in

---

[1] See 1.5 *Hic, hic*; and 11.3 (*dives*) *non putat sibi salvum ut iterum neget* (i.e., after his first denial—during that same murder trial); cf. Breij (2020, 225–26n368).

[2] Cf., e.g., Philostr. *VS* 1.pr.3.2 Stefec. On this motif in Roman declamation, see Santorelli (2014b, 16–22).

the victim (6.5–7.4). Rich Man, on the other hand, objects that Poor Man might still be capable of lying, in his determination to pin the murder of his son on his enemy (7.5–7). In contrasting these two positions, the speaker voices the two traditional approaches to the "commonplace on torture" (*locus de tormentis*): in rhetorical theory, proof by torture is admitted as a *probatio inartificialis* (i.e., not produced through rhetorical argumentation) and considered to be as reliable as any other statement under oath—or even more trustworthy; however, skepticism about the efficacy of torture was allowed, in view of the ability of some individuals to endure pain better than others, and therefore to lie or stay silent even amid their torments.[3]

The main obstacle Poor Man has to face is the law prohibiting him, as a freeborn citizen, from being tortured. This prescription is consistent with actual Roman procedure: torture was admissible only in the case of slaves above the age of fourteen and in general was only to be used in extreme cases;[4] among other limitations, evidence given under torture was not to be trusted in case of a preexisting feud between the involved parties.[5]

To win his case, Poor Man will have to prove that, although the letter of the law (*scriptum*) prohibits torture for any freeborn individual, the intention of the legislator (*voluntas*) was to prevent freeborn citizens from being

[3] Cf., e.g., Quint. 5.4.1–2. See Zinsmaier (2015, 204–6) on this rhetorical debate, and Breij (2020, 32–66) for a full discussion of torture in declamation.

[4] See *Dig.* 48.18 (*De quaestionibus*); Bernstein (2012, 167–68); Zinsmaier (2015, 213 and nn. 46–50).

[5] Ulp. *Dig.* 48.18.1.24, *inimicorum quaestioni fides haberi non debet, quia facile mentiuntur.*

tortured *against their will* (4.1–5)—which is not Poor Man's case.[6]

This is the structure of the speech:[7]

> PROEM 1.1–2.5
> NARRATION 3.1–3
> ARGUMENTATION
>   *Confirmatio* 3.4–6
>   *Refutatio* (ending with a long pathetic *excessus*)
>   4.1–12.7
> EPILOGUE 13.1–5

This speech has been often considered a *controversia figurata*: on this view, Poor Man does not actually want to be tortured, but "seeks to increase his credibility by displaying a *willingness* to be tortured";[8] however, this interpretation seems highly questionable especially in light of 12.5, where a metarhetorical "signal" clarifies that Poor Man is *not* asking for interrogation only to gain sympathy for his calamities.[9]

DM 7 is linguistically and stylistically close to *DM* 16; a dating in the mid-second century AD may be suggested for both speeches.[10] The only known reply to this piece is the speech on behalf of Rich Man by Patarol.[11]

[6] Cf. Breij (2020, 60–66).

[7] Breij (2020, 66–70).

[8] Zinsmaier (2015, 209). Thus already Bernstein (2013, 50–51).

[9] Cf. already Ritter (1881, 114): "It seems that the speaker is genuinely anxious to attain his torture"; and now—albeit with some remaining doubts—Breij (2020, 55–60).

[10] See General Introduction, §4.

[11] (1743, 229–42).

Tormenta pauperis

LIBERUM HOMINEM TORQUERI NE LICEAT. Pauper et dives inimici. Pauperi erat filius. Nocte quadam pauper cum filio revertebatur. Interfectus est adulescens. Offert se pauper in tormenta dicens a divite eum interemptum. Dives contradicit ex lege.

1. Sentio, iudices, plurimum detrahi calamitatibus meis miserationis, quod ad vos detulisse videor nimium fortem dolorem, et tristissimae orbitati hanc[1] quoque accessisse novitatem, quod, cum adversus me tam gravia et crudelia deposcam, patior invidiam hominis exigentis aliena tor-
2 menta. Non possum tamen vel hinc[2] vobis[3] approbare quid patiar, quod mihi non est relicta miseri patris infirmitas.

[1] -tati hanc *scripsi* (*cf. fere 5.1.1*): -tatis mihi (*codd.*) ‹hanc› *Wint.*[7] 145
[2] hinc *Bur.* (*cf. 7.11.3*): in *codd.*: inde *Sch.*
[3] vo- ς: no- *codd.*

Torture for a poor man

IT SHALL BE UNLAWFUL FOR A FREE MAN TO BE TOR-
TURED. A poor man and a rich man were enemies. The
poor man had a son. One night the poor man was coming
home with his son. The young man was killed. The poor
man offers to be tortured, saying his son had been murdered by the rich man. The rich man opposes, appealing
to the law.

(Speech of the poor man)

1. I am aware, judges, that very much of the pity that might
be felt for my calamities is forfeited by the fact that I seem
to have brought before you too brave a grief, and that to a
tragic loss has been added this novel element too, that, in
demanding such serious and cruel measures against *myself*, I am incurring the disfavor that attends one who demands torture for *another*. (2) But I cannot convince you
how much I am suffering precisely because I do not have
left to me the weakness of a wretched father.[1]

---

[1] He *cannot* portray himself as a weak and pitiable father: for
he has offered to be tortured, which is not a sign of weakness.

3   Percussorem filii mei vidi, et miserior sum quam si
nescirem quis occidisset. Fateor igitur, iudices: ipse miror
4 unde ad hoc probationis genus repente confugerim. Veneram tamquam nuntiaturus indubia, manifesta, nec alium
expectaveram[4] publicarum suspicionum de filii mei morte
5 consensum, quam si percussorem videretis omnes. Hic,
hic, ut torquerer, inveni; postquam satis non videbantur
explicare verba quod videram, confugi ad fidem doloris.
Quid faciam, si temeritates quoque nostras conscientia
6 reorum non potest pati? Intellexi miser ratione[5] factum,
qui[6] ut torquerer exegeram, ex quo me dives non putat
aliud in quaestione dicturum. Neque ego, iudices, quemquam vestrum dubitare crediderim, ex qua conscientia,
qua trepidatione descendat ut quis torqueri nolit inimi-
7 cum. Quos nunc putatis cruciatus divitem pati, quem dolorem, quod hoc mihi negat? Quam vellet ideo tantum
filium meum non occidisse, ut mihi posset indulgere tor-
8 menta! An[7] hoc creditis, iudices, divitem facere legum
libertatisque respectu, et reum pro exemplo esse sollicitum? Ille vero nunc laceratur, at sic[8] magis nostro dolore

---

4 expe- B (*def. Reitz.*[2] *36.1*): spe- V Φ
5 miser *Watt*[1], ratione *Wint.*[9] (*coll. 19.10.2*): miseratione *codd.*
6 quid D: quia *Håk.*[2] *62*
7 an ς: ad B V ψ: at *cett.*
8 at sic *scripsi*: etsi E: et sic *cett.*: sed sic *Wint.*[9]

---

2 Because I know who murdered my son, but I am not able to
convict him.

3 Torture.

4 I.e., in court, after he has realized his case is making no
impression.

5 Sc., as well as the accusation itself.

(3) I saw my son's murderer, and I am more wretched than if I did not know who killed him.[2] Indeed, judges, I confess that even I am surprised at the way in which I have resorted to this type of proof[3] so suddenly. (4) I had come here envisaging that I should be reporting to you facts beyond doubt, clear as daylight, and I had expected that members of the public, in their suspicions about my son's death, would take a unanimous view, exactly as if you could all see the murderer before your very eyes. (5) It is here, here[4] that I found the solution: that I should be tortured; after words did not seem to be making what I had seen sufficiently clear, I resorted to proof by pain. What am I to do if the guilty conscience of the defendants cannot endure my bold move either?[5] (6) I have come to realize (ah me!) that this has happened[6] for a good reason: I had demanded to be tortured, and from this demand the rich man deduces that I should not tell a different story if I were put to the rack. I hardly believe that any of you doubt the consciousness of guilt, the panic, that must lie behind unwillingness to have one's enemy tortured. (7) What torments do you think the rich man suffers now, what grief, in denying me this? How dearly he would wish not to have killed my son, just so that he could be in a position to indulge me with tortures! (8) Or can you believe, judges, that a rich man takes this course of action out of respect for laws and liberty,[7] that a guilty man is worried about a precedent being set?[8] In fact *he* is being torn now, but this

---

[6] I.e., Rich Man has opposed my demand to be tortured.

[7] I.e., of my rights as a free man.

[8] This murderer is concerned only to find a way to save himself, regardless of the unfair legal precedent he might set in the process (cf. 7.4.8) (AS).

fruitur: operae pretium est inimico negare tormenta, cum feceris ut velit ipse torqueri.

2. Illud igitur a vobis, iudices, infelicissimus omnium mortalium peto, ne, cum inaudita, incredibilia passus sim, misereri velitis corporis mei; crudelius et indignius est quam torqueri non impetrare tormenta. Est adversorum meorum et ista novitas, quod necesse habetis ea mihi ratione succurrere, qua odissetis alium, nec quicquam est 2 homine infelicius, pro quo tormenta sunt. Percussorem a me filii mei visum esse contendo; facinus est hoc vos non deprehendere, si mendacium est, facinus est hoc me non probare, si verum est. Quod ad me quidem, iudices, pertinet, orbitatis meae repeto praesentiam, et noctem illam rursus ante oculos meos cogitationes reponunt: iam mihi videor et in tormentis esse confessus.

3 Filium, iudices, habui, sicut erecti ac sublimis animi, ita qui nondum suos haberet inimicos, et quem nemo ad-4 huc nisi causa tantum mei doloris occideret. O parentum misera condicio, quam novis inusitatisque patemus insidiis! Nos exasperamus, nos offendimus, inimici tamen liberos nostros oderunt. Quis hoc umquam, iudices, simultatium timuisset ingenium, ut eodem aliquis excogitaret

---

9 Rich Man is waiving an opportunity to inflict pain on his enemy; this does torment him, but not as much as he enjoys seeing Poor Man's anguish as he asks in vain to be tortured.

10 I.e., not wish to relieve me of the agony of bodily as well as mental torture.

11 Sc., by allowing his torture, something which in the case of another would show the judges' hatred.

12 In that case, Poor Man should be charged with *calumnia*.

way he enjoys our suffering more: it is worth an enemy's while to deny torture when you have caused him to *want* to be tortured.[9]

2. So what I, most unhappy of all mortals, ask of you, judges, is that, though I have suffered things unheard of and incredible, you should not wish to feel pity for my body;[10] more cruel and more outrageous than to be tortured is to be refused torture. There is a further novelty in my adverse situation: you have to come to my aid in the way you would show hatred of another,[11] and no one is unluckier than someone for whom torture is a blessing. (2) I assert that I saw my son's murderer; it is a crime for your side not to disprove this, if it is a lie,[12] it is a crime for me not to prove it, if it is true. As far as I am concerned, judges, I am going over and over in my mind the moment when I was present at my own bereavement, and my thoughts keep bringing that night before my eyes once again. I feel as if I have already made my statement, and under torture too.[13]

(3) I had, judges, a son of upright and lofty mind, one, accordingly, who did not yet have enemies of his own, one whom no one would kill yet except to cause *me* grief. (4) How unfortunate we parents are, how open to novel and unheard of plots! *We* provoke, *we* offend, yet it is our children whom our enemies hate. Who would ever, judges, have feared a feud conducted with such ingenuity that a

---

[13] The crime scene keeps coming to my mind so vividly that I feel as if I had *already* given my statement—and under torture, so painful is it for me to remember (AS).

5 animo et quod parcit et quod occidit? Reliqua, iudices,
non debebam[9] nisi in quaestione narrare. Felices illos in
mei comparatione patres, qui perisse liberos suos nuntiis
credunt! Ego sum inaudita malorum novitate percussus,
cuius unicus ideo tantum occisus est, ut viderem.

3. Revertebamur nocte pariter, sicut omnia nos vitae
ministeria iungebant, et homines, quibus non servos prae-
stabat fortuna custodes, tuebamur pauperem mutua pietate comitatum invicem sustinentes, invicem innixi nec
nisi magna percussoris diligentia separandi, cum dives
medio noctis horrore stricto mucrone prosiluit et stupen-
tibus attonitisque miseris confodit illum fortiorem, illum,
2 qui fortassis aliquid in mea morte fecisset. Confiteor, iudices, nihil tunc oculorum meorum diligentia, nihil egit
3 cura miseri patris: percussor voluit agnosci. Vos nunc,
cives, vos, omnes humani generis adfectus, miserrimus
interrogo pater: suadete quid faciam. Hunc, quem videtis
circa me sanguinem, de filii vulneribus excepi; his manibus labentis unici membra sustinui. In oculis adhuc vultus
ille[10] morientis, haerent auribus verba super cadaver ha-
bita exultantis inimici.
4 Fidem tormentorum, quousque percussoris filii mei

9 -beam V D H: -beo E
10 ille B (*def. Hamm.[1] 58*): illius V E: illi D δ: filius β

___

14 I.e., kills the son but spares the father who saw him die:
equally cruel acts.

15 Because it is so painful to tell the story that it would have
to be forced out of him—and also (AS) because speaking under
torture would have enhanced credibility.

16 Cf. 7.9.5.

man should think up in the same frame of mind something that both spares and kills?[14] (5) The rest of the story, judges, I should not have had to tell except under interrogation.[15] Happy, compared with me, those fathers who believe that their sons have died because others report it! *I* am afflicted by an unprecedented twist of fortune: my only son was killed just so that I should be there to see him die.

3. We were coming home at night, together as we always were in the course of our daily routine, and, not being rich enough to have slaves to guard us,[16] we looked after our impoverished company with mutual affection, supporting each other, leaning on each other, inseparable unless a murderer took special pains.[17] Then the rich man, sword drawn, leaped out at the dead of night, and, while we stood there aghast and thunderstruck, stabbed the stronger of us, the one who would perhaps have done something in the event of *my* death. (2) I confess, judges, that the keenness of my eyes, the concern of a stricken father played no part: the murderer *wanted* to be recognized. (3) As a most wretched father, I question you, citizens, I question you, the combined feelings of humanity: advise me what to do. This blood you see upon me I took from my son's wounds; with these very hands I supported the body of my only son as his life ebbed away. I can still see his face as he died, ever in my ears ring the words of my jubilant enemy over his body.

(4) In the name of tortures:[18] for how much longer am

---

[17] Sc., to separate us, by the son's death.

[18] *Fidem tormentorum*, sc., *obsecro* or the like, amounting to: "I appeal to torture, in which I place my trust, to help me."

conscius ero? Aperite pectus istud et totum de visceribus
5 meis latronis egerite secretum. Vidi, et mihi non creditur!
Vidi, ita possim et in tormentis idem dicere! Aut[11] si com-
pono, si fingo, urar, lacerer, et non probem. Si videtur,
6 torquendus sum, iudices, ut hoc desinam dicere. Nec me,
iudices, fallit, quantam molem accusationis etiam in manifesta veritate susceperim: divitem detuli reum pauper,
inimicus, occisi pater, et postulo ut mihi credatur testimonium in mea orbitate dicenti. Itaque non deprecor
quominus mihi velitis irasci;[12] donec probem, torquete
tamquam mentientem.

4. "Lex" inquit "liberum hominem torqueri vetat." Per
fidem, iudices, quis non hoc eum respondere credat, cuius
2 tormenta poscantur? Nemini, iudices, credo dubium legem, quae torqueri liberum hominem vetat, hoc pro-
spexisse tantum, ne quis torqueretur invitus, et iura, quae
nos a servilium corporum condicione secernunt, impa-
3 tientiae tantum succurrisse nolentium. Omnium beneficiorum ista natura est, ut non sit necessitas, sed potestas;
quicquid in honorem alicuius inventum est, desinet pri-
vilegium vocari posse, si cogas. Cuncta, si videtur, iura
percurrite: nusquam adeo pro nobis sollicita lex est ut,
4 quod praestat, extorqueat. Dedit caeco talionis actionem:

---

[11] at *Franc.*
[12] *h.l. gravius dist. Håk.: post* probem *vulg.*

---

[19] For I know his identity yet am failing to get him convicted.
[20] = "If you deem it appropriate" (as in 7.4.3). Poor Man will
not cease his claims as to what he saw; so the judges should let
him be tortured, if only to silence him.
[21] Cf. 11.5.3.

I to be the accomplice of my son's murderer?[19] Open up this breast and dig the brigand's secret out of my inward parts. (5) I saw, yet I am not believed! I saw, so may I have the strength to say the same even under torture! Or if I am lying, if I am making it up, may I be burned, torn to pieces—and fail to prove it. If you will,[20] let me be put to the torture, judges, to make me stop saying this. (6) I am well aware, judges, how heavy a burden of accusation I have taken on, even where the truth is quite obvious: I have brought to court a rich man, though I am myself poor, his enemy, father of the man he killed—and here I am demanding to be believed when I give evidence on the death of my son! So I do not ask you not to be angry with me; until I prove my point, torture me as if I were lying.

4. "The law" he says "forbids a free man to be tortured." Heavens, judges: who would not think this was an objection raised by a man being summoned for torture? (2) I think no one, judges, doubts that the law forbidding the torture of a free man envisaged merely that no one should be tortured against his will, and that the rights that mark our bodies off from those of slaves brought help only to those unable and unwilling to endure it. (3) The nature of every concession is that it is not obligatory, but offers a possibility. If compulsion is applied, whatever was designed as an honor for someone will cease to deserve the name of privilege. Go through all the statutes, if you please: the law is never so anxious to promote our interests that it extorts what it grants. (4) It gave to the blinded man an action for like-for-like punishment:[21] but it surely does

[QUINTILIAN]

num manus recusantis impellit? Iniuriarum caesis[13] agere
permisit, sed non cogit invitos. Adeo paene[14] levius est
5 ultionem perire quam potestatem. Genus servitutis est
coacta libertas et eadem iniquitas, quicquid de invito homine facias. Vis scire quid lex ista prospexerit? Non exigo
ut[15] torquearis.

6   Quam multa, dii deaeque, non minus sunt iusta quam
lex! Exigit quarundam invidia rerum ut vinci se consue-
tudo[16] patiatur, et quicquid accidisse mireris, tantundem
poscit in ultione novitatis. Filius in conspectu patris occi-
7 sus est; torquete securi: nihil iniquius fieri potest. Ignos-
cant persuasiones, si facinus istud omnium inlicitarum
rerum consumpsit invidiam, et, unde tormentis salva iustitia est, plus est de quo quaeritur quam quo modo quae-
8 rendum est. Nullum debet iniquum[17] videri genus probationis esse quod solum est, et quicquid potuit prodesse
veritati[18] numquam nocuit exemplo. Sufficit libertatis

13 -sis *Obr.*: -dis *codd.*
14 *del. Sh. B.*[2] *198, Sh. B.*[4] *197–98*
15 ut <tu> *Wint.*[9], *fort. recte*
16 consuet- *Håk.*[2] *62–63:* magnit- *codd.*: mansuet- *olim Håk.*
necnon *Watt*[2] *24*   17 -iqu- *B. Asc.*[1] *xlvii v.*: -imic- *codd.*
18 ve- *Håk.*[4] *154–55:* seve- *codd.*

---

22 *Iniuria* covers all wrongdoings causing a physical or moral
offense. Against the wrongdoer an *actio iniuriarum* was available,
leading to monetary compensation and to the offender's loss of
social standing (*infamia*).

23 Rich Man. Poor Man does not demand (though he would
gladly do so) that Rich Man be tortured, because the law would
not allow him to be tortured against his will.

not force the hand of someone who declines to exact the penalty. It permitted those who are struck to bring an action for injury,[22] but it does not compel them to do so if they do not wish to. Indeed, loss of revenge is almost less burdensome than loss of freedom to choose. (5) Liberty under duress is a kind of slavery and at the same time an act of injustice, whatever you make a man do against his will. Do you want to know what this law had in mind? I do not demand that *you*[23] be tortured.

(6) How many things, gods and goddesses, are no less just than the law![24] The stigma attaching to certain things requires that customary procedure allow itself to be overridden, for every remarkable event demands an equivalent degree of novelty in its punishment. A son has been killed as his father looked on; torture away, have no fear!—nothing can be done that is more unjust.[25] (7) Let public opinion be understanding,[26] for this crime surpassed all illicit things in its hatefulness: what is being investigated is more important than the method of the investigation, and this justifies the use of torture in such a case. (8) No type of proof should be thought unjust if it is the only type available, and anything that is able to help establish the truth never forms a harmful precedent.[27] Sufficient respect for the status of a free man is shown by the fact that

[24] = Many things are fair and just, though not enshrined in law.

[25] The crime is so heinous that no way of dealing with it could be ruled out of order.

[26] I.e., forgive the use of torture in this case (DAR).

[27] Cf. 7.1.8 and n. 8.

reverentiae quod torquetis inviti, quod contra me non[19]
alius invenit.[20]

5. LIBERUM TORQUERI NON LICET. Hoc est, iudices,
propter quod filium meum dives coram me non timuit
2 occidere. Filium igitur meum in conspectu meo occisum
esse contendo. Quid dicitis? Ita non erat contra proclamationis huius fidem, si nunc agere possem quietum mo-
3 destumque miserum? Vultis, cum hoc viderim, tantum
testimonium dicam? Mirum hercules si scindo vestes,
nudo corpus, ignes, flagella deposco? Insaniat necesse est
4 pater, cum solus hoc sciat. Fallitur, iudices, quisquis hoc,
quod postulo, contemptum, quisquis audaciam vocat: filius urit, exagitat, et inter tormenta fugio dolorem. Si men-
tientis est velle torqueri, invenite quid facere debeat qui
verum dicit et non probat.
5 "Mentiris" inquit. Bene quod et tu fateris non esse mihi
sine quaestione credendum. Et quas, per[21] fidem, mendacio meo causas, dives, adsignas? Ignoro percussorem,
deinde te potissimum, de quo quererer, elegi? An scio,
et simultatibus nostris occasionem[22] orbitatis indulgeo?
6 Decipi me non potuisse manifestum est: filius meus, cum

---

[19] om. B (prob. Tos. 143)   [20] invenit codd. (cf. ThlL
VII.2.147.72–75): id petit (-iit Wint.[9]) Sch.
[21] quas per ς: qua spe codd.
[22] -ne Sh. B. teste Wint.[9]

---

[28] The judges.   [29] Except me.   [30] = choosing to be
tortured.   [31] Rich Man knew that the judges would not consider Poor Man a reliable witness (cf. 7.3.6) unless his evidence
was given under torture; but he was not afraid that this might
happen, since the law forbade that. See also 7.9.6, 7.12.6.

you[28] torture me against your will, that nobody else[29] has thought up against me what *I* have.[30]

5. IT IS UNLAWFUL FOR A FREE MAN TO BE TORTURED. This, judges, is why the rich man was not afraid to kill my son in front of me.[31] (2) Yes, I contend that my son was killed under my very eyes. What do you say?[32] Would it not damage the credibility of my assertion if I, in these circumstances, were able to play the part of a quiet and unassuming man in distress? (3) After I've seen this happen, do you want me merely to give evidence? Is it surprising, by heaven, if I rend my clothes, bare my body, call for flames and tortures? A father cannot but play the madman, when he is the only person who knows the facts. (4) Anyone, judges, who calls my request an act of contempt,[33] calls it reckless, is mistaken: it is my son who burns and harasses me, and amid my tortures I am escaping from my grief.[34] If wanting to be tortured implies that one is lying, then find out for me what a man ought to do if he is telling the truth but cannot prove it.

(5) "You lie," he says. It is excellent that even you confess that I am not to be believed unless I am tortured. And what reasons for my lying can you suggest, rich man, I ask you? Is it that I do not know the murderer, but then chose you in particular to accuse? Or that I do know, and am using my loss as an opportunity to pursue our feud?[35] (6) It is obvious I could not have been mistaken: my son

[32] Judges.   [33] I.e., making light of my torture, indifference to what happens to me.

[34] Under torture I will stop grieving for my son, for I will then be acting to avenge him.   [35] By prosecuting my enemy rather than the real murderer of my son. See also 7.11.4.

pariter rediremus, occisus est. An dinoscere percussorem
nocte non potui, cum percussor potuerit eligere, fugere?[23]

7 Quid ais? Iuvenem meum alius occidit, et tu mihi solacium ultionis imples? Te accuso scilicet, ut interim ne-
8 scioquis ille fugiat, evadat? Quod tu mihi genus furoris
adsignas, ut maximi sceleris ultio pereat falsae accusationis incerto! Homo, qui me vidisse contendo, cum occi-
deres filium meum, nisi de te vindicor, non reliqui mihi ut
hoc de aliis probarem. 6. O te extra omnes humanorum
pectorum adfectus, inimice, sepositum, nunc qui me putas
posse mentiri! Perdidi infelix illum cariorem pauperibus
2 adfectum. Succurrere mihi putas quod aliquando dissedi-
mus? Falleris, deciperis: hominis, cuius occisus est filius,
unus inimicus est. Sane possit aliquis hanc doloris simula-
tionem[24] mendacio perferre verborum; torqueri volo: nihil
3 est tanti, nisi verum. Videlicet inter ignes ac flagella sufficit mihi, si dixero: "Hic est inimicus, anime, qui nobis
subinde maledixit, hic ille contumeliosus, ille impotens"?
Ego nescio an mihi possit in quaestione sufficere quod
vidi![25]

4   Atqui inimicus me contendit odio velle torqueri, tor-

---

23 fugere *del. Wint.*[3]
24 si- *Sh. B.*[1] *76 (cf. 2.19.1, 3.13.5):* dissi- *codd.*
25 *gravius dist. Sh. B.*[2] *198*

---

36 Anxious as I am to have the real murderer convicted (see
7.5.4).   37 Poor men (more than rich men) need loving sons
to look after them.   38 The killer.

39 I cannot be lying: my wish to go as far as to be tortured
guarantees that.

was killed while we were coming home side by side. Was I not able to recognize the killer in the darkness?—after all the killer could see well enough to choose his victim, then run away. (7) What do you say? Another man killed my son, and you are giving me the revenge I need to console me? Can it really be true that I am accusing *you* now so that, in the meantime, some unknown can get away and escape? (8) What kind of madman do you suppose me, to lose the chance of revenging the worst of crimes for the sake of a false accusation with no certainty of success? I claim I saw what happened when you were killing my son; if I fail to have you punished, I have left myself no room to pin the crime on others. 6. How devoid you are, my enemy, of all human feelings! How do you imagine I can be lying *now*?[36] I have lost the source of affection that is more important for the poor.[37] (2) Do you think it occurs to me now that we were once at variance? You are wrong, you are deceived. A man whose son has been killed has only one enemy.[38] One might well carry through such a pretense of grief as long as one lies with *words*; but I want to be *tortured*: nothing is worth that except the truth.[39] (3) Of course, it suffices me if amid the fires and the whips I say to myself: "This, my heart, is the enemy who often cursed us, who insulted us, who is beyond reason"?[40] In fact, I don't even know if under interrogation it can suffice me that I was an eyewitness!

(4) But my enemy claims that if I want to be racked, if

---

[40] Ironic. The thought of his enmity with Rich Man will not help Poor Man to stand up to torture; nor (he goes on to say) may the thought that he saw Rich Man kill his son.

menta postulare.[26] En ad quod confugiat homo, qui se
5 sciat posse mentiri! Nulla est ratio quaestionum relicta
mortalibus, si adiuvant contra veritatem, et sublata est de
rebus humanis necessitatis huius utilitas, si causam[27] ultro
6 tuetur explicatque fingentibus. Hucusque durant ‹adversus›[28] artis ingenia mortalium ut,[29] licet sit aliquis secreti
firmitate compositus, hominem tamen ultra non sequa-
tur[30] animus. Non vacat adserere quae finxeris tunc, cum
vix prodest et verum fateri, et nemo non contra id torque-
7 tur, quod dixit ante tormenta. Non refert, cuius ad ecu-
leum nominis persuasionem, quas silentii adferas causas:
in quaestionibus tantum corpora sumus, et nemo non con-
8 tra aliquem torquetur adfectum. Exigam quaestionem an
recusem, quid interest tormentorum, brevi futurus similis
homini qui fateatur invitus?[31] Novum, iudices, inauditum-
que rebus humanis aperitur exemplum: 7. nemo umquam
ideo torqueri non debuit, quia mentiretur.

2   Sed etsi[32] fas est, iudices, dubitare de fide quaestionum, alius debet esse suspectus: ille scilicet, in quo servi-

---

[26] atqui . . . odio . . . postulare *Str.*[16] (*q.v. de interpunct.*): et
quod . . . ideo . . . postulo *codd.*   [27] si causam *Sch.* (*corrob.*
Håk.[4] 155): si iam B Φ: suam V   [28] ‹adversus› (*vel* ‹contra›)
Wint.[7] 145–46   [29] ut *Wint.*[7] 145–46: et *codd.*
    [30] -qua- *Wint.*[7] 145–46: -qui- *codd.*
    [31] exigam—invitus *dist. Sh. B.*[2] 198   [32] si S

---

[41] Sc., and that I would therefore lie under torture.
[42] Sarcastic = I'd hardly have asked to be tortured if I knew I
was capable of lying under torture (cf. what follows) (AS).
[43] I.e., "father"—which will not influence the torturer anyway.
[44] = his intentions and emotions.

I ask for torture, it is out of *hatred*.[41] Look at what a man who knows he is capable of lying is resorting to![42] (5) There is no point left for mortals in conducting interrogations if they help to counter the truth: the usefulness of this means of compulsion is lost to human affairs, if it goes out of its way to defend and expedite a case for people who make things up. (6) The natures of mortal men last out ⟨against⟩ the arts of torturers only so far that, even if someone is firmly resolved to keep a secret, the mind cannot go on beyond the limit of human endurance. There is no room to maintain a lie in circumstances where it scarcely helps even to confess the truth: everyone is tortured just to make him deny what he said before being tortured. (7) It makes no odds what authoritative name,[43] what reasons for silence you bring to the rack: on the rack we are only flesh and blood, and everybody is tortured precisely to break some frame of mind in him.[44] (8) Whether I demand or refuse to be questioned under torture, is of no concern to the torments:[45] before very long, I shall be just like a man who confesses against his will. Novel, judges, and unheard of is the precedent that is being set to human affairs: 7. no one was ever forcibly refused torture on the ground that he was lying.

(2) But even admitted, judges, that it is possible to doubt the reliability of interrogation, another person ought to be suspect:[46] one, that is, in whom the recesses

---

[45] I.e., the torments (personified, as in 7.7.7) will not be influenced by my spontaneous request to be tortured: they will aim at getting the *truth* out of me.

[46] Torture may sometimes fail to elicit the truth—but only when it is applied to a slave, used to corporal punishment.

lium pectorum recessus, in quo verniles excutiuntur artus.[33] Quotiens tortori est rixa cum membris, tum cruciatus
3 agnoscit adsiduis suppliciis durata patientia. At[34] homo cui
omnino[35] est nova res dolor, corpus applicat[36] quod scissa
lacerataque veste primum ferre non potest pudorem,
quod nescit ad flagellorum vices membra componere nec
ullo verbera frangit occursu. Nos, inquam, sumus, quos
4 leges supervacuum putavere torqueri. Unde nobis inter
ista secretum? In tormentis libero homini opus est patientia, ut verum dicat.
5   "Sed" inquit "ideo torqueri non debes, quia exigis ut
torquearis." Aliud sunt, inimice, tormenta, aliud velle tor-
6 queri. Felices illos, qui recusare voluerunt! Meretur clementiam et favorem quisquis ad illa tremens exanimisque
perducitur, quem vix a genibus tortor abducit, cui iam
7 scissas quoque difficile possis eripere vestes. Ego quemadmodum vultis deprecer, qui videor provocasse torto-
rem? Ille, ille sine ulla miseratione laceratur, cui ad singulos ictus dicitur: "Ipse voluisti," quem non decet rogare,
qui creditur fingere proclamationes, simulare gemitus, de

---

[33] -tes *Bur.*, sed cf. 7.12.3
[34] at *Sh. B.*[2] *198–99: et codd.*: sed *Bur.*
[35] homo cui omnino *Dess.*[2]: homini non *codd.*
[36] -cat (*sc. eculeo*) *scripsi*: -cari π: -citum A β: -citi *cett.*: -co
Breij[3] *15* (-cui *Sch.*)

---

[47] Sc., and so can endure.

[48] To the rack.

[49] Free men.　　[50] Let alone lies.　　[51] For all pain is
diminished when one can prepare for it in advance (cf. 11.8.2–
6)—which enables him to lie even under torture.

of a slave's breast, the limbs of a household servant are
under examination. Whenever a torturer is fighting with a
slave's joints, then patience hardened by constant punishments recognizes[47] the agonies as familiar to him. (3) A
man, on the contrary, for whom pain is something entirely
unusual, submits[48] a body which, once the clothes have
been rent and torn apart, cannot, before anything else,
stand the shame of it, a body which does not know how to
adjust the limbs to the alternating blows of the whip, and
does not lessen their force by any meeting of them half-
way. It is we,[49] I say, whom the laws thought it pointless to
torture. (4) How can we keep a secret amid all this? Under
torture a free man needs endurance to be able to tell the
truth.[50]

(5) "But" he says "you ought not to be tortured precisely because you demand to be tortured."[51] Tortures are
one thing, enemy, wanting to be tortured another.[52] (6)
Happy they who would have liked to refuse![53] Mercy and
favor are deserved by anyone[54] who is led to the interrogation trembling and frightened out of his wits, whom the
torturer can scarcely drag up from his knees, from whom
it is barely possible to tear off clothes that are already in
tatters. (7) How do you want *me* to beg myself off, when
it looks as if I have provoked my torturer? He, yes he, is
torn apart mercilessly to whom at each blow is said, "You
asked for it!", for whom it is not appropriate to beg, who
is believed to be feigning his shrieks, faking his groans, on

---

[52] Being tortured by choice is worse, because you do not have
the comfort of being pitied (DAR). Cf. 7.7.6–7.

[53] Sc., torture.

[54] But not me, who asked for it.

quo primum videntur vindicanda tormenta. 8. Non invenio, iudices, quid sperare possit, qui mentitur et exigit
quaestionem. Homini, qui vult torqueri, diu non creditur
2 nec verum dicenti. Nec est, iudices, quod putetis adeo
mihi tristissimam orbitatem omnis humanorum pectorum
rapuisse sensus, ut non intelligam petere me quo[37] dives
possit evadere, et paene magis pro percussore torqueri.
3 Sed quid me facere vultis? Non debeo posse mentiri,
homo qui, cum filius meus occideretur, interfui.[38] Veritati
tantum praesto patientiam: exigo quaestionem, in qua
quid dicturus sim, nescio; quid debeam dicere, "Vidi,"[39]
4 scio. Vultis post hoc argumentis, suspicionibus agam? Bre-
viora[40] tormenta sunt!
5   Non invenio, iudices, cur renuat tantopere dives
quaestionem, postquam[41] supersunt adhuc incerta ac du-
bia. Facinus est tamen me non torqueri, si mihi torto uti-
6 que credendum est. Quousque me, crudelissime mortalium, metus dissimulatione[42] deludis?[43] Ego magis, qui
postulo tormenta, timeo, ego, qui nihil facere potui, cum
7 viderem. Suspecta tibi est nostra patientia?[44] Vides enim,

---

[37] quo *Håk.*[2] 63: quod *codd.*   [38] *h.l. gravius dist. vulg.*:
post mentiri *Breij*[2]   [39] *sic dist. Wint.*[7] *146*: iudices (*i.e.* iud)
coni. Sch.   [40] levi- *Håk.*[3] *128*: veri- *Håk.*   [41] post quam
Håk.[2] *63–64, sed vd. 7.11.7*   [42] dissi- *Breij*[2] (*cf. 7.1.6–7*): si-
codd.   [43] -des *Håk.*   [44] *interrog. dist. Håk.* (*cf. 5.11.4–5*)

---

[55] By asking to be tortured one shows contempt for torture
and the pain it can inflict: so torture itself (here personified, as in
7.6.8) will need to take revenge on nobody more than him.
[56] Poor Man might well break down under torture and retract
his own statement (7.13.4; cf. 7.8.9); Rich Man would then be
acquitted precisely thanks to torture.

whom tortures themselves above all—it seems—have to exact their revenge.[55] 8. I do not see, judges, what someone who lies and then asks to be interrogated can be hoping to gain. A man who wants to be tortured is long disbelieved even if he is telling the truth. (2) Nor, judges, should you think that my tragic bereavement has so robbed me of my common sense that I fail to see that I am asking for something that might result in the rich man getting away, and that my being tortured is almost to the advantage of the killer.[56] (3) But what do you want me to do? I must be incapable of lying: I was there when my son was being killed. It is only to the truth that I am offering my endurance: I am asking for an interrogation in which what I *shall* say, I do not know; what I *must* say—"I saw him!"—, I do know. (4) Do you want me after all this to deal in proofs and conjectures? Tortures take less time!

(5) I do not see any reason, judges, why the rich man should so firmly reject an interrogation when there still remain points of uncertainty and doubt.[57] But it is outrageous that I am not tortured, if I am to be believed without question only after torture.[58] (6) How long, cruelest of mortals, do you mock me by hiding your fear?[59] Still *I*, who demand to be tortured, am even more a prey to fear, I who was unable to do anything when I saw what I saw. (7) You find my ability to withstand pain worrying? Of course you

[57] See previous note.

[58] Poor Man's testimony is not deemed trustworthy at present, but would be credible once confirmed by torture; it is thus outrageous that he should be denied the only possible way to earn the judges' trust.

[59] Sc., of what I could say under torture.

hortatur nos contra dolorem primae robur aetatis, solidum
8 plenumque corpus. Quam facilis, quam expedita res est
torquere[45] miserum! Adfero ad quaestionem iam planctibus membra liventia;[46] quantum animae, quantum sanguinis orbitas traxit, quanto imbecilliora sunt haec cotidianis
lamentationibus everberata vitalia! Quicquam ergo fingere potest hic pallor, haec macies et[47] iam torto similis
9 infirmitas? Adice[48] quod nihil minus in quaestione diu
possis dicere, si mentiaris, quam quod oculis scias, et bre-
vissimum confessionis est genus destituisse[49] quod videris.
9. Felices, dives, quos tortor interrogat, qui non habent in
sua potestate caedentis![50] Impatientissima res est posse,
cum velis, desinere torqueri.
2   "Quin potius" inquit "probas?" Fiduciam hominis, qui
3 sciat hoc me vidisse solum! Sine dubio, dives, multa te
poterant argumenta convincere, si deferret alius, et eras
manifestissimus reus, nisi[51] mihi percussor quaerendus esset. Quis enim credibilior in caede pauperis quam dives
inimicus, aut de quo facilius constare posset scelere,
⟨quam⟩[52] quod non habet nisi de sola ultione ⟨ratio-

---

45 -re *Håk.*[2] *64*: -ri *codd.*

46 liven- γ β: laban- B: liben- V H: laben- O

47 haec *Klotz*[1]   48 -ce V E: -cere *cett.*: -ce eo *Leh.*

49 destitui- *Leh.*: distuli- *codd.*   50 caedentis (-es) *Helm*[1]
364–65: credentis (-es V) *codd.* (*frustra def. Håk.*[2] *65.33*)

51 nisi *Russ.*[2] *147*: si *codd.*

52 *add.* π: -lere, quod ⟨testem⟩ n. h., n. de s. u.? *Dess.*[1] *89–90*

---

60 Ironic: he is in a poor state, as he goes on to say.

61 Once you are under torture, it is hard not to utter the simple words "I did not see" and so be freed from all suffering: cf.
7.3.5, 7.8.3.

do, for—as you see—the first strength of youth, a tough and robust body, encourage me to stand up to pain.[60] (8) How easy, how straightforward it is to torture a man in distress! I bring to the interrogation limbs already livid with the blows I have struck in my grief. How much life, how much blood has the loss of my son drained away, how much weaker are these organs that have been battered by daily laments! Can then this pallor, this wasted body, and a weakness so like the weakness of one who has already been tortured, manufacture a lie? (9) Add that under interrogation, if you are lying, there is no statement less capable of being maintained for a long time than a claim to ocular knowledge: the briefest sort of confession is to disavow what you saw.[61] 9. Happy, rich man, are those whom the torturer interrogates, who do not have those who flog them in their power![62] Most intolerable is to be able to stop being tortured when you wish.

(2) "Why don't you prove it instead?" he says. O the confidence of a man who knows I was the only person to see it! (3) Of course, rich man, many proofs could have refuted you if someone else were laying the charge, and you would be quite obviously guilty, were it not *I* who had to identify the murderer. For who would be a more likely candidate for a poor man's murderer than a rich enemy? What crime could be easier to agree about ⟨than⟩ one where ⟨the motive⟩ is revenge pure and

[62] The voluntary victim (the free man) is really in charge of the situation and can pull out if he wishes; but this is actually worse than being a purely passive victim (DAR).

4 nem>?[53] Non invenit multa verba vidisse, nec mihi debet
5 perire probatio ista quia poteras et ⟨alia⟩[54] accusari. Exigit
probationes, cum facinus sic disposuerit, ne possit pro-
bari. Quem mihi nox testem, quos praestare potuit oculos
6 nuda semper,[55] incomitata paupertas? Tibi servus a conscientia sceleris summovendus fuit et ista ratione, ⟨ne⟩[56]
quis interesset, quem putares posse torqueri, et[57] totum
facinus in has angustias redegisti, ut illud soli scirent qui
7 faciebat[58] et cui non crederetur. Numquid dubitaretis credere,[59] si alius sciret hoc scelus? Facinus est ideo filii mei
8 perire vindictam, quia pater vidi. Ego vero, iudices, et ex
hoc, quod recusat dives quaestionem, partem probationis
implevi: accusatoris tormenta numquam timebit reus, nisi
de quo credi potest et ante tormenta.

9   "Cur," inquit, "si mihi causae sceleris simultates nostrae erant, non te potius occidi?" Saeve,[60] crudelis: ego te
hoc maxime argumento percussorem probo, quod mihi
10 pepercisti. Tuum fuit hoc, inimice, commentum, occiso

---

[53] add. Håk. coll. 7.9.10   [54] add. Reitz.[2] 36: ⟨aliter⟩ Wint.[9]
[55] dist. Håk.   [56] add. Reitz.[2] 36
[57] del. Reitz.[2] 36: en Helm[1] 364   [58] -at Bur.: -ant codd.
[59] credere β (def. Håk.[2] 64–65): credi quaerere B: quaerere
vel que- V γ δ   [60] -di? saeve Håk.[2] 65 (-dissem? s. Dess.[2]):
-disse ve B: -dissem ve V Φ*

---

[63] In fact, only one: "Vidi" (cf. 7.8.3).

[64] I.e., on proofs and arguments. Compared to these, an eyewitness statement is a much quicker way of proving (cf. previous
note), not to be discarded lightly (AS).

[65] = eyewitnesses.

simple? (4) But it doesn't take many words[63] to say "I saw him," so this way of proving ought not to be lost to my case only because the accusation against you could also have been founded on ‹different evidence›.[64] (5) He demands proofs after so arranging his crime that it could *not* be proved. Could the night have provided me with a witness? What eyes[65] could poor people, always unguarded and unaccompanied,[66] have provided? (6) As for you, you had to prevent a slave of yours from being aware of the crime with this further aim, that ‹no› one should be present whom you thought[67] could be tortured: so you reduced the whole outrage to this narrow compass, that it should be known to two persons only—one who did it and one who would not be believed.[68] (7) Would you judges have any hesitation in believing him, if someone *else* had knowledge of this crime? It is outrageous for my revenge of my son to be thwarted just because it was I, his father, who saw. (8) However, judges, I have completed part of my proof by pointing to the very fact that the rich man refuses inter-rogation. A defendant will never be afraid of the accuser being tortured, except where belief can be accorded even before the torments begin.

(9) "Why" he says "did I not rather kill *you*, if the mo-tive for the crime was our feuding?" Ruthless and cruel man, I prove you to be the murderer with *that* proof above all, that you spared me. (10) This, enemy, was your design:

66 Cf. 7.3.1.

67 Rich Man had foreseen that a slave present at the crime scene was likely to be tortured, but not that a free man would *demand* to be.

68 Cf. 7.12.3.

filio servare patrem. Parcendi tamen mihi vel haec fuit
ratio, quod defendi non poteras, si duo perissemus. 10.
Audire mehercules mihi videor illas cogitationes, illa scelerum secreta consilia: "Quid mihi cum vulneribus, quid
cum cruore consumptae et iam paene abeuntis animae?
Occidatur potius ille iam iuvenis, iam inimicus; de sene
2 vindicabitis me, patris oculi." Vis mirer quod me nolueris
occidere? Queri mehercules te puto quod in senectute
3 magni doloris vita brevis est. Pepercisti mihi quomodo
excogitant artes detinere supplicia, et de pereuntibus magis saevitia fruitur[61] dolore suspenso. Agnosco noctis illius,
inimice, clementiam: quod me torqueri non vis ex hoc
venit, quod neque occidisti.

4   Temptat, iudices, efficere dives ut incredibile videatur
quod occisum ab eo contendo filium. Dicturum ⟨me⟩[62]
nunc putatis magis interesse securitatis ut quis facinus sibi
tantummodo credat, et id tutius esse inimico patrante[63]
5 quam conscio?[64] Plus est quod affirmo: filium in conspectu
patris occidere sic operae pretium est, si illud ipse facias.
Perdit plurimam[65] de sceleribus voluptatem qui mandat,

---

[61] fruitur *Gron.*: eruitur B Φ: eruit V
[62] *addidi* (*cf.* 2.23.2, 7.1.6, 8.9.5, 16.7.4, 18.8.4, 19.6.2)
[63] -trante *Sh. B.*[3]: -tre *codd.*   [64] *sic dist. Sh. B.*[2] 199
[65] -mam M: -mum *cett.*

---

[69] In addition to the cruel wish to have the father see the son
die and not die himself (7.10.1).   [70] For in that case Rich
Man would have been the prime suspect.   [71] Poor Man's.

[72] A "striking reminiscence" (Breij [2016, 280n21]) of Sen.
Thy. 895, *Quod sat est, videat pater* ("Let the father see it—that
is enough [sc., for my revenge]").

to kill the son and leave the father alive. But there was also[69] this motive for sparing me: you would have had no way of defending yourself, if we had both died.[70] 10. By heaven, I think I am listening in on those thoughts, that secret plotting of the crime: "What do I want with the wounds, with the blood of a worn out and almost departing life?[71] Rather let the victim be one who is by now a youth, by now an enemy. It is for you, a father's eyes, to avenge me on the old man."[72] (2) Do you expect me to be surprised that you did not want to kill me? By heaven, I think you are really complaining that, in old age, life subject to great pain is short.[73] (3) You spared my life in the same way as skilled torturers devise ways to prolong the punishment: when men are dying, savagery enjoys their pain more if it is held in suspense. I recognize, enemy, the clemency you displayed that night: you don't want me to be tortured now for the same reason that you did not kill me then either.

(4) The rich man, judges, is trying to make my assertion that he killed my son look incredible. Do you think <my> next move will be to say that it is less dangerous to entrust a crime to oneself alone, and that it is safer when an enemy does the deed rather than some accomplice? (5) What I in fact assert is more than that: to kill a son in front of his father is only worth the effort if you do it yourself. Much of the pleasure in a crime is lost to someone who merely commissions it, for things that are only reported provide

[73] Rich Man did not kill (the old) Poor Man because he wanted him to live on to suffer—but is sorry it will not be for very long.

[QUINTILIAN]

6 et minus gratiae rebus ex nuntio venit. Occidet alius te
   iubente, sed vulneribus illis non fruentur oculi, sed plus
   est ut singultibus abeuntis animae, ut cruore satieris, ut
7 conlapsum palpitantemque videas—ut me vidente. Convenit, iudices, quod ipse dives hoc fecit et quod ego vidi.
   Ratio saevitiae est ut aliquis coram eo[66] occidatur, propter
   quem occiditur.
      11. Fidem vestram, iudices, ne me ideo non putetis
   vidisse, quia nihil feci. Servulorum iste libertorumque
   dolor est occiso homine statim scire quid facias, excla-
   mare, procurrere, fidem deorum hominumque testari,
2 postea cum lacrimis venire.[67] Vultis percussorem invadam,
   vultis fugientem sequar? Interim deficientem quis exci-
   piet, cui se morientis imponet infirmitas? Scis profecto,
   percussor, facinus ordinare, disponere: filium occidere coram patre securum[68] est.
3   Miseremini, iudices, igitur, ut hinc quoque velitis aestimare divitis conscientiam, quod contentus est ne de scelere quaeratur. Non habet fiduciam hominis qui me sciat
   mentiri, et, quod non minus debetis attendere quam si
4 fateretur, non putat sibi salvum ut iterum[69] neget. Dis-
   simules licet, non est innocentiae metus, cum timentur

---

   [66] eo *Håk.*[3] *129:* me *codd.*   [67] -ire V (*vd. ad Angl. vers.*):
   -i B Φ   [68] -curum *Russ.*[3]: -cretum *codd.*
   [69] verum V, *sed vd. Håk.*

---

   [74] As opposed to free men, who—like Poor Man—are over-
   whelmed by sorrow in such situations and behave correspondingly
   (7.11.2). Immediate reaction was also demanded of servants by
   the law, when their master was in mortal danger or murdered: see
   Knoch (2018, 104–5) (AS).

less gratification. (6) Yes, another will kill at your command: but your eyes will not feast on those wounds, and it is more satisfying to be glutted with the last gasps of the departing life, with the blood, to see him prostrate and quivering his last—and all with me watching. (7) It is all of a piece, judges, that the rich man himself did this and that I saw it. The rationale behind sadism is this: someone should be murdered under the eyes of the man who was the reason for the murder.

11. I beg you, judges, not to think I *saw* nothing just because I *did* nothing. It belongs to the grief of slaves and freedmen,[74] when a man is killed, to know at once what to do, to cry out, run forward, call gods and men as witnesses, and only afterward come to the spot with their tears. (2) Do you want *me* to attack the killer, to go after him as he runs away? But who will support the dying man in the meantime, on whom will his weakness lean? You certainly know, murderer, how to order and arrange a crime properly: to kill a son in his father's presence is a safe thing to do.[75]

(3) Take pity then, judges, so that from this too you may gauge the bad conscience of the rich man: he is happy that there should be no interrogation as to the crime. He does not have the self-confidence of a man who knows I am lying, and—something you should notice no less than if he were making a confession—does not think it safe for him to make a second denial.[76] (4) Pretend as you may, when the torture of another causes dread, that fear is not the

---

[75] Rich Man had foreseen that Poor Man would think only of his son, without reacting to the assailant.

[76] I.e., after Poor Man has reiterated his charge under torture.

aliena tormenta. Quid ais,[70] dives? Orbitatem meam in tale scelus ausumque converti, et sic[71] paterni doloris auctoritas facinus impingit[72] alienum? Deinde non ipse adfers
5 eculeos, non ipse disponis ignes? Dicerem[73] mehercules te velle torqueri: ego scindo vestes, tu intremiscis; ego ad flagella nudo corpus, te facit pallor exanimem; ego eculeos, ego posco flammas, tu non habes in meo dolore patientiam. Rogo, quid aliud faceret qui occidisset?
6 Quid nunc agam miser? Gratiam confessionis ante tormenta consumpsi. Scio quanto credibilius fuisset, si hoc statim inter ignes, inter flagella dixissem, et multum de
7 auctoritate primae proclamationis amisi. Non est tamen quod supervacua putetis esse tormenta, tamquam[74] dixerim quicquid sciebam; 12. habeo adhuc ex illo multa referre secreto, quae argumenta faciet dolor. Non refert an me vidisse dixerim; tormentis hoc probaturus sum, debuisse mihi credi ante tormenta.
2 O quantopere nunc, inimice, torqueris, quod te coram iudicibus interrogo, quod hoc non potes mihi fateri! Sed si bene gaudii tui perspicio secretum, non putas te negare

---

[70] ais S (*def. Håk.[1] 318–19, Lund.[1] 69.6*): ait *cett.*

[71] sc- aus- con- et sic *Håk.[1] 318–19* (et *firm. Lund.[1] 69*): genus usumque convertet si *codd.*   [72] ‹tibi› im- *Dess.[2]*

[73] dicerem M: -re B V AD δ: dic E: discere β: diceres ς

[74] tam- *Håk.[2] 66*: quam- B V Φ*

---

[77] The "crime" is explained by the next clause.

[78] Cf. 7.5.5.

[79] If he has no reason to fear, Rich Man should wish that Poor Man be tortured and his allegations proved false.

[80] As at 7.7.7, 7.12.3–4: the screamed confession.

mark of an innocent man. What do you say, rich man? Have I made my loss the motive for such a daring crime,[77] is the authority of a father's grief thus pinning on you a deed that someone else committed?[78] Then aren't *you* bringing up the rack, getting the fires going?[79] (5) Heavens above, I should have said that it is you who wanted to be tortured: *I* rend my clothes, *you* tremble; *I* bare my body for the whip, *you* go deathly pale; *I* ask for the rack, for the flames, *you* cannot bear it while *I* feel the pain. I ask, what else would a murderer do?

(6) Ah me, what am I to do now? I have used up the favor accorded someone making a confession before the torture even starts. I know how much more credible it would have been if I had said this once the fires and the whips surrounded me: I have lost much of the authority attaching to the first shriek.[80] (7) But you should not think torture is superfluous, as if I have said all that I knew. 12. I have still much to recount from that private confrontation,[81] which pain will make into proofs.[82] Never mind whether I have already said I saw; it is by undergoing torture that I shall prove that I ought to have been believed *before* the torture began.

(2) O how sorely, enemy, are you now tormented, because I question you before judges, because you cannot confess your deed to me![83] But if I am right in guessing at the secret of your joy, you are not in your heart of hearts

---

[81] Cf. 7.8.5. This probably hints at the words shouted by Rich Man over the body of his victim in 7.3.3.

[82] Cf. 7.1.5, *confugi ad fidem doloris*.

[83] Sc., face to face. You would enjoy tormenting me yet more by such a confession; but you do not dare do this before the judges, for you would be convicted.

3 quia[75] vidi. Adrogantissime percussorum, evasisse te puta-
bas, quod illud duo tantum sciebamus? Meis, meis hoc
ignibus nega, et, dum me per singulos artus tortor inter-
4 rogat, perfer saltem non credendi patientiam. Cum ego
me vidisse proclamem, tu nullam adferas innocentiae
probationem,[76] non potes aliter absolvi, quam ut illud ego
negem.

5   Ne[77] tamen, iudices, putetis solo me calamitatium ambitu petere quaestionem, dabo propter quod me torquea-
6 tis irati. Filium meum, illum singulis vobis universisque
laudandum, iuxta quem felix, iuxta quem adrogans eram,
occidisti,[78] mea nimia[79] libertas. Ita ego te non eculeo af-
feram,[80] non super ardentis exuram[81] flammas? Nunc me
vindicas, nunc[82] tueris; modo modo coram me filium
7 meum dives[83] occidit fiducia tui. Concurrite, omnes liberi,
omnes parentes, urite, lacerate hos, hos primum patris
oculos, distrahite has manus, quae nihil pro pereunte fecerunt, hoc corpus, haec membra, quae de complexu latronis vulnera nulla retulerunt. Sive hoc poenam sive vultis

---

[75] quod *Wint.*[9], *sed cf. OLD*[2] quia §5.*a*
[76] patientiam—probationem *dist. Russ.*[3]
[77] ne *Reitz.*[2] 50: nec *codd.*   [78] -disti *Russ.*[3]: -di B: -dit V Φ
[79] nimium mea B   [80] aff- *Russ.*[2] 147: eff- *codd.*: off- W
et Obr.: inf- *Bur.*[1]   [81] -uram *Wint.*[7] 147: -uam *codd.*
[82] nunc . . . nunc *codd.*: num . . . num *Russ.*[3]
[83] *del. Sh. B.*[2] 200

---

[84] Sc., what happened. See 7.9.6.
[85] I.e., maintain that my statement should not be trusted—
rather than brag about what you have done to your enemy.
[86] Cf. 4.1.1.
[87] Metarhetorical: cf. Introduction to the present declamation.   [88] See next note.

denying that I saw. (3) Most arrogant of murderers, did you think you had got off free, because only two of us knew?[84] Deny this in the face of *my*, yes *my* fires, and, while the torturer questions me one limb at a time, at least keep on enduring the role of a disbeliever.[85] (4) When I cry aloud that I saw, and you can bring no proof[86] of your innocence, you cannot be acquitted unless *I* retract.

(5) But in case you think, judges, that I am asking for interrogation only to gain sympathy for my calamities, I will give you something to make you torture me in anger.[87] (6) My son, that object of praise by each and every one of you, in whose company I was happy, in whose company I was proud, was killed by *you*, O my excessive liberty.[88] Shall I then not put you on the rack, not scorch you over blazing flames?[89] Now you are claiming me for your own, now you want to protect me; but just a very little while ago, the rich man killed my son before my eyes because he trusted you. (7) Come to my aid, all free men, all parents, burn, rend these, a father's eyes, before all else, tear apart these hands that did nothing for him as he died, this body, these limbs, that took home no scratch after grappling with the brigand. Whether you call this[90] punish-

[89] It was Poor Man's *libertas* (= outspokenness) that provoked Rich Man to kill Son, and it is his *libertas* (= status of free citizen) that prevents him from being interrogated under torture to convict Rich Man—the reason why this latter could safely murder Son in the presence of Father (see below; cf. 7.5.1 and 7.9.6). Thus Poor Man has every reason to bring his *libertas* to torture—along with himself (= to be interrogated under torture though he is a free citizen) (AS).

[90] I.e., your cooperation in torturing me, which can be seen either as a punishment (for my taking no action when my son was killed) or as a mercy (in conceding what I ask) (AS).

esse clementiam,[84] debeo tam miser esse, dum probo, quam cum viderem.

13. Miserum me, si fas est in quaestione mentiri! Sine dubio dives hoc captavit recusando quaestionem, ne crederetur. Sed dura parumper, anime: vidisti. Nunc infelix ad nos, misera pietas, redi, quod fieri in ipsa orbitate non potuit, et vires, quas improvisus abstulit dolor, probatio restituet. Cum flammis urentur nuda vitalia, nox illa occurrat; cum membra fiduculae, flagella laxaverint, rursus ante oculos sit morientis unici vultus, haereant verba percussoris, mandata pereuntis. Filium spectasse morientem longa praesentia est. Nescis, infelix senectus, quanta tibi opus sit veritatis contentione, ut paeniteat divitem quod non duos occidit. Iam nunc tamen vobis, iudices, infirmitatem meam allego, commendo. Si me forte fiduculae, flagella mutaverint, ego tamen vidi. Si vocem in eculeis ignibusque perdidero, ego tamen vidi. Si totus undique dolor pariter admotus occiderit, ego tamen vidi. Alioquin, nisi hoc animo meo, nisi licuerit[85] oculis, moriar[86] hoc dolore, quo puto me posse torqueri.

[84] dem- *Gr.-Mer.* (*et cf. Sh. B.*[4] *198*), *sed vd. ad Angl. vers.*
[85] liqueret *Obr.*, *sed vd. Sh. B.*[2] *200*
[86] -riar *Sch.*: -rerer *codd.* (*def. Sh. B.*[2] *200*)

[91] By torture.

[92] There is an implied contrast between the strength demanded by the *contentio* and his weakness in the face of torture.

[93] I.e., what I say: cf. 7.8.2, 7.8.9.

[94] = are not permitted to testify to what they have seen.

[95] Perhaps = I shall commit suicide out of . . . Cf. 1.17.7–8, 2.24.7.

ment or clemency, I ought to be as pitiable while I prove
as when I saw.

13. How wretched I am, if it is possible to lie under
interrogation! Undoubtedly the rich man's aim in refusing
me an interrogation was that belief should be withheld.
But bear up for a while, my heart: you did see. (2) O unhappy fatherly devotion, return to me now, as was not
possible at the actual moment of my loss: the proof[91] will
restore the strength that unforeseen grief removed. When
my bared vitals are roasted, let that night come back to my
mind; when my limbs are loosened by cords and whips, let
there appear again before my eyes the face of my only son,
may the words of the murderer dwell in my ears, together
with the last instructions of the dying man. To have seen
your son die is something that abides with you for a *long*
time. (3) You do not know, unhappy old man, how valiantly
you need to contend for truth, to make the rich man
repent that he did not kill *both* of us. Yet now, judges, I
have to submit my weakness to you, commend it to you.[92]
(4) If the cords, the whips should by some chance change
me[93]—I did nevertheless see. If I lose the power of speech
on the rack and in the flames—I did nevertheless see. If
the whole pain, brought against me from all sides at
one and the same time, kills me—I did nevertheless see.
(5) Otherwise, if my mind, if my eyes are not to be allowed
to do this,[94] I shall die of[95] the very grief[96] that makes me
think I can be tortured.

[96] For the murder of his son. This sorrow is what prompts
Poor Man to believe he can legally be tortured despite his status
as a free man.

DECLAMATION 8

INTRODUCTION

A father of twins is accused of ill-treatment by his wife. Their children had both fallen ill, and all the doctors despaired of saving them—all except one, who promised he would save one child if he were allowed to vivisect the other in order to find a cure. Father consented: the son subjected to vivisection died, the other was cured. Mother blames Father for not involving her in the decision, and for not trying to find a treatment able to cure both sons.

A trial on a charge of ill-treatment, in itself, is a fiction conceived in the schools of declamation; Quintilian, however, regards it as the counterpart of a real-life procedure, intended to allow a wife to recover her dowry in cases of divorce.[1] The speaker in *DM* 8—Mother's advocate—offers his own interpretation of this connection between ill-treatment and divorce: a charge of ill-treatment is no doubt too trivial for a man who has killed his son; but this is the only legal proceeding available to a mother against her husband, when the very presence of children does not allow her to divorce (6.1–4).

The whole speech of the woman's advocate is built on a tragic doubt: since one of the twins was eventually cured,

[1] Quint. 7.4.11. See Stramaglia (1999b, 94–95n3) and Breij (2015, 60–70).

no one will ever know if the illness was actually incurable, as the majority of doctors had stated; indeed, since one of the twins died and the other survived, it will be impossible to tell whether they were even affected by the same disease (1.2). This calls into question the reliability of the doctors: both those who gave up hope of saving the twins, and the one who promised to find a cure by means of vivisection (3.3–4.4). Later in the speech, Mother's advocate will have an opportunity to question the validity of medical research in itself, especially when it aims at predicting an impending death rather than keeping hopes alive (9.3–10.5; also 21.1). After all, the speaker concludes, medicine can do very little to change what fate has decided for each mortal (9.4). The potential benefits and the legitimacy of vivisection in particular are obviously opposed by the speaker: this declamation seems to voice the criticism of the Empiric and Methodic medical schools against vivisection (e.g., 16.1–18.6), which we are informed about in Celsus' *De medicina* (pr.27ff.).[2] Additionally, to counter the claim that both twins may have been affected by the same illness and so were both doomed to die, the speaker engages in a discussion of the nature of twins: although their faces are indistinguishable, twin brothers have been allotted an individual character and a specific destiny (12.1–13.5).

A major task for the speaker will be to prove that, although Father and Mother have both lost a child, their condition is not comparable. Father trusted the doctors,

---

[2] See in detail L. Greco in Stramaglia (1999b, 4–9); Selinger (1999, 32–41); Guerrini (2003, 6ff.); cf. also Gibson (2013, 539–40).

agreed to have one son killed, and now takes pride in at least having saved one (2.1–2). Mother, however, could not settle for the death of a son to save the other (2.3) and now cannot be comforted by the survival of only one of them (3.1–2). What is worse, she was not informed of the therapy offered by the doctor, nor was she allowed any role in the decision (4.5–6); this leads to a lengthy discussion of what part mothers have, or should have, in the decisions affecting the life of their sons, in comparison with the role and authority of fathers (6.6–8.1).[3]

A crucial question raised in the speech on Mother's behalf is who decided which one of the twins should be vivisected. On the one hand, the speaker implies that Father made this choice, which is taken as a proof of his lack of affection for his children: he was able to choose which one to kill, because neither of them mattered to him (4.6–7). On the other hand, Father tries to hold the *doctor* responsible for the choice; but if the doctor could make a choice between the two patients, this would prove that their condition was not identical, so that the vivisection of one could not be a suitable course of action to save the other (19.4).

The facts are related in two narrations. In the first and shorter one, the speaker recalls the onset of the disease, the despair of most doctors, the proposal of vivisection, and the decision by the father (3.1–5.1). Mother is then quoted as explaining how she cured the surviving son with her maternal love: the son entrusted to her care was healed, and the same treatment should have been accorded the other (5.2–4). Later in the speech, the ad-

3 Cf. Bernstein (2013, 66–74).

vocate describes what happened in the room to which
Mother was not admitted: a gruesome second narration[4]
provides full details of the vivisection performed by the
doctor with Father's consent and implies that the doctor
aimed at furthering his medical knowledge more than at
curing the ill youth (19.5–21.9); additionally, in the peroration, Mother is made to recall the care she gave to the
remains of her son after the procedure (22.5).

The structure of the speech may be analyzed as follows:

> PROEM 1.1–2.6
> NARRATION (I) 3.1–5.4
> ARGUMENTATION
> > *Confirmatio* 6.1–9.2
> > *Refutatio* 9.3–19.4
> NARRATION (II) 19.5–21.9
> EPILOGUE 21.10–22.6

The needs of his argumentation lead the speaker into
some inconsistency with the theme: there, the twins are
said to be "infants"; yet in the speech they seem grown-up
enough to have already traveled and served in the army
(13.4), and each seems to be mature enough to be willing
to die for his brother (8.2).

DM 8 is particularly close to *DM* 5, in terms of language
and imagery; its author seems to know also *DM* 4 and 10.
Judging by language, style, and use of rhythmical clausu-
lae, *DM* 8 may be considered the most recent piece of the
whole collection, dating to the middle or to the second half
of the third century AD.[5]

---

[4] *Epidiegesis*: see Introduction to *DM* 5, n. 4.
[5] See General Introduction, §4.

DECLAMATION 8

The declamation inspired a short twelfth-century poem, *De gemellis*, ascribed to Bernard Silvestris or his circle in Tours.[6] A reply to *DM* 8 in Castilian was given by Gabriel Bocángel in his *Quintiliano respondido* (1647);[7] another one, in Latin, is included in the collection of *Antilogiae* by Patarol.[8]

[6] Now available, with English translation, in Wetherbee (2015, 247–55).

[7] Ed. Dadson (2000, 2:867–87). See Fernández López (2018, 236–45).

[8] (1743, 243–67). Full discussion in Martella (2015).

8

Gemini languentes

Gemini, quibus erat mater et pater, aegrotare coeperunt.
Consulti medici dixerunt eundem esse languorem. Desperantibus reliquis promisit unus se alterum sanaturum,
si alterius vitalia inspexisset. Permittente patre execuit
infantem et vitalia inspexit. Sanato uno accusatur pater ab
uxore malae tractationis.

1. Quamvis, iudices, plurimum infelicissimae matris adversis miserationis abstulerit, quod ex duobus liberis pari
desperatione languentibus alter evasit, et plerisque maximum dolorem prima fronte tractantibus videatur aviditas
gaudiorum, ut modo ad totius orbitatis redacta patientiam
iam non sit unius salute contenta, non possumus tamen
affectibus vestris non hanc primam tristissimae calamitatis
allegare mensuram, quae ex ipsa quoque solacii sui condi-

---

1 See Introduction to the present declamation.

8

The sick twins

Twin brothers, whose mother and father were both alive, fell ill. Doctors were called in and said their illnesses were identical. The others offered no hope, but one said he would cure one of the two if he first inspected the vital organs of the other. With the father's permission, the doctor cut the infant[1] open and inspected the organs. The other twin was cured. The father is accused by the wife of ill-treatment.

(Speech on behalf of the mother)

1. Although, judges, a great deal of the sympathy for the misfortunes of this most unhappy mother has been removed by the fact that of her two children, both equally despaired of, one escaped, and although to so many who look only superficially at her extreme grief it seems to show greed for happiness that, after having come close to suffering complete bereavement, she is now not content with the survival of one, nevertheless we cannot but lay before your sympathetic consideration, first of all, the following way of gauging this grievous disaster, a way which takes its rise from the very circumstance that gives her

cione descendit: minus misera quereretur de marito, si
sanari nec ille potuisset, pro quo est frater occisus; nunc
infelix par non est dolori, nunc non invenit ulla solacia, ex
2 quo sibi videtur filium perdidisse victurum. Super impatientiam tristissimae orbitatis increscit quod intellegit illum non sine sanitate fuisse languorem, nec persuaderi
miserae potest perituro[1] laborasse fato, in quo inventum
est quod sanaret alium. Captet licet crudelissimus senex
parricidii immanitatem metu maiore protegere, non invenio unde colligi possit utrumque fuisse moriturum: ex
duobus aegris non periit nisi qui occisus est.

2. Ante omnia igitur illud a vobis infelicissima mater
petit, ne maximi sceleris ideo decrescat invidia, quia pati
videtur et reus ex orbitate tantundem. Non perdidit fi-
2 lium, quisquis occidit. Explicat a dolore patrem quod sibi
videtur fecisse rem maximam, et in locum iuvenis amissi
3 substituit de vanitate solacium. Alia est, alia condicio matris, quae medico non credidit, apud quam saevissimae
condicionis immanitas fidem non potuit impetrare tempt-
4 tandi. Pro utroque timuit, pro utroque speravit. Facinus
est eum maioris pietatis videri, qui de morte filii potuit[2]
alterius vel certa salute transigere. Sic debetis odisse patrem, tamquam duos occiderit, cuius non interfuit uter
occideretur.

[1] -ri *Watt*[2] *25, sed vd. Sch. (coll. Petron. 119, v. 19)*
[2] potuit ⌐ *(corrob. Håk.*[2] *68–69)*: putavit *codd.*

[2] I.e., the survival of one son: she now realizes that the dead
son was curable, for the other survives, and this is cause of new
grievance (DAR).

[3] Clarified in the next words.

comfort:[2] the poor woman would have less to find fault
with in her husband if the child for whose sake his brother
was killed had proved incurable too. As it is, the unfortunate mother has not been able to bear her grief, she has
found no comfort, ever since she came to think that she
has lost a child who would have lived. (2) What makes her
tragic loss the more intolerable is her realization that the
illness was not incurable: the unfortunate woman cannot
be convinced that the child was doomed to die, seeing that
something was found in him able to cure his twin. Though
the sadistic old man is seeking to cover over the enormity
of his murder by conjuring up a greater fear,[3] I see no way
of inferring that both would have died: of the two sick
children, the only one who died was the one who was
killed.

2. First of all, then, a most unfortunate mother asks this
of you, that the revulsion felt at the worst of all crimes
should not be diminished simply because the accused is
thought to be suffering just as much as she is from this
bereavement. Someone who kills his son has not lost him.
(2) It relieves the father from grief that he is convinced he
has performed a great act: he has made vain pride a comforting substitute for the young man he has lost. (3) Quite,
quite different is the position of the mother, who did not
believe the doctor, who could not be brought to approve
of an experiment on such barbarous terms. She feared for
both her children, she hoped for both. (4) It is outrageous
if more affection is attributed to a parent who found it in
him to settle for the death of one son even to gain the assured survival of the other. You should hate the father as
being the killer of both, for it made no difference to him
which was killed.

5 Est tamen, sanctissimi iudices, quod de crudelissimo parricida queri possit non sola mater: adiecit humanis calamitatibus ipsam sanitatem, et morborum languorisque violentiam medicinae concessit. Filium occidit, si ipsi creditis, fortasse moriturum, et hominem, cuius caritas debuerat ipsa desperatione crevisse, in hoc solum impendit,

6 ut tantundem superesset incerti. Non exonerat, iudices, immanitatem saevissimi patris quod hanc rationem[3] credidit: de languente filio rem inauditam, rem facere crudelem unam rationem habet, si ipse sanetur.

3. O tristior indigniorque semper mensura calamitatum, magna felicitas! Huncine fecit exitum illa modo civitate tota conspicua mater, ille indiscretus ab utroque latere

2 comitatus, ille gaudentium dulcis error oculorum? Quid mihi mortem nuntiatis unius? Perdidit misera geminos.

3 Passi sunt enim languorem miserrimi iuvenes sine dubio pariter unaque non fraternitate, non animae corporumque consortio, sed condicione fragilitatis humanae, qua sic extranei quoque duo languere potuissent; non negaverim terribilem, gravem, et parentibus utique metuendum, de cuius tamen adhuc—ut parcissime dixe-

4 rim—remedio quaereretur. Quid refert an medici con-

---

[3] hanc -nem (*sc. esse*) *Håk.*[2] 69: hac -ne *codd.*

---

[4] But also for the human race in general.

[5] He made the attention of doctors as dangerous as illnesses.

[6] When one is used to a condition happier than normal, any misfortune will be all the harder to bear.

[7] Probably an echo of Verg. *Aen.* 10.391–92, *simillima proles, / indiscreta suis gratusque parentibus error.*

[8] Her special pleasure lay in having *twins*. Cf. 8.22.1.

(5) But there is a sense, most revered judges, in which it is not only for the mother[4] to complain of a most cruel murderer: he has added to the list of human disasters even the act of curing, by handing over to the art of medicine the violence associated with diseases and illness.[5] He killed a son who—if you believe his account—would perhaps have died anyway, sacrificing a human being who should have grown dearer to him just because he despaired of his life, merely so that exactly the same degree of uncertainty might remain. (6) It does nothing, judges, to mitigate the dreadful behavior of a barbarous father that he was convinced he was acting justifiably. To do something unprecedented, something cruel in the case of a sick son can only be justified if it is *he* who is then healed.

3. O great good fortune, always too sad and inadequate a measure of calamities![6] Is this what has become of that mother, just now so familiar a sight throughout the city, of those indistinguishable companions to left and right, of the sweet mistake made by the eyes that rejoiced to gaze on them?[7] (2) Why do you bring me the news of the death of one son? The poor thing has lost *twins*.[8]

(3) Indeed, there is no doubt that those most unfortunate young men fell ill in the same way and at the same time not because they were brothers, not because they were bound together body and soul, but because of the frailty of our human condition, which could have made two strangers also fall sick just like that. I do not mean to deny that the illness was frightening, serious, and certainly to be feared by parents, but (to use extremely measured language) it was one for which a remedy was still to be sought. (4) What does it matter if the doctors, having said

senserint utrumque periturum, cum eundem dixerint esse
languorem? Manifestum est de duobus non dixisse verum,
5 quos de altero constat esse mentitos. Iam tamen, iudices,
de tam perdita pronuntiatione non querimur, quod aegros, quos sibi videbantur explicare non posse, parentibus
crediderunt; innocentior est simplicitas desperare, si remedia non noveris, et hanc ignorantiae malo probitatem,
ut languorem quem nescias tantum neges posse sanari.
6 Maximi tamen virorum et quibus arti suae[4] solvendo non
sit humanitas, si sciebant hoc genus curationis et illud non
indicare voluerunt. 4. Vultis ut[5] illos mentitos breviter probem? Desperaverunt de languore, cuius remedium, si patri creditis, alius invenit.

2   Sive enim, iudices, vanissimus nescientium vidit hanc
patris in periculo liberorum rigidam nimiamque patientiam et hominem in filiorum languore sollicitum de remedio generis humani, sive captavit ex hoc velut[6] quandam
artis imaginem[7] imitari, quod sanare non poterat, et ignorantiae pudorem tegere magno temptavit incerto, sive, ut
aliud videretur dixisse quam reliqui, verba desperationis
incredibili vanitate variavit magnaque miseros parentes
ambage suspendens tutissimum putavit promittere quod

---

4 arti suae *Obr.* (*firm. Pi.*[1], *Str.*[10] 115–16.89): artis suae *codd.*:
gratias suas *Watt*[2] 25   5 et V Φ   6 velut *Sch.*: vultu
B V Φ*   7 *om.* B V γ, *sed vd. Håk.*[2] 70

---

9 I.e., they got it wrong. As one twin did survive, a remedy
must have been possible—and the doctors should have kept
searching for it.   10 If they *were* ignorant, they were right to
confess ignorance; but if they *did* know vivisection would help

that the illnesses were identical, agreed that both boys
would die? It is obvious they did not tell the truth about
both, for it is established that they lied[9] in the case of one.
(5) But now, judges, I am not complaining of such a despairing pronouncement, or that they left to the parents
the fate of children whose sickness they thought they
could not cure; it is more forgivable to express frank despair if you do not know the remedy, and I prefer the
principled confession of ignorance that makes you restrict
yourself to calling an illness incurable, when you cannot
identify it. (6) But[10] they are the greatest of men, ones to
whose art men of true humanity could not but be in debt,
if they knew this type of cure and yet would not reveal it.
4. Do you want me to prove in a word that they did not
tell the truth? They despaired in the case of an illness for
which, if you believe the father, another found a remedy.

(2) Maybe, judges, this falsest of ignoramuses observed
how unflinching and extreme was the stoicism shown by
the father when his children were in danger, and how
anxious he was, though it was his own sons who were ill,
to find a remedy for mankind in general; or maybe he at-
tempted to convey a certain air of professionalism by the
very fact that he could not find a cure, trying to cover up
the shame of his ignorance under a cloak of mystery;[11] or
maybe, in order to look as if he was saying something different from the others, he produced a variation on a bul-
letin of despair by including an incredible fiction, and,
keeping the wretched parents in high suspense, thought it
safest to promise something that no one would have to try

and did not say so, then we as humane men are much in their
debt.　　　[11] Cf. 8.15.6.

3   deberet nemo experiri: causas quidem se dixit ignorare
morborum, sed salutem spopondit unius, si licuisset alte-
4   rum occidere, lacerare, perspicere. En cui pietas patris,
cui credere sollicitudo debuerit: dixit se scire remedium,
et[8] nesciebat.

5   Vultis intellegere, iudices, nihil impatientia caritatis
6   fecisse patrem? Non retulit ad matrem. Adacta est a morte
filii vel sanitate discedere. Non propinquos consuluit, non
amicos, sed sua tantum persuasione medicique contentus,
quod nocentius est quam si ipse occidisset, alterutrum
7   potuit eligere. Dicat nunc parricida quid fecerit illud,
quod [etiam][9] de ⟨tam⟩[10] similibus,[11] tam paribus aegris
in alterum desperatio illa praevaluit. Si medici non interfuit utrum occideret, constabit vivere utrumque potuisse;
si interfuit, constabit non eundem fuisse languorem.

8   Qualis fuerit illa curatio, quid passus sit iuvenis in
morte, qua[12] medicus parabatur, omnium adfectibus, omnium cogitationibus liquere crediderim, ideoque parci-
mus auribus matris. 5. Breviter tamen longae crudelitatis
explicanda saevitia est: ex omnibus quae pertulit, levissi-
mum fuit quod occisus est. Non est quod veniam tris-

---

8 et V: quod B Φ   9 del. Wint.[5] 346   10 add. Bur.
11 del. Alm. necnon Scheff. 438–39 (ut plane sit de tam paribus)   12 quam . . . -bat Obr., sed de in non iterato cf., e.g.,
Sen. Ep. 93.1 in epistula, qua . . . , Nep. Att. 18.1

---

12 I.e., he thought that the parents would not take up the sug-
gestion. Cf. 8.2.3 (temptandi), where Mother rejected it; also
8.15.9.   13 Hysteron proteron: the killing is the result of the
dissecting and examining, but is put first for emphasis.

out.[12] (3) Whatever the case, he said he did not know what had caused the illnesses, but promised the recovery of one twin if he were permitted to kill, dissect and examine[13] the other. (4) You can see the kind of doctor an affectionate and anxious father had to trust: he said he knew a remedy—yet he did not.

(5) Do you want to see, judges, that the father did not act out of overmastering affection? He did not tell the mother. (6) She was compelled[14] to absent herself from the death, or the cure, of her son.[15] He did not consult relations or friends, but, content with his own conviction and that of the doctor, he proved (something more culpable than if he had killed the boy himself) capable of choosing between the two.[16] (7) Let the murderer[17] now explain to us how it came about that in the case of two patients ⟨so⟩ similar, so alike, the verdict "no hope" was passed on only one. If it made no difference to the doctor which he killed, it will follow that both could have lived; if it did matter, it will follow that it was not the same illness.

(8) What that cure was like, what the boy had to suffer in a death where[18] a doctor was called in, is—I should think—obvious to anyone of feeling or imagination; so I shall spare the mother's ears. 5. All the same, the barbarity of the long scene of cruelty needs an explanation, however short: out of all he suffered, being killed was the easiest to bear. There is no reason why the horrific cure should be

[14] Cf. also 8.19.6.   [15] I.e., from the decision about it (DAR).   [16] I.e., he was so insensitive as to be able to choose. Cf. 8.9.2.   [17] = Father.   [18] Amounting to "in the case of a death, in relation to which . . ." Doctors are usually called in to secure the life of a patient, not his death.

tissimae curationis paret, quod videtur in alio fratre explicata promissio: an alterum medicus sanaverit, fortuna
viderit; quod negari non potest, alterum medicus occidit.

2   Erumpit hoc loco mulier infelix et tota libertate procla-
mat: "Redde mihi," inquit, "marite, filium, quem tibi pariter medicoque commisi, recipe quem mihi credidisti.[13]
Hic est ille vester insanabilis, ille moriturus, hic quem
3 permiseras medico, si maluisset, occidere. Vides quid
profecerint anxia vota pietatis, sollicitae preces. Dum iam
frigidi pectoris calorem superpositis revocamus uberibus,
dum rigentia[14] membra continuis osculis et spiritu trepidae matris animamus, dum labentes oculi ad nostras
exclamationes nostrosque planctus admissa[15] paulatim
luce laxantur, dum multa mentior, multa promitto et fratrem dico sanatum, respexit ad vitam, convaluit, evasit.
4 Non tamen iacto pietatem, non arrogo mihi prosperae
curationis eventum. Quid hunc sanaverit, vis scire breviter? Quod potuit utrumque sanare."

6. Pudeat vos, o iura legesque, quod miserrimi sexus
dolorem his clusistis[16] angustiis. Ita maritum, quod occisus
2 est filius, malae tractationis uxor accusat? Perdiderunt
legis huius auctoritatem quae ad illam[17] uxorias querelas,

---

[13] recipe—credidisti *h.l. habent* Exc. Mon. *p. 366, 15 Lehnert*
(*vind. Reitz.*[2] *77*): *post* insanabilis *codd.*
[14] ri- *Wint.*[7] *148*: fri- *codd.*
[15] admi- π (ammi- ς, *quod def. Leh.*[1] *442*): ami- *cett.*
[16] clu- ς: elu- *codd.*
[17] -am *Plas. 67.5 (firm. Håk.*[2] *71*): -as *codd.*

---

[19] Compare the desperate efforts of another mother at 10.4.1.
[20] Sc., her tender loving care. Cf. 8.21.6.

forgiven just because the promise has (it seems) been made good in the other brother. Whether the doctor healed the one is a question for fortune; what is undeniable is that the doctor killed the other.

(2) At this point the unhappy woman bursts out and proclaims with complete openness: "Husband, give me back the son I entrusted to you and the doctor between you; take back the one you entrusted to me. Here is your incurable, your doomed son, the one you would have let the doctor kill if he had preferred him. (3) You see what a loving parent's anxious vows, her distraught prayers could bring about. While I was summoning back the warmth to his already chill chest by laying my breasts upon it, while I was bringing life to his stiffening limbs by continual kisses and a frightened mother's breath,[19] while in answer to my cries and my wails his drooping eyes were beginning to open again and gradually admit the light of day, while I was telling many a fib, making many a promise, and assuring him his brother had been cured—it was then that he turned his eyes toward life, grew stronger, came through. (4) But I make no boast of maternal devotion, or claim for myself the credit for a cure that proved successful. Do you want to know, in a word, what cured him? What could have cured both of them."[20]

6. Ordinances and laws, you should be ashamed to have placed such tight constraints on the grievances of those unfortunate enough to be females! So a wife is to accuse her husband of *ill-treatment*, when her son has been killed? (2) The authority of this law has been destroyed by women who so often appeal to it over wives' grievances,

matrimoniorum solent deferre delicias; ego illam datam
3 miseris tantum matribus puto. Potest autem[18] ab iniquo
coniuge explicare divortium, et contra maritales tuetur
iniurias ut nolis praestare patientiam. Illa his[19] succurrit,
quas nefas est abire, discedere, quas in pessimi coniugii
durum[20] perpetuumque complexum communium pignorum nexus artavit, quae malos maritos pariter et patres
4 nec relinquere nec ferre sufficiunt. Facinus est ideo evadere maritum, quia damnaretur si illa de[21] minore dolore
quereretur. Itaque[22] impudenter facit, quod pro detracto
matronae[23] cultu negatoque comitatu, fastiditis noctibus
pulsataque facie, filium complorat occisum?
5 Sileo adhuc illa, per quae parricidii crevit immanitas;
occisum filium obicio.[24] Puta[25] luxuriosum, perditum,
nocentem; fingite hoc patrem ira, indignatione fecisse.
Quantum facinus sit filium occidere, nemo magis fatetur
quam qui vult videri se[26] illud fecisse pro filio.

---

[18] puto. potest autem *Reitz.*[2] 67 (autem *fere* = enim, *cf. H.-Sz.*
490–91 et Håk.[2] *71*): puto potestatem *codd.*

[19] illa his *Wint.*[9]: illis *codd.*: ‹illa› illis *vel* illis ‹lex› *Sh. B.*[2] *200,*
cf. Sh. B.[4] *199* [20] dir- B V δ, *sed vd. Håk.*[2] *70–71*

[21] illa de *Wint.*[5] *346*: de illo *codd.* [22] itane *Sch., sed cf.*
e.g. 10.9.2 [23] -nae ⟨ (*genet.: cf. Håk.*[3] *129–30, qui et* -nali
coni.): -na *codd.* (*frustra def. Pi.*[2] *480*): -na *ante* impudenter
transp. Wint.[5] *346, post* facit *Bur.* [24] gravius dist. *Wint.*[9]
[25] -ate ⟨, *sed cf. e.g. 8.9.6* [26] del. *Leh., sed vd. Håk.*

---

[21] Cf. 19.5.2. [22] The law of *mala tractatio* is needed by
wives with children. For divorce is there to enable (childless)
wives to deal with bad husbands; but *mothers* need a different
sort of help, because they cannot just go away as divorcees can.

over the frivolous trifles of married life.[21] Personally, I
think that it was meant to apply only to *mothers* in a sad
plight. (3) Indeed, divorce can[22] free a woman from an
unjust husband: refusal to go on suffering guards a wife
against injuries inflicted by her spouse. That law[23] comes
to the aid of women who are forbidden to leave, to depart,
women whom the ties of children in common have locked
into the harsh and unending embrace of a bad marriage,
who can neither leave nor put up with bad husbands who
are at the same time bad fathers. (4) It is outrageous for
this husband to be let off the hook precisely because he
would be convicted if his wife were going to court over a
smaller grievance.[24] Is she then acting impudently in complaining of a son being killed, rather than of the loss of a
matron's trousseau or the denying of attendants or the
disdaining of night pleasures or a blow in the face?

(5) I do not speak yet of what aggravated the horror of
the murder; I accuse him of killing his son.[25] Suppose him
lecherous, a rake, a criminal; imagine the father acted out
of anger, out of wrath.[26] How great a crime it is to kill a
son is confessed by no one more than someone who wishes
it to be thought that he did it for the sake of another son.

[23] Viz., on *mala tractatio*.

[24] The husband would have been convicted for *mala tractatio*
had he been responsible for one of the minor offenses listed
above; it would be absurd if, by that same law, he could not be
condemned for having committed something more serious, i.e.,
killing his son. See also 19.5.2.   [25] Pure and simple, with
(for the moment) no aggravating circumstances.

[26] I.e., that would be better than to do it for the reason he did.

6   Ecquid,[27] iudices, vel ex hoc totus animus mariti, tota
tristissimae coniugis calamitas perspici potest, quod se
negat matri communium liberorum debere rationem?
7   Placet ergo, mortales, ut de hominibus, in quos plus ex
harum sanguine, ex harum transit anima, non habeant partem nisi tantum doloris? Solos ergo communicabit misera
planctus, et ab omnibus consiliis quibus ordinatur iuventa,
vita disponitur, extranea vilitate seposita circa maerores
tantum lacrimarumque consortium orbitate iungetur?[28] 7.
Si mehercules fas est aestimare utri plus parenti debeatur
ex liberis, non improbe totam potestatem sibi vindicabit
adfectus qui decem mensibus ante vestram incipit diligere
notitiam, et, cum vos patres gaudium primum faciat oculorum, ante sunt conscientia matres. Facinus est ideo tantum illis minus licere, quia minus facere sufficiunt.

2   Vos estis, qui crescentes adhuc in peregrinationes, qui
iam adultos in castra magnorum[29] parentum[30] vanitate
dimittitis. Erubescitis desideriis tamquam infirmitate, et,
unde velocissimus transitus est in rigorem, liberos vultis
amare patientia.[31] Quam multa ideo tantum de filiis facitis,

[27] ecquid ⊊: haec quid B V δ: et quid γ β
[28] -etur ⊊: -entur (-un- J) *codd.*
[29] magna cum *Kuy., sed genetivos iuxta positos nec conexos*
(magnorum | parentum) *item praebet e.g. 17.19.7*
[30] imperatorum *Watt*³ *51*
[31] pote- *Bur.*

[27] Sc., than from the fathers: a variation on the prevalent opinion that both parents transmit their blood to the child (cf., e.g.,
Ov. *Fast.* 1.471; Stat. *Silv.* 3.3.119–21).
[28] Whereas this seems to be conceded to *fathers* (cf. 8.7.5).

(6) Judges, cannot the whole attitude of the husband, the whole plight of his grieving wife be discerned precisely from this, that he says he is not accountable to the mother for the children they have in common? (7) Is it then your judgment, humankind, that, except in grief, women have no part of those beings into whom more passes over from *their* blood, from *their* soul?[27] Shall then a poor woman take a share only in laments, and, excluded, like a worthless outsider, from all the discussions about the regulation of her son's youthful years and the planning of his life,[28] will she be regarded as a partner only when a child is lost, when sorrows and tears unite both parents? 7. If, by heaven, it is proper to calculate to which parent children owe more, absolute precedence will rightly be claimed by the affection that begins to feel love ten months before you[29] make their acquaintance: while *you* are made fathers only by the first joyous glimpse of the child, *they* are mothers before that in their inmost thoughts. It is scandalous that less should be allowed them just because they are able to do less.

(2) It is you who in the foolish pride of parenthood send off your sons on foreign trips while they are still growing up, and, when they *are* adults, dispatch them to do military service under the grandees.[30] You blush at the idea of missing them in their absence, as though that were a weakness, and your wish is to make love of your children an endurance test: a short step, indeed, away from being harsh. How many things you do with your children just

---

[29] Sc., you fathers (so too in 8.7.2), who do not get to know your child till he is born.

[30] Cf. 3.5.1.

3 quia licet! Et frequentius potestatis vestrae iactatione tamquam aliquo gravitatis genere delinquitis. Non habet orbitas vestra lacrimas: super ardentes rogos tenetis incon-
cussam rigidamque faciem, itis obviam consolationibus,
et, quod omnem modum feritatis excedit, captatis in
4 magna calamitate laudari. Quicquam ergo erit quod de
communibus pignoribus non pari mente, pari patientia,[32]
vel, si necessitas postulet, pari rigore faciatis?
5   Mali tantum patris interest ut matri minus liceat. Sane
cedat vobis circa regendas communium pignorum mentes
sexus infirmior: vos mores, vos vitae genus, vos matrimo-
nia ceterosque actus vestra persuasione firmetis; numquid
arrogans consortium, numquid impotens societas est libe-
6 ros communes esse languentes? Si quis immo pudor est,
cede nunc tota potestate matri, illius sit in aegri toro proxi-
7 mus locus, haec adhibeat fomenta, porrigat cibos. Si quid
impatientia, si quid flagrantium viscerum poscit infirmitas,
mater neget, mater indulgeat. Illas quas immodicus ardor
discutit vestes haec super fatigatos reponat artus, illas iac-
tatas toto lectulo manus ‹haec›[33] sedulo contineat affectu.
8. Frustra captas videri ultionem[34] magnae[35] caritatis ab

32 pa- *Håk.*[2] *71–72*: impa- *codd.*
33 *add. Reitz.*[2] *40 (corrob. Str.*[3])
34 ultionem *codd.* (*an* ‹vel› ul-?): velut timore *Håk.*
35 maternae *Håk., sed vd. Str.*[3]

---

31 For your steadfast firmness.
32 Sc., as this deplorably insensitive father.
33 Sc., than a father who can act so arbitrarily.

because you have the power! (3) And all too often you act
improperly to show off your power, as if that made you
look important. Losing a child does not make you weep:
over the burning pyre your expression remains unshaken
and rigid, you snub those who try to comfort you, and,
most inhuman of all, you look for praise[31] at a time of great
misfortune. (4) In short, will there be anything that you
fathers would not do, in regard to the children you share,
in the same frame of mind, with the same self-control,
and, if need be, with the same harshness?[32]

(5) It is in the interests only of a wicked father that a
mother should have less power.[33] Certainly the weaker sex
should give way to you in the exercise of control over the
children you have in common: *your* views should dictate
their behavior, their manner of life, their marriages and
their other activities; but is it an abuse of your partnership,
a sign of your union being stretched too far, if your children are held in common when they are ill? (6) No, if you
have any sense of shame, you should yield the mother full
power at such a time: *she* should have the place nearest
the bed of the sick child, *she* should apply the cold compresses, offer the food. (7) If intolerable pain, if a failure
of inflamed organs causes demands, it is for the mother to
deny, for the mother to grant. If his bedclothes are disor-
dered by the heat of fevers, it is for her to rearrange them
over weary limbs; if his hands are flung all over the bed, it
is ⟨for her⟩ to put them back under the covers with ever-
vigilant love. 8. It is in vain that you seek to be thought to
have banished your wife from any role in the children's

133

omni curae ratione seposuisse:[36] cum circa curationes liberorum non consentiunt parentes, curationis est culpa,
non matris.

2   Quid, quod filium occidit innocentem, cui nihil obicere, nihil poterat irasci? Filium—si ipsi creditis—pro
fratre mori paratum, cuius suprema ferre non poterat?
3 Novum, iudices, et incognitum rebus humanis audite facinus: iam parricidium pietas, caritas et impatientia orbitatis
admittit! Malo odium, querelas, execrationes, quam ut
4 quis liberos affectu, quo servantur, occidat. Quid refert an
per hoc alterius filii anima redimatur? Si parricidium fas
est ullas accipere causas, filius propter se tantum debet
occidi.

5   Adicite, iudices, immanitati, quod occidit aegrum.
Omnibus equidem mortalibus maiorem crediderim de
languore venire reverentiam, et illorum quoque, quos inter supplicia pereuntis avido spectamus assensu, iuxta
valetudines tamen morborumque violentiam quodam in-
6 nocentiae favore miseremur. In carceribus et in illa pro-
funda nocte poenarum, religiosius ille anheli pectoris pallor inspicitur; non sic confundunt obvios gravibus catenis

---

[36] -suisse *scripsi* (*de clausula heroa q.d. vd. Str.[15] 57.131*):
-situs *codd.*

---

[34] Father claims that he excluded Mother from any decision
in the "cure" for fear she could halt his project by appealing to a
court (seeking "revenge"), out of love for both sons.

[35] It is a cure that should not be tried (like vivisection in the
present case).

[36] See Introduction to the present declamation.

cure to forestall a revenge prompted by her huge love:[34] when parents do not agree about the cure of their children, that is the fault of the cure,[35] not of the mother.

(2) What of the fact that he killed an innocent son, whom he had no possible reason to reproach or feel angry with?—a son who, if you credit his own account, was ready to die for a brother[36] whose last moments he could not bear to witness. (3) Judges, I must tell you of a crime novel and unparalleled in human history: now a sense of duty, affection, and inability to bear bereavement allow parricide![37] I prefer hatred, complaints, curses, rather than that someone should kill children out of the same sentiments as those which normally prompt us to keep them alive. (4) What difference does it make that the life of a second son is saved by these means? If it is right for any motive to justify parricide, a son should be killed for his own sake alone.

(5) Add, judges, to the enormity of the offense that he killed a *sick* man. Personally I incline to think that all mortals deserve greater respect if they are sick: even when we look on with eager approval at the deaths of men being executed, yet we pity them, with the sort of favor accorded to innocence, if they are in ill health and suffering serious disease. (6) In prison cells, in that profound night where punishment is exacted, the pallor of a man gasping for breath is treated with more respect. Those who meet with convicts are not so disconcerted by necks clanking with

[37] Parricide is here the killing of a child. Father committed it in order to save at least one son, and so to avoid complete bereavement. Cf. 8.14.2.

colla stridentia et diutino squalore concreta facies ut ille,
quem ad singulos conatus gressusque labentem vix trahit
impellitque longus ordo vinctorum, et inter tot destinatos
totque perituros omnium tamen in se retorquet oculos
unus aeger. 9. Quid ais? Tu illum, quem nunc nefas est
castigare, reprehendere, cuius auribus parcere debuerunt
saeviora verba, quem,[37] si quid negares, videreris occi-
2 dere, ferro, vulneribus aggrederis? Non potest hinc tibi
venire defensio, ut hoc sis pro alterius salute commentus.
Inter duos liberos pari desperatione languentes da bonum
patrem: non praeponderabit alterutrum,[38] non eliget, sed,
ut incertum orbitatis evadat, ipse morietur.

3   Temptat hoc loco, iudices, crudelissimus senex excusationem temeritatis suae de medicorum trahere consensu:
"Desperaverant" inquit "de duobus." Sepono paulisper
immanitatem patris, qui credidit: [et][39] de arrogantissimae
persuasionis hominibus queri [de][40] totius generis humani
4 nomine volo. Quam multas artes, misera mortalium sollicitudo, fecisti! Fato vivimus, languemus, convalescimus,
morimur. Medicina, quid praestas, nisi ut iuxta te nemo
5 desperet? Dicturum me putas: "Non credo renuntianti-

---

37 quem β: om. cett.   38 dist. Reitz.[2] 68: post -rabit vulg.
39 del. Wint.[7] 148 coll. 8.16.1   40 del. Gron. (firm. Håk.)

---

38 Cf. 16.8.6–7.

39 "[T]he repeated use of the connective -que evocatively
mimes the sick man's stumbling gait" (Schwennicke [2018, 500]).

40 Contrast 8.4.6.   41 Cf. 10.4.1.

42 Artes here hints at "arts" (such as medicine) as well as
"tricks" (like the cruel procedure devised by this doctor).

43 Cf. Petron. 42.5. All that medicine can offer is hope, since

heavy chains and faces crusted[38] with long-accumulated
filth as by a man who stumbles at every attempt to take a
step forward, and can scarcely be dragged or[39] pushed
forward by the long line of the chain gang; and among so
many who are doomed, so many who will die, one sick man
nevertheless draws the attention of all. 9. What do you
have to say? Do you assail with knife wounds someone
whom it is in his condition wrong to chide or find fault
with, someone whose ears should have been spared from
overharsh words, someone whom, if you denied him anything, you might seem to be killing? (2) You cannot plead
in your defense that you devised this to save the life of the
other. When two children are suffering equally desperate
illnesses, suppose their father to be a decent man: he will
not come down either way, he will not choose, but to avoid
the uncertainty attending his bereavement he will die
himself.[40]

(3) At this point, judges, our elderly nonpareil of cruelty attempts to find an excuse for his own recklessness by
appealing to the agreement of the doctors: "They had despaired of both," he says.[41] I put aside for the moment the
barbarity of a father who believed this: I wish, in the name
of the entire human race, to complain of men so arrogant
in their convictions. (4) Wretched anxiety of mortals, how
many arts[42] have you contrived! It is according to *fate* that
we live, fall ill, recover, die. Medicine, what have you to
offer except that no one should despair when you are on
the case?[43] (5) Do you think I am going to say: "I do not

everything is governed by fate; so the doctors should not have
despaired of the sick twins, but helped the parents by keeping
hope alive.

137

bus, non accedo, cum deserunt relinquuntque languen-
6 tes"? Ego vero medicis non credo sperantibus. Aspicite
maiorem partem generis humani et, si me interroges, illam robustiorem, illam adhuc in prima rerum naturae
veritate[41] viventem: nullos[42] artis huius novit antistites,
nec minus tamen bellorum vulneribus morborumque me-
detur incursibus; non disputationum vanitate sollerti, sed
experimentis et, invicem per similes dissimilesque casus
7 observatione ducente, tradita ratione succurrit. Non medicina sanat, sed quicquid videtur sanasse medicina est.

10. Quo vultis animo feram quod ars, quantum dicitis,
inventa pro vita, ⟨sic,⟩[43] si dis placet,[44] auctoritatem fa-
mamque[45] captat ut longe ventura suprema prospiciat, ut
adesse fata denuntiet quae nec timentur, et maxima[46] sci-
2 entiae pars esse coepit sanare non posse? Quisquamne ab
homine qui adhuc loquitur, spirat, intellegit, sic recedit
quemadmodum relinquitur exanime corpus, et ibi finem
vitae putabit, ubicumque scientiae substiterit infirmitas?
Si fragilitatem mortalitatis incertosque velimus aestimare
3 casus, tantundem periculi habet omnis aeger. Iniquissi-
mum est desperationes vocari, quotiens remedium medicina non invenit, et angustias sive artis seu mentis humanae ad invidiam referre fatorum. Nihil magis interesse
omnium puto, quam ut spes pro homine tam longa quam

---

[41] viriditate *Alm.* (*prob. Watt*[3] *51*)   [42] -los ς: -lus (-lum
S) *codd.*   [43] *add. Wint.*[7] *148:* ⟨tantam⟩ *Hine ibid.*
[44] dis placet V: displicet B Φ*   [45] fam- *Watt*[2] *26:* form-
codd.   [46] -ma ς: -me *vel* -mae *codd., unde* ⟨cum⟩ -me *Håk.*

---

[44] "[T]he idea is that nature ceased to be truly nature when it
was corrupted by man" (Watt [1991, 51]).   [45] Doctors.

believe in their verdicts of despair, I do not go along with them when they give up hope and abandon sick patients"? In fact, I don't believe them even when they hope. (6) Look at the greater part of mankind, and—if you ask me— the stronger part, those still living in the true primeval state of nature:[44] they know no high priests of this art, yet they can heal wounds caused by war and counter the onset of disease; they bring succor along traditional lines, not by the futile ingenuity of theoretical disputes but by experiment and the observation that leads such men alternately through cases similar and dissimilar. (7) It is not medicine that cures; rather, everything that is seen to have cured in the past is medicine.

10. How do you want me to feel about the fact that an art which was, as you[45] assert, invented to preserve life is (heaven help us!) looking for authority and repute ⟨by⟩ claiming to foresee deaths well in advance, to announce that ends are at hand when they are not even feared, and that the greatest part of the science is coming to be its inability to cure? (2) Does anyone, when he sees a man still talking, breathing, understanding, go away as though it is a lifeless corpse that he is abandoning? Will he think the end of life comes at any point where feeble science is brought to a halt? If we care to bear in mind the vulnerability of mortal men and their uncertain fortunes, every sick man is in exactly the same danger. (3) It is quite wrong for cries of "no hope" to be raised every time medicine cannot find a remedy, and for the limitations of art or the human mind to be ascribed to the malevolence of fate. I think nothing is more in the interests of everyone than that hope for a man should last as long

4   vita sit. Unde putatis inventos tardos funerum apparatus, unde quod exequias planctibus, plangore[47] magnoque semper inquietamus ululatu, quam quod facinus videretur credere tam facile vel morti? Vidimus igitur frequenter ad

5   vitam post conclamata suprema redeuntis. Plerique convaluerunt neglegentiae bono, quosdam explicuit quicquid alios fortassis occideret; hos indulgentiae temeritas, illos adiuvit desperationis audacia.

    11. Detur[48] fortassis huic arti perspicere morbos, profutura meditari: sed unde sciret quantum intra[49] viscera latentesque pectoris sinus unicuique animae natura concesserit, quam proprietatem spiritus, quam corpus acce-

2   perit? Non tam variae mortalibus formae, nec in vultibus nostris sedet tanta diversitas, quanta latet in ipsis dissimilitudo vitalibus. Inenarrabile, indeprehensibile est quicquid nos elementorum varia compago formavit, et, prout in nos plura seu rariora de terrenis seminibus caelestibusque coierunt, ita vel duramur tacita ratione vel solvimur.

3   An desperantibus credi debuerit, vos aestimabitis; qui negarunt aegros posse sanari, nec in hoc probaverunt qui evasit, nec in illo quem non languor occidit.

4   Iustas mehercule haberet mulier causas querelarum, si

---

47 pl- B V δ (*vind. Beck.*[2] *79.4*): cl- γ β (*def. Dess.*[1] *80*)
48 dat- Φ
49 intra W (*vind. Wint.*[7] *148*): inter *codd.*

---

46 A reference to the ritual of *conclamatio*: after the funeral wake, the relatives would direct repeated cries at the deceased, to awaken them from a possible apparent death before proceeding to bury them. Cf. *Decl. min.* 246.4; Pasetti (2014, 21–22).

as life. (4) How do you think it came about that preparations for funerals are so slow, that we always disturb the
proceedings with breast-beating, wailing and shrieking?[46]
It is because it was thought outrageous to believe so easily
even[47] in a death. We have in fact often seen people returning to life after their last rites had been performed.
(5) Many have recovered thanks to being neglected, some
have been saved by what might perhaps kill others; some
have been helped by reckless indulgence, others by the
boldness born of despair.

11. Maybe it is granted to this art to see deep into illnesses, to think out what will treat them effectively:[48] yet
how could it know the length of life nature has conceded
to each individual within the guts and the secret recesses
of the breast, what particular feature a spirit, what a body
has been given? (2) Shapes are not so various in mortals,
nor is such diversity imprinted on our faces, as the difference that lies hidden in the vital organs themselves. Beyond description, beyond detection is the form, whatever
it may be, that we have been given by the various structur-
ing of our elements, and, in so far as more or fewer earthly
and heavenly seeds have come together to construct us, so
we are mysteriously made to endure or to break up. (3) As
to whether the doctors who offered no hope should have
been believed, *you* will judge; those who said the patients
could not be cured proved their point neither in the case
of the boy who escaped, nor in the case of the other who
was not killed by *illness*.

(4) The woman would indeed have good reason for her

[47] Death being apparently so final a thing.
[48] Cf. 8.16.2.

141

nova incognitaque ratione vel utrumque servasses. Numquam ex magno venit affectu incredibilia vel profutura
temptasse, et, in re quae plus de incerto habet, temeritas
5 experimenti solam probat desperationis audaciam. Quid
refert cuius sit condicionis aeger, quantum adhuc spei,
quantum videatur habere de vita? Sacrosancti sint parentum metus. Dii non sinant ut ex liberis vilior incipiat esse
6 periturus. Medici desperaverunt: quid istud ad patrem?
Spera tu, iube⁵⁰ sperare matrem, tuis potius affectibus,
7 tuis crede votis. Et hoc de parricidii facilitate est:⁵¹ circa
filiorum languorem ad desperantes potius accedere. Fidem habes hominibus, quos mentiri alius affirmat, contra
8 quos iterum credis uni?⁵² Pessime mehercule⁵³ de tua
feritate sentirem, si in quacumque filii curatione non ad-
hiberes propinquos, non interrogares amicos, non respi-
ceres ad matris animum. Non hanc primam impatientiam,
9 non hunc consulis timorem? De nullo filio minus debet
soli sibi permittere pater, quam qui videtur utique⁵⁴ moriturus.

12. "Fratres" inquit "et gemini erant, ideoque credibile
est illis eundem fuisse languorem." Rogo, quis in ullo mor-

⁵⁰ ⟨tu⟩ spera, tu iube W: spera tu, ⟨tu⟩ iube *Wint.*⁷ *148*
⁵¹ *dist. Gr.-Mer.*   ⁵² *dist. Håk.*² *72*
⁵³ pessime mehercule *vel sim.* ς (*def. Håk.*² *72; adde Cic.* Phil.
14.18): praesertim si me hercule *codd.*
⁵⁴ utrique (*ut* soli sibi *opponatur*) *Håk.*² *72*

⁴⁹ I.e., to the doctors who predicted death. Instead, a good
father should have consulted friends, relatives (8.4.6), and especially his wife (8.7.6–7). Compare the attitude of another father
at 10.4.1.

charge even if you had saved both of them by a new and untried treatment. Great affection never leads to trying out far-fetched methods even if they prove successful, and in a case so full of imponderables a risky experiment proves nothing but the audacity of the desperate. (5) What difference does it make what the condition of the sick youth was, how much hope, how much life he seemed still to have? The fears of parents should be sacred. God forbid that of two children the one on the verge of death should begin to be less valued! (6) The doctors had no hope: what is that to a father? *You* must hope, tell the mother to hope, trust rather in *your* feelings, *your* prayers. (7) This too is a sign of readiness to commit parricide: to prefer to turn to the no-hopers when your sons are ill.[49] Do you then trust people whom another asserts to be liars, then turn round and believe in that single individual? (8) I should think very poorly of your barbarity if, whatever cure was in question for your son, you did not summon relations, did not ask the opinion of friends, did not pay regard to the views of the mother. Do you not first consult *her* passionate emotion, *her* fear? (9) A father should allow himself the sole say least of all where a son looks as if he is going to die in any case.[50]

12. "They were brothers, and twins at that," he says, "and so it is likely enough that they had the same illness." I ask you, who would tolerate such a combination of igno-

[50] If a son seems to be going to die in any case, a father has less reason than ever for trusting the question to his own sole judgment (DAR).

2   talium ferat ignorantiam pariter et adfirmationem? Quisquis nescit quod genus languoris sit, non potest scire an idem sit. Nihil, iudices, in rebus humanis voluit esse rerum natura tam simile, quod non aliqua proprietate secerneret. Quid refert an ex isdem prima illa duorum cor-
3   porum animorumque compago seminibus oriatur? Sibi quisque firmatur,[55] sibi quisque componitur, et duo pluresve fratres nascuntur fato singulorum. Hanc ipsam in-
4   differentiam, quam mirantur occursus, stupent civitatis oculi, parentum tamen agnitio dinoscit, separat notitia nutricum, et, fallentibus notis, est rursus quod faciat ipsa similitudo dissimile. In plerisque, quamvis sit indiscreta facies, invenitur tamen alius oris sonus, habitus, incessus, seu,[56] ut ipsa[57] consentiant, diversa mens, contrarii mores et vitae genera rixantia.

5   Quid, quod non eandem esse naturam geminorum probat etiam fortuna dissimilis? Hunc pressit paupertate perpetua, illum insperatis opibus excoluit; huius[58] per titulos, honores, illius per ignobiles obscurasque sordes totam
6   duxit aetatem. Simile est quicquid accipiunt ex homine gemini, dissimile quicquid ex fato. Nec enim tam pariter in lucem de maternis exiluere visceribus, ut illos eadem origo signaverit. 13. Quantum putas interfuisse temporis,

---

[55] for- π, *sed vd. Håk.*
[56] seu *Dess.²* (*firm. Håk.²* 72–73): sed *codd.*
[57] ita δ: ista W *necnon Franc.*
[58] huius *scripsi, cf. supra* hunc . . . illum (*nisi chiastice h.l.* illius, *mox* huius *malis*): illius *codd.*

---

[51] Sc., for both twins.
[52] Cf. Quint. 10.2.10.

rance and assertiveness in any mortal being? (2) A person who cannot identify an illness cannot know if it is the same.[51] Nature, judges, wished nothing in the realm of humanity to be so alike that it did not mark it off by some special feature.[52] (3) What matter if that original combination of two minds and two bodies takes its rise from the same seeds? Every one is built up individually, is formed individually, for two or more brothers are born with separate destinies. (4) Their very likeness may make those who meet them marvel, it may astound the eyes of the city; but their parents can tell them apart, nurses who know them well can distinguish them, and, for all the misleading features they have in common, there is nevertheless something that their very similarity makes different. In most cases, though the face is indistinguishable, yet there can be discerned a different tone of voice, bearing, walk, or, even if those are similar, a different mentality, a contrasting character, a manner of life at variance.

(5) What then of the fact that different fortunes too show that twins do not have the same nature? Fate oppresses this one with continual poverty, that one it favors with unexpected riches; throughout life it bears one along in a succession of titles and public offices, the other amid the undistinguished obscurity of low degree. (6) What twins get from man is similar, what they get from fate is dissimilar. The truth is that they did not spring from their mothers' wombs at the same time, so that the same origin could set its seal on them.[53] 13. How much time do you

[53] I.e., so that they could have the same horoscope (= disposition of the stars at their birth), and thereby the same destiny (cf. Introduction to *DM* 4).

dum primum uteri pondus egeritur, dum parumper exonerata vitalia altero rursus homine laxantur? Breve fortassis exiguumque videatur immortalibus oculis, sed, si ter-
rena mente perspicere velis orbis huius vastitatem, scies
2 multum esse, quod inter duas transcurrat animas. Volvitur
super nos haec caeli siderumque compago et,[59] praecipiti
per proclive decursu totius diei noctisque brevitatem[60]
emensus, orientis occidentisque cursus diversis siderum
⟨intervallis⟩[61] in primo statim ortu rotato se rursus axe
3 consequitur. Hoc tu parvum[62] credis esse spatium,[63] quod
diversis pariter rebus impletur? Quantum inter illa trans-
4 currentis horae momenta nascitur, perit! Igitur quando
umquam peregrinati sunt una, militavere pariter? Quid
non diducti[64] separatique fecerunt? Quando illos languor,
5 quando suprema iunxerunt? Et quandoque sit necesse est
⟨aeger⟩[65] alter ex geminis:[66] quod pariter languerunt non
sic accidit quomodo fratribus, sed quomodo duobus. Non
eodem fato languere geminos quemadmodum vultis bre-
vius probem, quam quod nec uterque occisus est nec uterque sanatus?

[59] ⟨sol⟩ *post et add.* ς (*i.a. B. Asc.*[2]), *post* decursu *Franc.*
[60] -tem *Sch.*: -te *codd.*   [61] -sis s. ⟨intervallis⟩ *Hüb.*: -si s.
codd.: -sorum s. ς   [62] -rvum ς: -rum *codd.*
[63] (parum . . .) -tii *Wint.*[9]   [64] ded- V Φ
[65] *suppl. Håk.*[3] 130   [66] *dist. Obr.* (*et vd. Håk.*[3] 130)

[54] Every day the sun completes its revolution around the
earth, while all the heavenly bodies follow their own courses; the
rotation of the celestial axis then makes it possible for the sun to
"catch up" in time to start its course anew by the new day, though
the distances between the planets have meanwhile changed.
These crucial astronomical movements take place every single

think elapsed between the ejection from the womb of its first burden and the point when the vital organs, after a period of relief, opened again to bring forth a second human being? It may seem short and tiny in the eyes of the gods, but if you care to gaze at the vastness of this globe from an earthling's perspective, you will realize that there is a considerable gap between the birth of the two souls. (2) Above us this framework of heaven and stars rolls on, and the course from east to west measures out in its headlong descent the short period of a complete day and night; then, just where the new dawn is at its very crack, that course catches itself up despite the now different ‹distances› between the planets, thanks to the renewed rotation of the celestial axis.[54] (3) Do you think it is a small time that is filled with so many different things at once? How much is born and perishes between those moments of the passing hour! (4) As a result, when have they ever gone abroad together, gone to war alongside each other? What have they not done apart and separate?[55] When did illness, when did death join them together? (5) Sooner or later, it must be that one of two twins falls ‹ill›: their sickening together did not happen to them as brothers, but as two persons. When a couple of twins are ill, it is *not* because they share the same fate—how should I prove this more briefly than by reminding you that the two of them were neither both killed, nor both cured?

instant, so it is no wonder that the horoscopes of two twins may change dramatically from each other in the interval between their births, short as it may seem. Cf. Favorin. fr. 27.26 Amato; August. *De civ. D.* 5.2–3.

[55] See Introduction to the present declamation.

6   Sed fingamus hoc esse verum, quod desperaverunt
medici; relinque nobis, pater, innocentiam calamitatis.
Salva solacia sint de liberis, quos tibi videris non perdidisse nisi fato.[67] Quis ex parentibus nescit in hanc[68] se
7   mortalitatis procreare legem?[69] Sed indigni exitus supra
orbitatem sunt. Ideo magis flemus illos quos bella rapue-
8   runt, hausit incendium, naufragia merserunt. Fortius fe-
ras inter adsidentium manus, inter suorum officia labentes, cum se invicem oscula, cum se satiavere sermones,
cum data[70] suprema mandata sunt, et se scit pietas omnia
fecisse pro vita. Igitur verum dixerim: illos mori credimus,
hos perire.

14. Non invenio quemadmodum excusationem pater
de consensu possit accipere medicorum. Hoc est quod
omnem comparationem feritatis excedit: filium pater
propter hominem occidit,[71] quem non putavit posse sa-
2   nari. Quod tu monstri portentique genus es? Habes parricidii patientiam, non habes orbitatem; ita demum potes
3   ferre filii mortem, si facinus adieceris. Tu occidis quia
desperavere medici? Quererer mehercules si reliquisses,
4   si quid de continuatione curae sollicitudo laxasset. Nihil
ergo plus facies quam illi, qui nunc plures circumeunt
fortassis aegros, quos distrahit,[72] quos avocat alia curatio?

---

[67] nisi ex f. V   [68] hanc V (*def. Håk.[2] 73*): hac B Φ

[69] -em B V (*def. Håk.[2] 73*): -e Φ   [70] *del. Leh., sed vd.*
Håk.[2] 73   [71] -dit *h.l. habet* β (*def. Håk. coll. 8.19.3*): *ante*
propter π: *post* sanari ς: *om.* B V γ δ

[72] distrahit A (-ait V), *cf. ThlL V.1.1542.17ss.*: detrahit *cett.*

---

56 Lawyer and client (cf. 1.1.3 with n. 6).

(6) But let us pretend that the doctors were right to despair; leave *us*,[56] father, our innocence in this catastrophe. Let our comfort remain unaffected, regarding children that—in your opinion—you have only lost by fate. What parent does not know that he begets children subject to the law that men must die? (7) But undeserved deaths[57] are worse than bereavements. That is why we grieve more bitterly for those whom war has taken from us, fire engulfed, shipwreck drowned. (8) You can bear it more bravely when people slip away in the arms of their carers, with the household doing its duties, when there has been kissing enough, talk enough, when the final instructions have been given, and dutifulness knows it has done everything to keep them alive. That is why it is true to say that these people die, those others perish.

14. I do not see how the father can look for an excuse to the agreement of the doctors. What goes beyond any comparable instance of barbarity is this: a father killed his son for the sake of another human being he thought could not be cured. (2) What kind of prodigious monstrosity are you? You can tolerate killing a child, but not losing one; you can only bear your son's death if you add a crime to it. (3) You kill because doctors despaired? Heavens, I should be accusing you if you had *neglected* him, if you had in your stressful situation been in some way remiss in persevering with a treatment. (4) Do you intend, then, to do no better than doctors who perhaps at this moment have many patients to visit on their rounds, who are diverted and called away by another case? At least entrust your sons

[57] I.e., violent or premature deaths, as opposed to ordinary natural ones.

149

Filios saltem committe vel matri; de fortuna queratur, diis
5 faciat invidiam. Mulieri, quae ferre non potest quod videris desperasse, numquam ex hoc rationem reddas, quod
occideris.

6   Quis hanc, iudices, impudentiam ferat? Temptat pater
ut et huic rei credatis, quod desperaverunt[73] omnes et
7 quod speravit[74] unus. Nostrae quidem querelae sufficit
non convenisse medicis, et, cum inventus sit qui contra
sensum desperantium genus aliquod sanitatis adferret, fas
erat, iudices, ut adhuc inveniretur alius qui laetiora, uti-
8 liora promitteret. Hoc nunc me queri putatis, quod in re,
de qua credere nec omnibus debuisset, accessit uni? Non
interest an supersit remedium quod temptare non debeas,
et ubi tantundem periculi spes[75] quantum desperatio ha-
9 bet, melior exitus est qui facit miseros innocentes. Quid
invidiam prioribus medicis paramus? Nemo magis despe-
rat quam qui se negat nosse languorem.

15. Quid ais, pater? Ita tecum quisquam sic audet
agere de duobus filiis tamquam de duobus aegris?[76] Tu ex
2 geminis alterum occidendum dabis? Non ferrem si sepa-
rare expositurus auderes, si contentus esses educaturus

[73] -rint B V A
[74] -arit *Gand. 321*
[75] spes *Gr.-Mer.* (*firm. Håk.*[2] *74, Håk.*): speres *codd.*
[76] servis *Håk.*[3] *130–31, sed vd. Bur.*

[58] Your wife does not forgive you for giving up hope of curing
both twins; still less could she forgive you for killing one of them.
[59] If innocence is to be preserved, so uncertain a remedy
should be excluded a priori (AS).

to their mother; let her complain of fortune, curse the gods. (5) To a woman who cannot bear it that you, as it seems, despaired, you could never justify yourself by saying that you killed.[58]

(6) Who, judges, would tolerate such impudence? The father tries to make you believe even this, that all lost hope and one retained it. (7) It is enough for our charge that the doctors did not agree; when one was found who, against the opinion of those who held out no hope, offered some kind of cure, the right course, judges, was to go on looking for someone who could suggest a happier and more practical solution. (8) Do you think my present complaint is that, in a matter concerning which he should not even have believed a unanimous opinion, he went along with just one doctor? No, it makes no difference whether there is still a remedy available if it is one that you ought not to try out: when hope involves as much danger as despair does, the better way out of the problem is one that makes the unhappy innocent.[59] (9) Why do we reproach the earlier doctors?[60] No one has less hope than someone who says he does not recognize the illness.

15. What do you say, father? Does then anyone dare to discuss two sons with you as though they were two patients?[61] Of two twins, will you give one to be killed? (2) I should not put up with it if you had the temerity to make a choice between them as candidates for being exposed, if you were content to raise one or the other as your son; I

[60] For having no hope; in fact (see the next sentence) the doctor who advised vivisection had as little hope as they.

[61] I.e., just two ordinary sick persons, not related to each other or to you.

alterutrum; non ferrem a piratis captum filium alterius
vicaria servitute redimentem. Tu de orbitate facies vices,
3 et casum singulorum per utrumque diffundes? Parricidium vocarem si, promittente medico quod sanaret unum,
posses eligere periturum. Paene crudelius est geminos
dividere quam perdere.

4   En scientia cui debeat credi! Negat se scire causas languoris, deinde promittit quicquid licere non deberet nec
5 intelligentibus. "Occidam," inquit, "deinde sanabo." Me-
mineris, pater, in hac condicione prius esse, ut occidas.
Non est tanta pietas servare filium, quantum facinus occi-
6 dere. Tu nunc hoc putas profundae artis esse secretum?
Verba tantum desperationis involvit, et homo cautissimae
vanitatis captat illam novissimam circumire veritatem.[77]
7 Vides quanta promissum suum experimentumque caligine
medicus involverit: numquam constabit an fuerit languore
8 moriturus aeger, qui aliter occiditur. "Non novi" inquit
"languoris genus." Post hanc vocem mehercule non de-
beres committere aegros, etiamsi vellet[78] experiri potionis
9 haustus, ciborum fomentorumque novitates. "Nescio," inquit, "sed si permiseris alterius aperire vitalia, pectus ef-
fringere, remedium fortassis inveniam." Iam excusatus es,
medice, matri: sperasti ne tibi crederetur.

---

[77] veri- *Håk.*: brevi- *codd.*
[78] -et 5: -ent *codd.*

---

[62] This doctor prescribes a treatment that should not be permitted even to one who, unlike him, is confident of its efficacy.

[63] Literally, "now": i.e., in the light of all this, with an ironic
nuance.

[64] = that he could not cure them both. Cf. 8.4.2.

152

should not put up with you ransoming a son in the hands
of pirates by sending the other twin to be a slave in his
place. Will you play fast and loose with the loss of children,
spreading the fate of one between both? (3) I should call
it parricide, if the doctor promised a cure for one and you
were able to choose the one to die. It is almost more cruel
to part twins than to destroy them.

(4) Here indeed we have a science worthy of confidence! He says he does not know the causes of the illness,
then he prescribes things that not even people understanding those causes should be allowed to do.[62] (5) "I will
kill," he says, "then I will cure." Remember, father, that
the first stage of this arrangement is that you kill. It is not
so great an act of fatherly affection to save a son as it is a
crime to kill one. (6) Do you really[63] regard this as a secret
of a deep art? All he is doing is camouflaging his verdict
of despair: this master of cautious deceit is trying to avoid
revealing the ultimate truth.[64] (7) You see in what dark
words the doctor wrapped his promise and his experiment: it will never be established if the sick man was going
to die of his illness, for here he is, killed in a different way.
(8) "I do not know" he says "the kind of illness." After this
avowal you should not, by heaven, have entrusted him
with sick men, even if he wanted to[65] test the correct dose
of a potion, or novel diets and compresses. (9) "I do not
know," he says, "but if you let me lay bare the vital organs
of one of them, break open his chest, I shall possibly find
the remedy." You are excused by now, doctor, in the mother's eyes: you hoped you would not be believed.[66]

[65] Sc., no more than to.
[66] Cf. 8.4.2

16. Differo paulisper quod de fratribus, quod de geminis, quod pater hoc facit[79] non consentiente matre;
publico potius mortalitatis contendo nomine non debere
genus istud curationis admitti. Peractum est velut de genere humano, si nobis pro salute aegri opus est morte
hominis alterius, et paene[80] ratio sanitatis intercidit, si
2 consumit medicina tantundem. Ego quemquam dicentem
feram: "Ut inveniam valetudinis causas, date mihi corpus
aliud, alia vitalia; occidam, deinde salutaria quaeram, profutura meditabor"? Ita non facilius est nosse languorem?
3 Quae haec est impudentia crudelissimae vilitatis? Aegrum
placuit occidere, ut inveniretur cur non debuisset occidi!
4   Nullum, sanctissimi iudices, natura morborum genus
solis visceribus abscondit, et quicquid causas valetudinis
de vitalibus trahit, in corpus emanat. Inde pallor, inde
macies, quod ad interiorem dolorem superposita con-
5 sentiunt. Non invenio cur hominem vulneribus exquiras,
cum[81] remedia quoque vitalibus per corpus immittas, et
in latentes meatus ‹per›[82] haec, quibus tegimur, medicina
descendat. Cur ergo non eadem ratione languor admittit
6 intellectum qua sanitatem? Prodit abditos profundosque
morbos aut citatior clausi sanguinis cursus aut crebrior
anhelitus laborantis animae. Crede de his ante omnia sensibus, oculis tuis, et ipsos, de quibus agitur, modo singulos,
modo pariter interroga, cui potissimum parti grave tacitae

---

[79] fec- *Gr.-Mer., sed cf. e.g. 8.15.1*
[80] plane *Håk.*   [81] cum *Sch. (firm. Håk.² 74): cur codd.*
[82] *add. ⟂*

---

[67] Cf. 8.15.3.
[68] The particular case of the twins is envisaged here.

16. For the moment I pass over the point that the father is doing this to sons, to *twins*,[67] without the mother's consent. Rather, in the name of all men in general, I assert that this type of cure should not be countenanced. We may as well say goodbye to the human race, if to save a sick man we need the death of another human being: the rationale of curing is virtually annihilated, if medicine destroys as many as it heals! (2) Shall I tolerate someone saying: "So that I can find the causes of an illness, give me another body, other vital organs; I will kill, then I will look for ways to heal, I will think out what will help"? Can one then not get to know an illness more easily than that? (3) What is this impudence on the part of a contemptible sadist? He thought it proper to kill a sick man to find out why he ought not to have been killed!

(4) Most respected judges, nature hides away no type of disease in the inward parts alone: anything that derives causes of disease from the vital organs spreads on to the surface of the body. Pallor and wasting away are the result of the outer parts being in sympathy with the internal pain. (5) I see no reason why you should have to pry into a man by cutting him open, for remedies too can be passed into the vitals through the body, as medicine descends into the hidden passages ⟨through⟩ the parts that cover us. Why then can illness not admit understanding in the same way as it admits cure? (6) Hidden and deep-seated diseases are betrayed by swifter flow of the blood within the body or more frequent gasps of the troubled breath. On these matters you should put your trust primarily in the senses, in your own eyes, and interrogate the patients in question—sometimes individually, sometimes together[68]—as to where in particular the oppressive weight of the hidden

155

pestis pondus insederit, unde prorumpat in gemitus
7 conscius dolor. Medicus, qui per haec non potest invenire
languorem, non invenit nec remedium.

17. Quodsi[83] aliquid laniatus[84] medicinae[85] potest praestare[86] rationis, sufficit quod, aliquando iam facta exanimis[87] hominis inspectione, ad totius intellectum naturae
medicina profecit. Quid adlaturus huic aegroto es[88] quod
non tot saeculorum, tot languentium experimenta depre-
2 henderint? Vis tu potius hac audacia, qua secreta languoris
exquiris, remedia temptare? Brevior via sanitatis huma-
3 nae, propior nostrae salutis utilitas est. Si viscerum nimius
ardor stricta circa se membra duravit, adhibe remedia
laxantia. Si fluitat nimis aeger humoribus, praesto sint per
quae pressis clusisque venis in novas vires corpus arescat.
4 Si parum prodest abstinentia, rursus ciborum qualitate
foveatur. Si spiritus receptis premitur alimentis, ad pu-
5 riores meatus ieiunio fameque tenuetur. Contigit tibi
magna experimentorum materia, medice: aegri duo et
languor idem. Non est opus ut expectes quando se per[89]
unius hominis patientiam explicet profuturorum magna

83 quod si π: quid si *cett., at vd. Sh. B.[1] 76*

84 laniatus *scripsi (vel subst. abstract., cf. 12.27.1; vel partic.
vi subst., cf. 8.17.9)*: sanato *codd. (frustra def. Håk.[2] 74–76)*: ⟨ex⟩
laniato *Reitz.[2] 64*: ⟨ex⟩ secto *Wint.[7] 148–49*

85 -nae *(dat.) Sch.*: -na *codd.*

86 laniatu . . . praestari *olim ego, invitis numeris*

87 exanimis *Håk.[2] 74–76*: ex unius *codd.*: [ex] unius *Reitz.[2] 64,
Ellis 336*   88 es *Gron. (ut vid.)*: est B V Φ*

89 se per ς *(corrob. Bur., Håk.[2] 76)*: super *codd.*

---

69 Sc., by cutting up another's body.

bane has settled, where the pain they are aware of is coming from, that makes them groan aloud. (7) The doctor
who is unable to identify an illness by such indications
doesn't find its remedy either.

17. Anyway, supposing that butchery *can* provide medicine with some basis of method, the art surely has made
sufficient progress toward understanding the overall nature of man once it has inspected, now and then, a *dead*
person. What in fact will you bring to this sick man[69] that
has not been found out through the experience of countless patients[70] over countless years? (2) Will you not rather
test out *remedies*[71] with the same boldness with which you
propose to pry into the secrets of an illness? There is a
shorter route to human health, a way of curing us that is
closer at hand. (3) If excessive heat in the bowels has
hardened organs by knotting them up, administer laxa-
tives. If the sick person is unduly awash with humors,
make available means to compress and close the veins, so
that the body can dry out and acquire new strength. (4) If
abstinence does not do the trick, then try coddling the
patient with appetizing food. If the breathing is affected
after taking nourishment, let the patient be made thinner
by fasting and hunger to clear the passages. (5) Doctor,
you have come upon a wealth of material for your experi-
ments: two sick patients, and the same illness. There is
no need to wait for a great variety of potential remedies
to unfold itself as a single man suffers; you can try out

[70] I.e., the experience doctors have drawn from the observation of individual cases.

[71] To be found on the principles described in 8.17.2–4, as
opposed to vivisection.

diversitas; potes experiri pariter eadem, consentanea, di-
6 versa, pugnantia. Nulla ratio est vulnerum, sanguinis, su-
premorum. Quemadmodum sanari debeat alius aeger,
scire non possis nisi ex homine sanato.

7   Quid, quod, etiam ut idem sit valetudinis genus, necesse est tamen duorum corporum diversitate varietur?
Numquam in alienis visceribus invenias totum quod de
8 altero quaeras, et alius languor est ⟨si⟩[90] alius aeger. Cur
maximum nefas alterius filii salute defendis? Homo, in
quo sola quaeritur causa languoris, propter medicum occiditur.

9   Adice quod nec deprehendi ex laniato[91] potest ullius
causa languoris. 18. Quicquid nos in vitia morborum a
naturali sanitate commutat, facit aut nimii sanguinis pondus exaestuans aut superfluens calor aut ultra naturalem
modum humor exundans aut spiritus per tacitos meatus
2 non solita laxitate discurrens. Quid horum, si vitalia ferro
vulneribusque resecentur, salvum potest esse languentibus, cum compressi spiritus laborem protinus ille reserati
pectoris meatus emittat, sanguis isdem pariter deprehen-
datur egrediaturque vulneribus? An fas putatis ut suam
servent viscera nudata faciem, ut nihil perdat ex priore
natura illud pectoris vitaeque secretum, cum admisit ocu-
3 los? Plurimum in nobis etiam timore mutatur. Quantum
aufert[92] sollicitudo, gaudium, dolor et aliquis subitus

---

[90] add. Wiles 69   [91] laniato Reitz.[2] 64.3 (cf. ad 8.17.1):
sanato codd. (frustra def. Håk.): secto Str.[3] (-cato Watt[2] 26)
[92] aufert V: off- B δ: aff- γ β

---

[72] Because there are two patients.
[73] Denying the possibility raised at 8.17.1.

simultaneously[72] treatments that are the same and compatible with each other, or unlike and conflicting. (6) There is no justification for using wounds, blood, deaths. You can only know how another sick person ought to be cured by looking at someone who *has* been cured.

(7) What then of the fact that, even if it is the same kind of illness, there must be variation arising from the differences between two bodies? You'd never find in the internal organs of one person all that you are looking for with regard to another: <if> the patient is different, the illness is different. (8) Why do you try to defend an extreme crime by adducing the cure of the other son? When a man is investigated only to discover the cause of an illness, it is for the satisfaction of the doctor that he is being killed.

(9) Besides, there is no illness[73] whose cause can be detected from the butchering of a body. 18. Any change from the health natural to us into the disorder of disease is the result either of a seething mass of excess blood, or of undue heat, or of moisture overflowing its natural limit, or of breath not traveling through its secret passages with its normal freedom. (2) Which of these processes can be preserved if the sick man's vital organs come under the knife? The passage made by the opening up of the chest instantly allows the escape of the labored breath that had been confined within, and blood comes out through those same gashes the instant it is revealed. Or do you think it possible for the inward parts to retain their appearance once they are exposed, for the secret life of the breast to lose nothing of its former nature when it has let eyes in to see it? (3) Fear, too, causes extreme alterations in us. How much is taken away by anxiety, joy, grief, or any sudden

4 adfectus! Quotiens, dum ad curationem praeparatur aeger, dum componitur ad sua remedia corpus, medentium
manus anima destituit! Iam vero ad singulos ictus et lon-
gissimas vulnerum moras quantum ex toto homine conver-
5 titur clamore, gemitu! Necesse est omnis perire, quibus
continetur vita, causas, quotiens ipsa vita consumitur, et,
cum homine qui propter intellectum languoris occiditur,
6 ipse quoque paulatim languor emoritur. Differ saltem,
pater, hanc crudelitatem; quicquid ex filio facis, facies ex
cadavere. Si potest deprehendi languor, dum occidit, facilius, cum occiderit.

7   Interrogare mehercules hoc loco libet, utrumne peri-
8 turum pater an medicus elegerit. Negavit[93] sua interesse
quem occideret. Hoc,[94] si et alter perisset, probaverat
utrumque fuisse periturum; cum convaluerit, probat
9 utrumque victurum. Ad saevissimam curationem[95] potuit
aegrum facilius mehercules explicare, si esset unici pater.
Sufficit[96] ergo comparare, decernere? Non iterum ille tibi
pretiosior, ille melior incipiet esse victuro?[97] 19. Ubi est
impatientia,[98] qua vix[99] dimittitur cadaver in rogos, qua
2 corpus exanime detinetur amplexu? Dii immortales, quam

93 ‹uterque› n. *Håk.*: ‹ille› n. *Russ.*[3] (hic *mox recepto*)
94 hic *Wint.*[9]   95 at -ma -ne *Sch.*
96 -is *Håk.*   97 sufficit—victuro *dist. Håk.*
98 impa- 5: pa- *codd.*
99 vixit V Φ

---

74 Cf. 8.19.8.
75 Father, probably (cf. 8.18.9); the speaker will later state that
Father was in fact able to choose, thanks to his lack of affection
for his children.

emotion! (4) How often, while a sick man is being made ready for treatment, while his body is being prepared for the remedy appropriate to it, does the patient's breath escape the healers' hands! Or, to be sure, how much of the whole frame is altered by the screams and groans uttered at every cut, at the long-drawn-out incisions![74] (5) Everything that serves to keep life going must perish whenever life itself is destroyed, and, as well as the man who is being killed to throw light on his illness, the illness itself too dies a gradual death. (6) At least delay this cruel process, father! Anything you do with your son you will be able to do with his dead body. If an illness can be identified while it is in the process of killing, identification will be easier when it has killed.

(7) I should dearly like to ask at this point whether it was the father or the doctor who chose who was to die. (8) He[75] said it made no difference to him whom he was to kill. If the other too had died, he would have proved thereby that both would have died; since one got better, he proves that both would have survived. (9) Heavens, he could more easily have exposed a sick man to a horrendous treatment if he had been the father of one son only.[76] Is he in a position, then, to compare, to decide? Will not that one in turn become more precious, become better in your paternal eyes, than the one who will live? 19. Where is the overwhelming love that makes one hardly able to allow the corpse to be taken off to the pyre, so that he goes on embracing the dead body? (2) Immortal gods, how savage,

---

[76] If he had had only one child, he would not have had to choose and would have found it easier to use harsh measures to try to cure his son (DAR).

saeva, quam crudelis est ipsa cunctatio! Dum deliberas,
dum unumquemque detrectas, parricidium in utroque
3 consummas.[100] Duorum vilitate fit ut ex fratribus possit
alteruter occidi. Numquam, iudices, res tam horribilis
inauditaeque[101] feritatis admissa est: filium pater propter
4 eum occidit, quem etiam ipsum poterat occidere! Trans-
fert, iudices, reus in medicum electionis invidiam: "Ille"
inquit "aestimavit, ille decrevit." Ergo manifestum est non
parem fuisse languorem: ex duobus aegris plus habuit
spei, propter quem debuit alter occidi.
5 Recede paulisper, mulier infelix: filii tui nobis refe-
renda curatio est. Felices aegri qui languore moriuntur,
qui supremos anhelitus inter suorum amplexus, inter suo-
6 rum adloquia posuerunt! Ut erat iuvenis primo ipso com-
parationis incerto, mox electione cruciatus, abacta est a
perituro prima mater, et modo sedula ministeria servorum
repente mutata sunt in mortis officia. Detrahuntur tre-
mentibus velamenta membris et, ut grassaturas manus
totum corpus admitteret, nudatur miserabilis ac deflenda
7 macies. Toto deinde tenditur toro, et ad immobilem rigidamque patientiam per omnia lectuli spatia duraturus
exponitur. Accipit carnifex ille telum, non quo dextera statim totum vulnus imprimeret, sed quo[102] leviter paula-

---

100 -mmas *B. Asc.*[1] *lvi r.* (*cf. 11.11.4, Curt 6.10.14*): -mis *codd.*
(*errat ThlL IV.617.50–51*)
101 inauditaeque M D[2] P: tam inauditae E: mandatique S:
inauditae *cett.*: <et> inau- *Sh. B.*[2] *201*   102 quo *Wint.*[7] *149*
(*qui et* quod dex- . . . quod lev- *coni.*): quod *codd.*

---

77 Cf. 8.4.7.
78 I.e., from court.

how inhuman is the very delay! While you ponder, while you reject each in turn, you are completing your murder in the case of both. (3) It is because of your low valuation of both that either of the brothers can be killed. Never, judges, has an act of such horrific and unheard of cruelty been perpetrated: a father kills one for the sake of the other, whom he might have killed as well! (4) The accused, judges, is seeking to shift the invidious choice to the doctor: "*He*," he says, "weighed the issue, *he* decided." So[77] it is obvious that the illness was not identical: in the case of two sick men more hope was entertained for the one for whose sake the other had to be killed.

(5) Withdraw[78] for a while, unhappy woman: I have to describe your son's "cure." Happy the patients who die from illness, who succeed in gasping their last amid the embraces of their family, amid their comforting words! (6) As for that youth, tortured as he was first by the very suspense of the comparison, then by the choice, before anything else the mother was driven away from the doomed man;[79] right after, the solicitous services of the slaves were abruptly changed into preparations for death. The clothes are stripped from the trembling limbs, and, so that the whole body should lie open[80] to the hands that will attack it, the emaciated frame is stripped naked, pitiful and lamentable. (7) Then he is stretched the full length of the bed, and put on display all over it to hold out against what he had to suffer unmoving and stiff. The dreaded executioner takes up his weapon, not to make the whole incision at once with a single stroke, but by light and gradual cuts to

[79] Cf. 8.4.6.
[80] Cf. 8.19.8, *patienter admitte*.

timque discindens[103] animam in confinio mortis ac vitae
8   librato dolore suspenderet. Haec exhortatio,[104] hoc fuit
perituri iuvenis adloquium: "Fortiter dura, patienter admitte; sanabitur frater. Non est quod exanimeris metu,
dolore deficias. Cave viscera exclamatione ne lasses, anhe-
litu gemituque concutias, ne remedium pereat alienum."

9   Passus est miser discurrentem per omnia reserati pectoris improbum vagae[105] artis errorem. 20. Contentum
fuisse medicum toto[106] homine discentem primo putatis
aspectu? Egesta saepe vitalia, pertractata, diducta[107] sunt;
2   fecerunt manus plura quam ferrum. Stat iuxta medicum
pater apertis visceribus inhians; stillantem animae sedem
cruentis manibus agitantem ne festinet hortatur, iubet
altius diligentiusque scrutari, interrogat, dubitat, contendit, adfirmat et accipit de filii morte rationem.

3   At mulier infelix, clusis advoluta foribus cruentumque
secretum toto corpore effringens, velut super busta tumu-
losque clamabat: "Audi, miserrime iuvenis, si quis adhuc
tibi superest sensus, exaudi: non permisit hoc mater, crede
orbitati meae, crede lacrimis; nec frater hac vellet ratione
4   sanari." Inter haec reficiebatur miser haustibus, detineba-
tur adloquiis, comprimebatur residuus cruor, cludebantur
aperta vitalia. Nemo umquam tam nova pertulit com-
5   menta saevitiae: tamquam sanaretur occisus est. Ite nunc

---

103 descen- Φ, sed vd. Håk.² 77   104 exortatio E (exho-
ϛ), def. Håk.² 77–78: exoratio (exho- S) cett.
105 vanae Sch., sed vd. Beck.² 77–78
106 ⟨de⟩ vel ⟨ex⟩ toto Wint.⁷ 149, sed vd. Tr.-B. 139
107 did- π (cf. 8.22.5): red- O: ded- cett.

---

81 Cf. 8.18.4.   82 Cf. 8.21.1.

regulate the pain and keep the patient's breath on the borderline between life and death. (8) This was his exhortation, these were the words he addressed to the doomed youth: "Endure bravely, let me enter you patiently: your brother will be cured. You need not be terrified, or faint from pain. Make sure you do not tire your organs by crying out, do not shake them by gasps and groans:[81] otherwise another's remedy may come to nothing."

(9) The wretched youth endured, as it roamed through every part of his gaping breast, the reckless wandering of a fumbling skill.[82] 20. Do you suppose that a doctor intent on his inquiries all over the body was satisfied with a first glimpse? The vital organs were often drawn forth, handled, separated; hands did more than scalpel. (2) Next to the doctor stands the father, transfixed at the sight of the exposed guts; as the doctor scours the dripping abode of life with bloody hands, he urges him not to hurry, tells him to make his examination deeper and more careful, asks questions, raises doubts, argues, makes assertions—is instructed in the rationale for his son's death.

(3) But the wretched mother, prostrate at the closed doors and trying with all her might to break a way in to the bloody secret, cried as though over the pyre, the tomb: "Hear me, most unfortunate youth, if you have any sensation left, listen: your mother did not sanction this, believe me as I lose you, believe me as I weep; not even your brother would want to be cured by this method." (4) Meanwhile the poor boy was being revived with drinks, kept going by comforting words; the remaining blood was staunched, the exposed vitals were closed up again. No one ever endured such novel devices of savagery: he was killed as if he were being cured. (5) Go on now, ask whether

165

et quaerite an potuerit medico sanante vivere, qui tamdiu vixit dum occiditur.

21. Vos tunc[108] putatis illius tantum languoris medicum quaesisse causas? Quaesivit quicquid nesciebat, et usus occasione rarissima in omnem voluit proficere novitatem.

2 Dii immortales, quantum infelix iuvenis animae, quantum sanguinis, quantum habuit ex vita, qui pertulit ordinem longissimae curationis! Vix, aegre[109] misero licuit mori, vix

3 a cruciatibus suis anima dimissa est. Inventum putatis esse

4 languorem? Inventum est illum potuisse sanari. Agedum commento tuo, senex, superbus exulta; habes quod liberis, quod parentibus, quod imputare saeculo possis: fecisti medicum parricida[110] meliorem.

5 Libet mehercules intueri par illud: ⟨illinc⟩[111] aegrum videtis hominem, qualem non salutares medentium manus, non ars inventa pro vita, sed diri ferarum rabidique morsus et animalium fames satiata destituit; hinc alium, in novas vires recensque robur reddito vigore surgentem.

6 Vultis scire, iudices, unde venerit tanta diversitas? Illum

7 pater curavit, hunc mater. "Quantum" inquit "misera pertuli laborem, dum tam magnam foveo tristitiam! Non fuit mihi rixa cum morbis nec cum repugnantis valetudinis

8 rigore contentio. Totus in lacrimas maeroremque resolutus oderat lucem; respuebat cibos, fastidiebat haustus, et

---

108 nunc B   109 -ro π A, *sed vd. Beck.*[2] *78–79 et Str.*[3]
110 -dio *Sch., sed vd. Str.*[3]
111 *suppl. Bur.* (*cf.* §6 illum… hunc)

---

83 The speaker invites the audience to form a visual reconstruction (*diatyposis*).   84 Cf. 8.5.3–4.

he could have survived if the doctor had been *curing* him: you see how long he lived while he was being killed!

21. Do you think that on that occasion the doctor looked only for the causes of the illness in question? He looked for everything he did not know: taking advantage of this quite unique opportunity, he was anxious to make progress toward any new piece of knowledge. (2) Immortal gods, how much breath the unhappy youth must have had, how much blood, how much life, if he could withstand the successive stages of so extended a "cure"! Scarcely, only with great difficulty, was the poor boy allowed to die, scarcely was his soul released from its torments. (3) Do you think the illness was discovered? What was discovered was that he could have been cured. (4) Go ahead, old man, exult in pride over your discovery; you have something to claim credit for with children, with parents, with a whole generation: by killing your son you made a doctor better!

(5) Heavens, I am of a mind to survey[83] the pair of them: <on the one hand> you see a sick man, looking not like one given up for lost by the healing hands of doctors, by the art that was designed to preserve life, but like one left over from the dreadful bites of rabid beasts and the sated hunger of animals; on the other, a man with restored vigor, rising to new strength and fresh energy. (6) Do you want to learn, judges, the source of such a difference? The one his father cured, the other his mother.[84] (7) "What pains I took," she says, "trying to comfort a son in such deep sorrow! My struggle was not with diseases; I did not have to battle with an obstinate illness. (8) Wholly given over to tears and depression, he loathed the light of day; he rejected food, he was disgusted by drinks; he was in

vitam parricidii pudore fugiebat. In omni proclamatione
gemituque frater, ille diebus ac noctibus cogitationes, ille
9 torquebat oculos." De quibus tu aegris, impotentissima[112]
medicina, mentita es![113] Non fuit, non fuit solo languore
periturus, quem non potuit nec mors fratris occidere.

10 "Quid igitur," inquit miserrima feminarum, "saevis-
sime senex, ex hac recordatione tristissimae orbitatis ad
hos vultus faciemque converteris?" Sine dubio filius est et
post gravissimas denuntiationes redditus vitae, 22. sed
ignoscat natura,[114] pietas: non est solacium matri unus
2 ex geminis. Felicior ille dolor est, quo[115] transigi saltem
cum oculis potest; ⟨hic⟩[116] renovatur, accenditur, et in
his vultibus illum cotidie putat videre pereuntem. Sed et
ipse gaudio redditae vitae laetitiaque non fruitur, nec se
credere potest caritate praelatum, quem medicus elegit.
3 Sentit infelix cuius orbitatis unicus sit, quibus lacrimis per-
fundantur oscula, quam magnis profundisque suspiriis
concutiatur amplexus. Misera verecundia sanitatis ingra-
tae: pretium[117] sibi videtur fratris occisi.

---

112 inpotentissima π (*def. Håk.*[2] *78*): in <u>potentissima</u> potissima
S: impotissima (pot- O) *cett.*

113 *exclam. dist. Str.*[3]

114 -rae πM E, *sed vd. Håk.*[2] *27–28*

115 quo *Sh. B.*[1] *77*: qui *codd.*

116 *add. Bur.*   117 praemium *Russ.*[3]

---

85 He blamed himself for his father's killing of his brother.

86 Literally, "have you, overconfident medicine, lied about"—
sc., when claiming that the twins were doomed to die: the surviving youth was in fact able to endure both the illness and the remorse for being alive at his brother's expense; it is implied that
the other too was strong enough to live.

flight from life out of shame at the parricide.[85] All his shouts and groans were of his brother: day and night, it was he that tormented his thoughts, he that tormented his eyes." (9) *What* patients has this overconfident doctor lied about![86] He was not, no, he was not, going to die just from illness: not even the death of his brother could kill him.

(10) "Why then," the most wretched of all mothers says, "cruelest old man, do you put the memory of this grievous loss behind you, and turn to this[87] face here, this countenance here?" A son, it is true, has been brought back to life, and after the direst prognoses; 22. but let natural affection pardon her:[88] one of a pair is no comfort to a mother. (2) Happier is the pain that at least lets one have done with one's eyes;[89] ⟨*this*⟩ pain gets renewed and inflamed: every day, in the face of the one, she thinks she sees the other dying. But even this twin does not reap the fruits of the joy and happiness of a life restored to him: he cannot believe that he was preferred out of affection, when it was the doctor who chose him.[90] (3) The unfortunate man feels the full extent of the bereavement which has made him an only child, is aware with what tears his mother's kisses are mingled, with what deep sighs she is wracked when she embraces him. He feels, poor wretch, ashamed of a cure he did not welcome: he thinks himself the reward for the killing of his brother.

[87] Sc., your surviving son's; he is taken to be present in court.

[88] I.e., for not being consoled by the survival of at least one son.

[89] I.e., a pain not renewed by seeing the surviving twin.

[90] Cf. n. 75. Here it is implied that the doctor chose, not the father.

[QUINTILIAN]

4   Convertitur hoc loco, iudices, mulier infelix et velut ad
quandam praesentiam amissi iuvenis "Sive" inquit "tandem securitate mortis explicitus in aliquo[118] sedis aeternae
nemore[119] requiescis, sive exclusus ac vagus [et][120] inter
fabulosa supplicia, metuendus adhuc laceratione, per stu-
pentes horrentesque manes umbra discurris, audi miser-
5   rimae matris iniquissimam complorationem. Non quidem
licuit mihi in illud cubiculum, conditorium[121] tuae mortis,
inrumpere, nec supra carissima membra prostratae meis
vulnera tua tegere visceribus; quod solum tamen potui,
corpus quod medicus, quod reliquerat pater, hoc sinu misera collegi ac vacuum pectus frigidis abiectisque visceribus rursus implevi, sparsos artus amplexibus iunxi, membra diducta composui et de tristi terribilique facie tandem
6   aegri cadaver imitata sum. Hoc est tamen, quod de tris-
tissima orbitate praecipue ferre non possum: propter fratrem videris occisus, nec tamen umquam constare poterit
an tu sanaveris fratrem."

118 al- ‹angulo› (*mox* pudore *recepto*) Axel., Sh. B.[2] 201
119 nemore Bur.[1] coll. Verg. Aen. 6.638–39, 703–4: pudore
codd.
120 delevi (et om. V)
121 cub- -rium (subst.) ⟨ (def. Bur.): -rum (-rium O[2]) cub-
codd., unde -rium (adiect.) cub- Tos. 143 (et vd. Str.[3]): -rium
[cub-] Sch.: [-rum] cub- Leh.

(4) At this point, judges, the unhappy woman turns, and as though speaking to her lost son in person says: "Whether, at last freed by death, the banisher of care, you are at peace in some grove of the eternal realm, or whether, shut out from there and condemned to wander among fabled punishments, still an object of fear for your mutilations, you range, a shade yourself, through ranks of ghosts that recoil from you in amazement: listen to the most bitter complaint of your all-wretched mother. (5) True, I could not burst into that room, your dead body's funeral chamber, or, prostrate on your darling limbs, cover your gashes with my own flesh; but the only thing I could, I did: in my wretchedness, I brought together in the fold of this dress what the doctor and the father had left behind, and replenished your empty breast with the organs they had discarded, now grown cold. I made the scattered members embrace each other, put the limbs together again, and out of that grievous and ghastly spectacle finally contrived the semblance of the sick youth's corpse. (6) But one part of my tragic loss I find especially impossible to bear: you were killed, it seems, for your brother's sake, but no one will ever be sure if it was you who cured your brother."

DECLAMATION 9

INTRODUCTION

Rich Man and Poor Man are enemies, while their sons are friends. Rich Man's son experiences the fate of most travelers in declamation: he is captured by pirates and writes home about a ransom.[1] His father, however, delays taking action, and the pirates sell the youth to a manager of gladiators.[2] The youth follows the gladiatorial school troupe to the city where a show was to be offered: when he is already resigned to meet his fate in the arena,[3] Poor Man's son rescues him by taking his place; in return, he asks the rich youth to support his poor father, should he be in need. The poor youth dies fighting; the rich youth returns to his city,

---

[1] Cf. Introduction to *DM* 6, n. 1.

[2] The speaker distinguishes between the *lanista*, manager of the gladiatorial school, the *magister*, who trains the gladiators in preparation for the fights, and the *munerarius*, who promotes and funds the games, for which he hires the gladiators from the *lanista*. Cf. Wallner (2008, 311).

[3] According to Carter (2015), the young man was sold to the *lanista* not as a gladiator supposed to engage in an actual fight, but as a captive to be executed in the arena: yet the youth states that he was trained as a gladiator (5.6) and exposed to some practice in killing (8.6), and his friend—who replaces him—will eventually engage in a real combat, in which he dies with honor (9.4–8).

finds Poor Man in need and starts maintaining him. This disappoints his own father, who has not forgotten his enmity with Poor Man, and now disowns his son. Rich Man's son challenges the disownment. *DM* 9 gives his speech.

Like any son arguing against a parent,[4] the speaker must present himself as a devoted son, who avoids opposing his father and his choices directly. So Father is not blamed for not intervening to ransom his son (his friends were responsible for this: 5.1); indeed, the speaker devises some flattering interpretations to explain his disownment: Rich Man may have resented his son supporting Poor Man without asking *him* to do so (2.2–4); or perhaps he brought this case to court just to pardon his son in public and himself support his (former) enemy, so as to show off that *his* household is generous too (e.g., 2.6, 21.3).

The whole case is presented as arousing public interest: "common people" accuse Son of cruelty, for letting his friend die in his stead (1.3); some people think that Rich Man is not really upset about his son, but is just seeking attention (2.6); and prejudiced observers are ready to pin on Rich Man the responsibility for the feud with Poor Man (2.7).

The enmity between the two characters must be accounted for too: in the speaker's interpretation, it did not arise from personal reasons, and it continued more by force of habit than because of real rivalry between the two; also, there had been signs that both sides were willing to call a truce, such as the friendship between the two sons, which the fathers did not try to stop (3.1–4.1, 15.1–5).

---

[4] Cf. General Introduction, §2 with n. 31.

The narration of the facts stresses the adversities Rich Son had to face in his imprisonment, so as to emphasize the merits of the poor friend and the value of his sacrifice (4.2–7.3); the description of the rich youth's bonds (4.3), his surprise on seeing his rescuer (7.4–7), and his resistance to the exchange (8.5–10) all follow the recurring pattern of topics on this subject;[5] the account of Poor Son's heroic combat against a veteran gladiator suggests that he could have survived: but he was not prepared to go on living the life of a gladiator—a role he had taken on for his friend's sake (9.3–9). Such a pathetic climax emphasizes the debt of gratitude that the rich youth owes his friend and his duty to grant him the only request he made before dying: to support his poor father (9.2).

For most of his argumentation, the speaker aims at countering two charges: on the one hand, he is accused of doing something against the wishes of his father (i.e., supporting his father's enemy); on the other, the youth thinks he should be charged with not doing *enough* for Poor Man, in comparison with what his friend did for him (1.5, 10.1–2, 19.2–8, etc.).

In reply to the first charge, the speaker argues that he has been supporting Poor Man at very limited expense, not even comparable to what other sons spend for their pleasures, and certainly not enough to justify disownment (10.2–7); nor is disownment the way for a father to welcome home a son unexpectedly restored to life (11.1–5). Praise of friendship (13.1–14.1), a plea that the enmity between fathers should not be passed down to their children (14.2–6), and a hint at the inescapable duty of solidarity

[5] Cf., e.g., 6.5.3–6.9, 16.8.6–9.8.

between human beings (15.6–17.8) provide the son's case with "philosophical" foundations. As for the charge of not doing enough for the father of his benefactor, the speaker cannot deny the disproportion between the good he has received and what he has done, but this is turned into a further argument against his disownment (e.g., 19.1–8).

Like the other earliest pieces of the collection (see below), this speech makes use of Roman *exempla*, to invite Rich Man to have mercy on his enemy (17.7, 20.6); examples from myth are exploited as well, to present the sacrifice of the poor youth as a gesture that surpasses all legends concerning friendship (22.1–4).[6]

The structure of the speech can be analyzed as follows:[7]

> PROEM 1.1–2.7
> NARRATION 3.1–9.9
> ARGUMENTATION
>   *Confirmatio* 10.1–11.5
>   *Refutatio* 11.6–22.8
> EPILOGUE 23.1–7

This piece may be included in the earliest group of the *Major Declamations* and shows a particular resemblance to *DM* 6 in theme, argumentation, and language. A(n) early Hadrianic date may be suggested.[8] A reply to the speech is included in the collection of *Antilogiae* by Patarol.[9]

---

[6] Cf. Krapinger (2007b, 19–22).
[7] Krapinger (2007b, 24–26).
[8] Cf. General Introduction, §4.
[9] (1743, 268–90).

9

Gladiator

ABDICARE ET RECUSARE LICEAT. Pauperis et divitis inimicorum filii iuvenes amici erant. Filius divitis, cum in
piratas incidisset, scripsit patri de redemptione. Illo mo-
rante profectus pauperis filius, cum amicum apud piratas
non invenisset, quia lanistae venierat, pervenit in civitatem, in qua munus parabatur, sub tempus ipsum, quo
pugnaturus erat divitis filius. Pactus est cum munerario
pauper adulescens ut vicariis operis redimeret amicum,
petitque ut, si egeret pauper pater, alimenta ei praestaret.
Ipse in pugna occisus est. Divitis filius reversus egentem
invenit pauperem. Palam coepit alere; abdicatur.

1. Neminem umquam, iudices, intra tam breve aetatis
suae spatium plura terra marique perpessum, quam quae

9

The gladiator

IT IS TO BE LAWFUL TO DISOWN AND TO CHALLENGE DISOWNMENT. The youthful sons of two enemies, a poor man and a rich man, were friends. The rich man's son, after falling into the hands of pirates, wrote to his father about a ransom. The father delayed, and the poor man's son set out; after failing to find his friend with the pirates, for he had been sold to a manager of gladiators, he came to a city where a show was in preparation at the very moment when the rich man's son was about to fight. The poor youth made an agreement with the promoter[1] to ransom his friend by taking his place, and asked that if his poor father was in need his friend should give him sustenance. He himself was killed in the fight. The rich man's son, on his return, found the poor man in need. He began to maintain him openly. He is disowned.

(Speech of the son)

1. Judges, it is, I think, easy to prove that no one has ever suffered more, by land and sea, in so short a stretch of his

[1] On the *munerarius*, see Introduction to the present declamation, n. 2; below, n. 22.

proxima peregrinatione vel tuli vel timui vel vidi, facilis,
ut opinor, fides est, cum ex omnibus, quos novimus, mortalibus unus nominari me miserior possit, quem infelicem
2 ego feci. Tamen in hac quoque omnia excogitantis in me
fortunae violentia confiteor numquam hunc me con-
cepisse animo metum, ne post redemptum per alienas
3 manus filium displiceret patri meo misericordia. Illas ve-
rebar magis iam non tacitas vulgi opiniones, quibus crudelitatis atque saevitiae reus peragor.[1] Apud plerosque
sanctos et graves homines nondum excusare potui quod
redemptus sum; obicitur mihi orbatus senex et ille, qui
modo salvo filio etiam contra divitem steterat, amissis in
4 uno iuvene omnibus bonis inimicae domus supplex. Licet
enim totas advocemus in odia fortunae vires et unum
egentem senem universa gratiae mole calcemus, confiten-
dum est tamen: plus amici nocuimus quam inimici. Quin
ipsa prorogatae cotidiana stipe infelicis animae videtur
quodammodo maligna clementia; quod enim beneficium
5 est efficere ut vivat orbus? Unum tamen vel gravius crimen infelix haec abdicationis meae fortuna defendit, quod
vix ad sustinendum spiritum sufficientis cibos, prorsus
tantum mortis impedimenta avara manu dederim. Puto,
iam ignoscetis omnes, si plus praestare non potui invito
patre.

2. Quamquam, iudices, oboritur animo meo nonnum-

---

[1] *dist. Håk.*[2] *79–80 cum* M[2]: *post* homines *vulg.*

---

[2] A reference, perhaps sarcastic, to the judgmental "observers" (cf. 9.2.7) who are spreading these rumors about the youth.

life than I bore or feared or witnessed in my late journey, since, out of all the mortals we know, only one can be named who is more unfortunate than I: and that is he whose unhappiness was *my* doing. (2) Yet even while this violence of fortune was devising everything it could against me, I confess that it never occurred to me to fear that, after his son had been ransomed by another's hands, an act of mercy might displease my father. (3) What I feared more was the opinion of the common people—now openly expressed—as a result of which I am being pursued as one guilty of cruelty and savagery. In the eyes of so many decent and important persons,[2] I have not yet been able to justify my being ransomed. The bereavement of an old man is held against me, and with it the fact that one who only recently had stood up even to a rich man while his son was alive now has to beg from an enemy family because he has lost all he had in the person of a single youth. (4) For though we may summon all the forces of our wealth to counter these animosities, and trample a single needy old man under the whole weight of our influence, it has to be confessed: we have done more damage as friends than as enemies. Indeed, the very clemency I show in prolonging his unhappy life by giving him money every day is seen as something spiteful: for what sort of a good deed is it to enable him to go on living after losing his son? (5) But there is *one*, still graver charge that my misfortune in being disowned in this manner can answer: I have indeed been stingy, giving food barely sufficient to keep him alive, just enough, indeed, to stop him starving to death; yet I think you will all forgive me now for not being able to give more: my father did not wish it.

2. All the same, judges, the further suspicion arises in

quam et illa suspicio, quod patrem non alimenta uni seni
parce vivere adsueto nec liberaliter data nec diu danda in
offensam meam compulerint: quantulum est enim ⟨ex⟩[2]
facultatibus divitis, quod sub patre sane tenaci filio fami-

2 liae superest! Ac si foret maius forte momentum, quis tamen parens tam durus est, ut propter aliquam impensam
carere filio velit? ⟨Nisi hoc iram movit,⟩[3] quod ipse celatus
sit, quod non suae misericordiae pauperem commiserim,
non rogaverim, praesertim qui, quicquid umquam petii a

3 patre, exoravi. Sed neque haec ultimo fulmine castigari
meruit in differendis precibus verecunda cunctatio. Qui[4]
dum tempus opportunum, faciles aditus, hilariorem ani-

4 mum capto, interim volui superesse qui[5] ignosceret. Neque infitior tamen fuisse me lentiorem quam oportuit,
tametsi hoc praecipue habere videor patris simile. Sed si
ulla emendatio paenitentiae est, hic in publico vobis adhi-

5 bitis rogabo. Non ego aes alienum luxuria contraxi, nec
profusus in vitia fortuna nostra male usus sum. Redemp-

6 tionis meae pretium debeo. Si impetro, intellegam verum
esse quod quidam opinantur, ambitiosum patrem publi-
care voluisse domus suae misericordiam, ne viderentur

7 pauperes tantum vitam inimicis suis dedisse. Si[6] perseve-

---

[2] add. *Håk.*   [3] *lac. stat. Sch., supplevi e.g.:* ⟨irascitur
(*Håk.*), puto,⟩ *Wint.*[7] 150   [4] -tatio, quia . . . ignosceret, neque *Russ.*[3], *sed cf. B. Asc.*[1] lviii v.   [5] qui *Wint. ap. Kr.*[2]: cui
codd.   [6] sin *Russ.*[3], *sed item 9.14.4 si innoxius = sin i.*

---

[3] Pathos: the old man will soon be dead. Cf. 5.22.5.

[4] Disownment: cf. 9.10.5; *Decl. min.* 259.17.

[5] I wished that Poor Man might survive, to forgive me—for
causing his own son's death.

[6] Not to be disowned.

my mind that what turned my father against me was *not* the support I have given sparingly, and will not give for long,[3] to a single old man used to a frugal existence. What a tiny part ⟨of⟩ a rich man's resources is left over for his son—at any rate if the father is stingy! (2) And if there were conceivably a greater sum involved, what parent is so hard as to want to lose a son because of some item of expenditure? ⟨Unless he got angry⟩ because *he* was kept in the dark, because I did not entrust the poor man to *his* compassion, did not ask *him*, especially considering that I have always got from my father everything I asked for. (3) But nor did the respectful hesitation that led to my putting off my request deserve to be punished by the ultimate thunderbolt.[4] While I was waiting for the right moment, when my father should be accessible and in a comparatively cheerful frame of mind, my wish in the meantime was that he might survive—to forgive.[5] (4) But I am ready to admit that I was unduly slow—though this is something I seem especially to have in common with my father. Still, if penitence can do any good, I will make my request[6] in public, in front of all of you who are summoned here. (5) I did not run up debts by living a dissolute life, nor did expensive vices lead me to fritter our wealth away. I am in debt—but only for my ransom money. (6) If I obtain what I ask, I shall recognize the truth of what some people think, that my attention-seeking father wanted to show off the mercy of his household, to avoid it looking as if only *poor* men gave life to their enemies.[7] (7) If instead he

---

[7] Father may have disowned Son just to have an opportunity to take him back and allow him to support Poor Man publicly, in order to show that he was no less generous than his (former) enemy.

rat ut porrectos egenti cibos mea fame rependat, expulsum ab omnibus bonis filium similem faciat inimico, vereor ne iniquis aestimatoribus inexpiabilis illius et saepe reprehensi odii[7] culpa videatur penes patrem, qui tam facile irascitur.

3. Verum enim, si placet, fortunae magis moribus dissedere[8] quam suis; nam et paupertatis est proprium, quando alia deficiant, exerere[9] libertatem et, dum contemptus fama vitatur, potentiores vel ambitiose offendere, et nacta bonam conscientiam magna fortuna indignius 2 imparem adversarium patitur. Ergo conseruit, ut solet, casus duratura longius a parvis initiis odia, dum contumeliam humilitas facilius intellegit, dignitas gravius. Neque ulla fuit aemulatio (quae enim esse inter impares potest?), sed fato quodam similis ex diversis causis contentio: hic ‹in›[10] irascendo pertinax erat, ille in cedendo contumax. 3 Quamquam, nisi ultimam exprimere confessionem victi utique[11] placuisset, multa iam pridem signa dederant veniae[12] finemque pugnae petentis. Nam quo pertinuisse credimus quod pauper adulescens relictis omnibus solum

[7] -si odii O[3]: -sio de *codd.*   [8] -sed- *Dess.[1]* 97: -sid- *codd.*
[9] -rere *Dess.[1]* 97 *post Bur. coll. 13.6.6*: -rcere B V Φ*
[10] *suppl.* 5   [11] utri- *Bur.*   [12] -am *Sch.*

[8] Poor Man: Son would be reduced to hunger like him (DAR).

[9] Apologizing for the subsequent, unusual interpretation of the feud with Poor Man.

[10] Poor men like to show their independence by offending their betters, and *honest* rich men find this particularly hard to swallow—they feel they do not deserve such treatment (DAR). Cf. 7.12.6.

persists in wanting me to pay with *my* hunger for the food
I handed to a needy man, if he persists in wanting to expel
his son from all he has and make him resemble his enemy,[8]
then I am afraid that in the eyes of prejudiced observers
the responsibility for such an inexpiable and often criti-
cized feud may seem to lie with a father who is so easily
moved to anger.

3. On the other hand, if I may say so,[9] their quarrel
arose from a difference of income rather than of character.
It is characteristic of poverty, in the absence of anything
else, to assert its freedom, and, in order to avoid being
thought contemptible, to be positively ostentatious in giving offense to more powerful people. Equally, a million-
aire blessed with a good conscience is disinclined to bear
with an adversary beneath his level.[10] (2) So, as often happens, chance produced hatreds that would endure despite
their small beginnings, the inferior having less difficulty
with insult,[11] the superior taking it more seriously. There
was no rivalry (how could there be any between persons
so unequal?), but a kind of fate led to tension that was
similar on both sides though it arose from different causes:
the one was pertinacious ⟨in⟩ growing angry, the other
contumacious in yielding. (3) Yet, were it not for their
resolution to extort a final confession of defeat[12] at all
costs, they[13] had for a long time given many signs of forgiveness and of looking for an end to the feud. For what
else do we think was meant by the poor youth choosing

---

[11] Poor men "understand" insults better, since they are more
used to being insulted (AS).   [12] I.e., to make the other confess
he had been defeated.   [13] What follows concerns Poor Man
only; but we do come to Rich Man at 9.4.1 (see also 9.3.5).

4   me, quem coleret, quem amaret, elegerat? Sine dubio a
primis aetatis annis iunxerat nos potentissimus amor ille
puerilis, dum aut nulla erant inter parentes odia aut a
nobis non intellegebantur. Post diductas[13] tamen domos
perseveravit, immo impensius laboravit, et, si quid mihi in
eo satis perspectum est, nihil horum fecit invito patre.

5   Quantum intellegere potui, pauper sine dubio pudore
cedendi, ne damnasse causam suam videretur, simul quod
nulla ipsi dabatur gratiae via, stare visus in suscepto, cir-
cuitu tamen quodam[14] molliores temptavit aditus, et, dum
firma tandem pax impetraretur, filium nobis obsidem dedit. 4. Ac ne meus quidem offendi visus est pater; certe
numquam reprehendit, numquam prohibuit. Nec clam
feci, nec contumacem adversus patris imperia umquam
fuisse me vel ipse rerum declarat ordo.

2   Nam quamvis infestum latronibus mare iussus intravi,
neque dissimulaverim magnas fuisse causas patri cur hoc
mihi imperaret, quod ipse facere non potuerat. Ego, etsi
nesciebam, non interrogavi; satis plena ratio fuit patrem

3   velle. Felix navigantium condicio, qui procellas modo et
saevos tempestatis incursus et albentes fluctibus scopulos
aliaque pericula tantum maris pertulerunt! Ego miser
naufragis invideo: captus barbaris manibus, nec tam nexu
catenarum vinctus quam pondere, inundatum carcerem

---

[13] diductas 5: ductas B Φ: duras V
[14] -od- δ (*def. Leh.¹ 433*): -o`s´d- V: -osd- *cett.*

---

[14] He let his son keep up the friendship: thus the son became,
as it were, a hostage in the enemy camp.
[15] Yet in 9.5.1 Father is anxious to go to the rescue in person.

me alone, to the neglect of all others, as an object of his
attention and love? (4) Of course we had from our earliest
years been joined by the love that is so powerful between
boys, at a time when there were no feuds between our
parents—or, if there were, we did not understand them.
But even after the rift between our families, he continued
his friendship, indeed became even more committed to it;
and, if I had any insight into him, he did none of this
against his father's will. (5) So far as I could see, the poor
man, no doubt ashamed to give way for fear he might seem
to have condemned his own cause, and at the same time
because no means were available for winning over the rich
man, *seemed* to stand firm in his resolution; but by a sort
of roundabout route he essayed gentler approaches, and,
looking to the day when peace might be firmly established,
he gave his son to us as a hostage.[14] 4. And my father did
not appear to be offended either; certainly he never re-
proached me, never put a stop to it. I did not act covertly;
and that I was never disobedient to my father's commands
is made clear by the actual sequence of events.

(2) It was in fact under orders that I embarked on the
sea, infested by pirates though it was, and I shall not pretend that my father did not have excellent reasons to command me to do something he had not been able to do
himself.[15] I did not know why, and I did not ask: it was
sufficient reason that my father wished it. (3) Happy the
lot of seafarers if they have had to bear only hurricanes,
and the onrush of violent storms, and rocks white with
waves, and other perils which are only perils of the deep!
I am unlucky enough to envy the shipwrecked: I fell into
the hands of barbarians, and, laden with chains as tight as
they were heavy, I had to endure a prison washed over by

4 tuli et vincula macie laxavi. Quis non ignosceret omnibus,
qui post hoc exemplum navigare timuissent? Ergo, qua
una spe misera trahebatur anima, litteras de redemptione
5 scripsi patri—testor deos—soli. Quid enim sentire viderer
de parentis adfectu, si hoc incolumi redemptionem ab alio
petivissem? Nam quod unum mihi secundum patrem fortuna videbatur parasse praesidium, hoc sperare in illa
sorte non poteram; quid attinebat amico scribere, quem
sciebam non habere unde redimeret?

5. Numquamne mihi dabitur liberum tempus conque-
rendi apud patrem de amicis suis,[15] qui proficisci volentem
retinere temptarunt, qui piae festinationi attulerunt moras? Profectus esset tamen vel invitis omnibus (quis enim
non hoc praestaret filio pater?), nisi quod interim amicus
2 antecessit. Illum non pericula maris, non infesti latronibus
sinus, non vicinum meae fortunae documentum prohibuit.
Minus haec miror de amico; illud est, quod pensari nullis
3 beneficiis possit: proficiscentem non retinuit pater. Immo,
si quid in subsidia vitae seposuerat parca frugalitas, id
omne in impensas itineris contraxit et contulit. Infelicis-
4 sime senex, sic egere coepisti! Dicam nunc ego[16] per quos
iuvenis praestantissimus navigaverit fluctus, quos accesserit scopulos, quantos lustraverit sinus? Faciliora ista pu-
5 tant qui numquam navigaverunt. [In][17] Omnia praeceps,

---

[15] istis *Russ.*[1] 45, *sed vd. Set.* 70–71   [16] ergo V
[17] *del. Russ.*[3]

---

[16] Cf. 5.16.5, 6.4.1, 16.8.6–7.
[17] Emphatic: Father's very friends discouraged him from res-
cuing his son, rather than urged him to do so (as good friends
should have done).   [18] Like my father.

the sea, making my bonds looser only by growing thin.[16] (4) Who would not forgive all those who after this precedent might have shrunk from setting sail? So, as this was the only hope that kept me going in my misery, I wrote for a ransom to my father—and to him only, I swear by the gods. (5) For how would people have judged my opinion of my father's feelings, if I had asked ransom money from anyone else while *he* was still in good health? I could not, indeed, in that crisis rely on the single support that fortune seemed to have provided for me next after my father: what was the point of writing to my friend, when I knew that he did not have the means to ransom me?

5. Shall I never be given the opportunity to complain to my father about the friends of his[17] who tried to hold him back when he wanted to be off, who delayed his affectionate haste? Still, he would have set out despite all their objections (what father would not do that for a son?), except that meanwhile my friend got in first. (2) *He* was not deterred by the perils of the sea, the bays haunted by robbers, or the all too recent lesson of my own misfortune. I am the less surprised by this in my friend; but here is something that can be paid for by no services: his father did not try to keep him back as he set forth. (3) Instead, he got together and contributed to the expenses of the journey all that his parsimonious frugality had set aside to support himself. Most unfortunate old man, that is how you started to be in need! (4) Shall I tell now of the waves over which the excellent young man sailed, the rocks he encountered, the bays he traversed? Such things are thought easier by those who have never been to sea.[18] (5) Rushing headlong,

sine respectu sui, quem iam tum apparebat vitae non parcere, adiit,[18] exploravit; et tamen ille quoque, qui tanto
opere festinabat, sero pervenit.

6   Audite, audite, iudices, novam captivi querelam: iam
miser apud piratas non eram; alebat devotum corpus gravior omni fame sagina, et inter dedita[19] noxae mancipia
contemptissimus tiro gladiator,[20] ut novissime perderem
calamitatis meae innocentiam, discebam cotidie scelus.
Haec tamen omnia sustinui, tuli; adeo difficile est etiam
sua causa mori. 6. Et iam dies aderat, iamque ad spectaculum supplicii nostri populus convenerat, iam ostentata
per harenam periturorum corpora mortis suae pompam
2   duxerant. Sedebat sanguine nostro favorabilis dominus,
cum me, cuius, ut interiecto mari, non fortunam quisquam
nosse, non natales, non patrem poterat, una tamen res
faceret apud quosdam miserabilem, quod videbar inique
comparatus; certa enim harenae destinabar victima, nemo
3   munerario vilius steterat. Fremebant ubique omnia appa-
ratu mortis: hic ferrum acuebat, ille accendebat ignibus

18 (in omnia . . .) abiit *B. Asc.[1] lix v.*

19 dedi- *Valla* eleg. 6.35 (*cf. Char. 401*): debi- *codd.* (*frustra
def. Bur., Beck.[2] 29*)

20 tiro, gladiatoris *Russ.[3]* (*voce -toris cum seq. scelus conexa,
unde gladiatorium coni. Wint.[9]*)

19 Gladiators were overfed on a poor quality diet, high in
calories (*gladiatoria sagina*: Tac. *Hist.* 2.88.1). See also 9.22.6.

20 I was being trained to kill, so that in the end I might lose
the innocence of one suffering undeserved misfortune (cf. 9.8.6).

21 I.e., by suicide.

with no thought for himself (it was obvious even then that he had no regard for his own life), he went everywhere, searched everywhere; yet even one in such haste arrived too late.

(6) Listen, judges, listen to a novel complaint from a prisoner: by now I was unlucky enough not to be with the pirates any more. My doomed body was being crammed with food worse than any hunger,[19] for I was now the most contemptible among the slaves suffering for their misdeeds: a trainee gladiator, learning to be a criminal every day—to make sure that I should last of all lose even the innocence of my calamity.[20] Yet all this I endured, all this I suffered: so difficult is it to die even in one's own interest.[21] 6. And now the day had come, now the people had gathered for the show that was to put an end to us, now the bodies of the doomed, after being displayed in the arena, had led the procession that marked their own deaths. (2) The master of the games, who sought popularity by means of our blood,[22] had taken his seat; as for me, whose fortune, birth and father no one could know with all that sea in between, only one thing could make me pitiable to some: I appeared to be unequally matched; there was no doubt of the fate that awaited me in the arena, and no one had ever been worth less to the promoter. (3) On all sides, everything hummed with preparations for death: one man was sharpening a sword, another heating up plates with fire; on this side rods were being

---

[22] The *munerarius*, promoter and funder of games, who aimed at earning the favor of the public by offering them a slaughter of gladiators.

laminas, hinc virgae, inde flagella adferebantur. Homines[21]
4 piratas putares. Sonabant clangore ferali tubae, inlatisque
Libitinae toris ducebatur funus ante mortem. Ubique vulnera, gemitus, cruor; totum in oculis periculum. Si quid
est in me abdicatione dignum, iudices, unum crimen
agnosco: quod in haec amicum meum misi.

5 Est quidem felicibus difficilis miseriarum vera aesti-
matio; figurare tamen potestis qui tunc animus mihi, quae
cogitatio fuerit. 7. Namque et natura redit in extremis
tristis praeteritae voluptatis recordatio, et mihi cum generis conscientia, cum fortunae conspicuus[22] aliquando fulgor, cum liberales artes, cum omnia quondam honestiora
munerario meo, domus, familia, amici ceteraque numquam videnda in ultima mortis expectatione succurrerent
tenenti servilia arma et ignominiosa morte perituro, tum,
si ulla miseris fides est, quid horum omnium ignari agerent
propinqui, nihil peius de fortuna mea suspicantes quam
2 quod scripseram. Illud tamen gravissimum, quod patrem,
qui tamdiu non veniret, captum putabam. Ergo tota cogi-
tatione intentus in mortem expectabam cruentum illum
3 confectorem. Quis enim dubitet quid futurum fuerit, si
ego pugnassem? Ille quoque occisus est, qui inter nos, ut
apparet, fortior fuit.

---

21 homines *Håk.*[2] 80 (*corrob. Kr.*[2]): omnis B V: omnes Φ
22 -spicuus *Håk.*[2] 80–81: -scius *codd.*: -gruus *Gron.*

---

23 The speaker strays into the "commonplace on tortures" (cf.,
e.g., 18.11.5–6), perhaps because he thinks of the ways gladiators
were forced to fight (cf. Tert. *De spect.* 21.4).
24 Sc., in comparison.   25 The *confector* was an attendant
who finished off any badly wounded beasts (Sen. *Ir.* 3.43.2) or

brought, on that whips.[23] The pirates, you might have thought, were human beings.[24] (4) The trumpets brayed their funereal tune, and the couches of Libitina were brought on, a funeral preceding death. Everywhere wounds, groans, gore; the peril was in full view. If there is anything in me that merits disownment, judges, that is the one crime I acknowledge: I sent my friend into all this.

(5) The fortunate find it hard to assess misery aright; but you can imagine what I felt at that moment, what I was thinking. 7. It is natural that at the last there comes back to a man the sad recollection of past pleasure; so in the final moments before death, bearing a slave's arms and on the verge of coming to a shameful end, I thought of my lineage, the brilliance of my fortune—once so illustrious—, my liberal education, everything in the past that had been more honorable than my promoter: house, family, friends, all the rest I should never see again. I thought too, if the wretched can be believed, of what my nearest and dearest were doing, in complete ignorance of all this, not imagining I was suffering anything worse than I had described in my letter. (2) But the hardest thing of all was the thought that my father, who had failed to come for such a long time, must have been captured. Thus, concentrated entirely on the prospect of death, I had nothing to look forward to but the cruel dealer of the final blow.[25] (3) For who could doubt what would have happened if I had gone into battle? Even the man who, as is evident,[26] was the braver of the two of us, was killed.

people sentenced to death in the arena (Euseb. *Hist. eccl.* 4.15.38). The youth, as the next sentence makes clear, looks beyond the fight to its inevitable end.   [26] Cf. 9.9.5–6.

4 His cogitationibus attonito et in mortem iam paene demerso inopinata subito amici mei species offulsit.[23] Obstupui totumque corpus percurrit frigidus pavor, neque aliter, quam si vana obiceretur oculis imago, mente captus
5 steti. Ubi primum lux rediit laxatumque est iter voci, "Quid tu?" inquam, "Quo casu pervenisti huc, miser?
6 Numquid et te vendidere piratae?" At ille complexus cervices meas, effusis in pectus meum lacrimis solutus, intercepto prope iam spiritu meo,[24] iam trepidante me, pri-
7 mam vocem et diu solam edidit: "Satis vixi." Ut vero causas itineris reddidit et venisse se ad redimendum indicavit, "Et unde" inquam "tibi pecunia,[25] nisi redistis in gratiam, et te pater meus misit?"

8. Audite gentes, audite populi! Non solita iudicium nostrum corona circumstet, sed, si patitur natura rerum,
2 totus ad cognitionem talis exempli orbis circumfluat. Tacete, priora saecula, in quibus tamen a primordio generis humani paucissima amicitiae paria admirabiliora fecerat[26] longa temporibus nostris fides intercepta.[27] Quicquid historiae tradiderunt, carmina finxerunt, fabulae adiecerunt,
3 sub hac comparatione taceant. Quis crederet, si dubitari posset, inter duos amicos, quorum alterum immunem malorum omnium fortuna fecerat, alterum piratis ac lanistae tradiderat, meliorem condicionem fuisse captivi?

[23] off- *vel* obf- V H S (*def. Beck.*[2] *29–30*): ref- A: conf- O: eff- *cett.*

[24] meo *scripsi* (*cf.* meas . . . meum . . . me): sero *codd.* (*frustra def. Pir. 546*): misero *Håk.*

[25] -am γ

[26] -rat *ϛ*: -rant (-runt E) *codd.*

[27] -rempta *Str. ap. Kr.*[2], *sed vd. Pas.*[5] *606–7*

(4) I was stunned by these thoughts and already almost sunk in the grave, when suddenly there burst upon my eyes the unexpected sight of my friend. I was struck dumb, and a cold dread ran through my whole body. I stood there bemused, just as if an empty phantom were being set before my eyes. (5) As soon as light returned and my voice found a way through, I said: "*You*? By what chance have *you* come here, poor wretch? Did the pirates sell you as well?" (6) But he flung his arms round my neck and dissolved in a flood of tears on my breast; my breath was by now almost taken away, I was by now trembling, when he spoke his first and for long his only words: "I have lived long enough." (7) But when he had told me the reasons for his journey and revealed that he had come to ransom me, I said: "And how did you get the money, unless—that is—you[27] have been reconciled and my father sent you?"

8. Listen peoples, listen nations! Let not the normal circle of onlookers stand round our trial, but, if nature allows it, let the whole world flock around to learn of such an exemplary act. (2) Fall silent, past ages: in them, from the very start of the human race, lasting loyalty—terminated in our times—had produced only a very few pairs of friends more to be wondered at. Whatever history has handed down, poems have invented, fables have added, let them keep silent in comparison with this. (3) Who would believe, if there could be any doubt about it,[28] that when, of two friends, fortune had made one immune from all evils, while handing the other over to pirates and a manager of gladiators, the better lot was that of the pris-

---

[27] Plural: the pair of you, your father and mine.
[28] Cf. 12.9.6, *incredibile, nisi nossemus*.

4   "Si dives essem," inquit, "pecuniam pro te attulissem.
Quod unum pauperibus praesidium est, manus habeo.
Has piratis daturus fui, has pro te in pugnam vicarias
dabo."

5   Ignosce, pater, quod nimia contentione adfectus paene
tibi orbitatis vulnus impresserim. Testor deos non per me
6   stetisse quod vivo. Neque enim ita me efferarat[28] ludus,
aut in tantum duraverat animum caedis longa meditatio,
ut eum amicum vellem occidi, qui pro me mori poterat.
7   Vindicabam mihi fortunam meam et adhuc necessitatis
gladiator depugnare etiam volebam, neque ullis precibus
poteram evinci; quamquam se non superfuturum alioquin
minabatur idque unum adfirmabat interesse, utrum vicarium mallem habere mortis an comitem,[29] non vicit.[30]
8   Quid igitur actum sit quaeritis? Duxit me ad munerarium,
9   iudices. Quas ego illius preces, quam pertinaces lacrimas,
quam miserabilem obtestationem vidi! Nemo umquam sic
10   rogavit missionem. Transferuntur in illum detracta corpori meo arma, et male aptatis insignibus festinatum[31] par
producitur.

[28] -rarat ⟨ : -rabat V D: -rebat (off- E, aff- O) *cett.*
[29] evinci—comitem *sic dist. Sant.*[3]
[30] -it *Wint.*[9]: -i *codd.*
[31] des- *Bur.*[1] *et Bur., sed vd. Wint.*[7] 150

---

[29] For a comparable paradox, see 16.3.4.

[30] Taking your place as prisoner, as in *DM* 6 (cf. 6.9.4).

[31] I demanded to keep the role that fortune had given me, i.e.,
to go on being a gladiator.

[32] I.e., he threatened to commit suicide.

oner?[29] (4) "If I were rich," he said, "I should have brought money to redeem you. All that poor men have to help them, *I* have—my hands. These I was proposing to give to the pirates,[30] these I shall give for you, to fight in your stead."

(5) Forgive me, father, if by an excessive rivalry in affection I almost inflicted on you the wound of bereavement. I ask the gods to witness that it was not *my* doing that I am still alive. (6) The gladiatorial school had not so brutalized me, nor had long practice in slaughter so hardened my heart, that I desired the killing of a friend who was ready to die for me. (7) I claimed the right to fulfill my own destiny,[31] and, hitherto a gladiator by necessity, I now positively wanted to fight it out, and I could not be won over by any prayers; although he threatened that he would not survive in any case,[32] and asserted that the only point at issue was whether I preferred to have a substitute in death or someone to share it with, he did not prevail.[33] (8) You ask what happened then? He took me to the promoter, judges. (9) What prayers on his part, what stubborn tears, what pitiful protestations did I witness! No one ever asked for *release* from combat[34] so urgently. (10) The weapons were taken from my body and transferred to him, and the hurriedly arranged pair was brought on with ill-fitting blazons.[35]

---

[33] Sc., he still failed to persuade me to accept the exchange.

[34] Sc., let alone for *permission* to combat, as the young man was now doing; cf. 6.5.6 and 16.9.2–3 for a similar paradox. On *missio*, see 9.9.7 (AS).

[35] The "insignia" of the gladiators: Poor Son had to use those that had been got ready for his friend.

9. Quid me admonetis supremarum amici mei precum, quibus haec alimenta caro empta inopi patris senectuti petit?[32] Adiutorium hoc ad causam putatis? Me pudet
2 quod rogatus sum. "Per hanc" inquit "mihi lucem ultimam, per notissimam[33] amoris nostri fidem, non[34] sinas mendicare parentem meum. Sustineas, adiuves, praestes
3 affectum. Si mereor, tu sis illi vicarius meus." Nec plura dicendi tempus fuit, iamque suprema per galeam dederam oscula, digressisque in diversum ministris permissus
4 Mars erat.[35] O quam sollicitus spectavi! Quam attonita
5 mente! Quam simili corporis motu! Quotiens ad infestum mucronem, quasi ipse peterer, me[36] summisi, quotiens ad conatus erectus sum! O misera cogitatio, o crudelis natura
6 metus! Merito tu, amice, pugnare maluisti. Facinus indignum illum animum, illum ardorem non contigisse castris, non bellicis certaminibus, ubi vera virtus nulla pugnandi lege praescribitur.[37] Qua vi proelium invaserat iratus
7 etiamnum tamquam adversario meo![38] At[39] omnis impetus excipiebatur callide,[40] veterani gladiatoris astu; omnes conatus contra se erant. Nec difficilem tamen sub illo praesertim auctoramento habuisset missionem: sed noluit

---

[32] -tit *Wint.*[3] (-tiit *Franc., aeque bona clausula*): -tita *codd.*
[33] nov- *Franc.*   [34] ne *Sch., sed cf. 4.21.2, 8.11.5, 13.18.2*
et fort. 9.17.2   [35] fuerat B   [36] me M: *om. cett.*
[37] praescr- J (*def. Wint. ap. Kr.*[2]): praemium scr- B V Φ*
[38] dist. *Håk.*   [39] at *Håk.*: ad *codd.*
[40] -do *Franc., sed vd. Håk.*

---

[36] Addressed to the judges, or, better, to unnamed supporters.
[37] I.e., the signal was given for battle.
[38] Sc., rather than to watch, which is even worse than fighting.

9. Why do you[36] remind me of the last prayers of my friend, by which he sought for his father's poverty-stricken old age this nourishment so dearly bought? Do you imagine this helps my case? I am ashamed I had to be asked. (2) "By this my last glimpse of the light," he said, "by the celebrated sincerity of our love, do not let my father have to beg. Sustain him, help him, give him your affection. If I merit it, be my substitute in caring for him." (3) There was no time to say more; I had already given him my last kisses through his visor, the attendants had scattered to do their various tasks, and Mars was let in.[37] (4) O, with what anxiety did I look on! How frantic my mind! How I moved as *he* moved! (5) How often I ducked to avoid the hostile blade, as though I myself were the target, how often I stood upright to make a new onslaught! O unhappy thoughts, o fear cruel by nature! My friend, you were quite right to prefer to fight.[38] (6) It was a crying shame that that spirit, that ardor did not find its proper place in the army, in martial engagements, where true courage is not trammelled by any rules of combat! How violently he had plunged into the fray, angry even now as though with *my* adversary![39] (7) Yet every onslaught was cleverly parried by the cunning of a veteran gladiator; all his efforts turned against themselves.[40] He would not have found it hard to win release from combat, though, especially under *those* terms of engagement;[41] but he had no desire to live—as a

[39] I.e., angry as though the adversary was threatening *me*. Poor Son is even now more worried about his friend than about himself.   [40] Cf. Quint. 2.12.2.   [41] His heroism when facing an experienced opponent would probably have led the *munerarius* (and the public) to spare him, had he surrendered.

8   gladiator vivere. Igitur iam nudum corpus vulneribus of-
ferens, ut totam pro me⁴¹ mercedem semel solveret, stans
periit. Cui licuit in patria, in domo, inter propinquos
securo consenescere aevo, cui tranquillam sine reprehen-
sione agere vitam, iacet confectus vulneribus, et primo
9   iuventae flore fraudatus periit miser fato meo. At ego, qui
debebar illi fortunae, quem mors sibi destinaverat, emis-
sus ludo nocentior quam venditus, etiam viatico illius infelicis revertor. Placeamus licet nobis fortuna nostra, pater,
pauperi solvendo non sumus.

     10. Si qua est fides, iudices, pudet me contra indicare
mea beneficia, nec videor vobis rationem posse reddere
2   quod mihi tam parum obiciatur. Redemptoris mei patri in
pretium meum orbo, egenti, quid praestiti? Quod pirata
capto, quod lanista gladiatori: exiguam stipem et cibos
semper petendos. Quantulum enim dari poterat, quod
3   non sentiret dominus tam curiosus! De hac re consedistis,
hoc concitavit istam iudicii scaenam, panis datus mendico:
ut⁴² dilatata hac impotentiae nostrae opinione videamur⁴³
4   amicos ferro occidere, inimicos fame. Computemus totam

---

⁴¹ pro me *Bur.* (*firm. Håk.²* 81): prope *codd.*: propere *Sch.*
⁴² ut *Sch.*: et *codd.*
⁴³ -eamur V: -emur M E: -ebamur *cett.*

---

⁴² = he died, but without being defeated. The phrase recalls
gladiators who were in exceptional circumstances *stantes missi*,
i.e., released after a valiant combat in which they did not prevail,
but did not surrender either. See Brescia (2009, 306–9).

⁴³ Sc., to my father's charges.

⁴⁴ He is now accused "only" of supporting Poor Man; but his
contribution was very limited, and he thinks he should really be
accused of not giving Poor Man enough (cf. 9.1.5, 9.19.2).

gladiator. (8) So, baring his body now to the blows, he perished where he stood,[42] to pay my ransom in one installment. He who might have grown old quietly in his homeland, in his house, among his relatives, who might have lived a tranquil life without reproach, lies there overcome by his wounds; robbed of the first flower of youth, the poor boy perished there, meeting *my* fate. (9) Instead I, to whom that stroke of fortune was due, whom death had marked out for itself, go back home, more guilty when released from the school than when I was sold into it: I even used the unhappy man's travel money. We may pride ourselves, father, on our wealth, but we cannot pay what we owe to the poor man.

10. If you can believe me, judges, I am ashamed to reply[43] by pointing out my good deeds, and I feel unable to explain to you why I am being charged with something so tiny.[44] (2) What did I offer my ransomer's father when, to pay the price for me, he had lost his son and fallen into need? What a pirate offers a captive, what a manager offers a gladiator: a pittance, and food that needs always to be asked for.[45] For how little could I give that was not noticed by so pernickety a lord and master! (3) This is what you are sitting here to consider, this is what has summoned up the panoply of the law like this: bread given to a beggar—so that the gossip here about my "unbridled behavior"[46] has become so inflated that I am imagined to put friends to the sword and starve enemies to death. (4) Let

[45] But see for gladiators' diet 9.5.6 with n. 19.

[46] Another sarcastic reference to alleged rumors hostile to the speaker: cf. 9.1.3, 9.2.7.

istam meae luxuriae impensam, audite summam et mira-
mini, si hos sumptus ne divitiae quidem sustinent. Tanti
constat patri captivitas mea, cum tam caro redemptus sim.
5 Quo tandem patereris animo si delicatus adulescens, praesertim splendidis opibus,[44] vel ex aetate mores vel ex fortuna traxissem, et tempestiva convivia et pervigiles iocos
advocata sodalium turba solutus atque affluens agerem,
tantumque impenderem, quantum non posset te igno-
rante consumi (quae tamen ipsa boni patres libenter annis
remiserunt), cum abdicatione dignum putes et ultimo
patriae potestatis fulmine coercendum, quare mendico
seni porrexerim—ut parcissime dicam—quod illi filius
6 misit? Non redempta meretrix, non egestum conviviis faenus, non lenonum parasitorumque cara adulatio in crimen
venit; cibaria senis, nempe unius, aetate ac malis confecti.
7 Hoc divitias tuas concutit? Hoc fundatam paternis avi-
tisque opibus domum exhaurit? Si tam avarus es, com-
puta: adhuc de alieno vixi.

11. At haec fortasse, quae circumstat iudicium, corona
et omnis ignara causae turba magnum nescioquid et por-
tento simile crimen expectat. Abdicas me, pater, tam cito?
2 Modo tibi ex illa funesta peregrinatione insperatus revertor, unde ut venirem vix optare potuisti; nulla adhuc pro

---

44 opi- 5: operi- *codd.*

---

47 Son, instead, was supporting Poor Man with small sums,
without Father noticing: cf. 9.2.1–2.   48 Cf. 9.9.2. The speaker
is taking the place of Poor Man's son in supporting him.

49 First, at the expense of the pirates; then, of the gladiators'
manager; finally, at the cost of his friend's life.

us reckon up all this profligate expenditure of mine: listen to the total, and be surprised if these are sums even the rich cannot afford. *This* is all my captivity costs my father, though I was ransomed at so high a price. (5) What, I wonder, would now be your reaction if, as a young man pleasure-bent, especially one born to glittering riches, I had made either my youth or my fortune the basis of my behavior, and, dissolute and rolling in money, I were throwing parties before sundown and passing nights of revelry in the company of a bunch of cronies, spending so much that it could not be got through without you knowing[47] all about it (though decent fathers are normally happy to overlook all this in sons of my age), when you think it a case worthy of disownment, of blasting with the ultimate weapon in a father's armory, that to an old beggar I offered—to put it at its lowest—what his son sent him?[48] (6) The charge against me does not include buying the freedom of a mistress, interest incurred on the expenses for banquets, the high price of the flatteries of pimps and parasites: just the cost of food for an old man, only one, broken down by age and misfortune. (7) Does *this* shake the foundations of your riches? Does *this* drain the resources of a house built firm on the riches passed down by father and grandfather? If you are as miserly as that, do the sum: so far, I have lived at the expense of others.[49]

11. But perhaps these onlookers around the court and the whole crowd of people ignorant of the case are looking for some great and portentous charge. Do you disown me, father, so quickly? (2) I have only just returned unexpectedly from that fatal trip, from which you could hardly have imagined I would come back; no vows for my safe coming

reditu meo soluta sunt vota, non percussae diis immorta-
3 libus hostiae; redemptori certe gratiam non retulimus. At
ego expectabam ut desiderio incensus affectus vix posset
expleri, ut post infaustam profectionem velut obiurgatus
tanto periculo numquam me post hoc saltem peregre
dimitteres. Vix salutatis laribus expellor, et apud plerosque
4 dubitari potest an admissus sim. An hoc agis, ne quid tibi
praestitisse videatur qui me redemit? Saevus enim, credo,
et impius et, quod maximum omnium vitiorum signum
est, ingratus beneficia patris non aestimo; fortasse, cui
vitam debeam, nescio, nulla est apud animum meum me-
5 moria meritorum. Miserum me, quod non possum tantum
solvere quantum accepi!

6   Quamquam causas abdicationis pater altius repetit et
ultra peregrinationem meam inquirit, idque ratione du-
plici: primum ut reum, quia premere atrocitas criminum
non potest, turba confundat; deinde ut gravius videatur
iudicium patris, cum is damnet, qui soleat ignoscere. 12.
"Cur," inquit, "cum ego inimicum haberem pauperem, tu
amicum filium eius habuisti?" Volo, iudices, omissa omni
contentione, si licet,[45] sic agere: peccavi, veniam peto; et
2 errare hominis est et ignoscere patris. Duxit me similis
aetas, evicerunt officia, cepit fides. Amantem odisse non
3 potui. Nihilominus satis habundeque poenarum [est][46] et,

---

[45] si licet V (*def. Ellis 337, Kr.*[2]): scilicet B Φ
[46] *secl. Håk.*[2] 81–82

---

[50] Sarcastic.
[51] Cf. 9.20.7.
[52] I.e., my being still alive: his friend in contrast to his genetic
father.

have yet been paid, no victims sacrificed to the immortal gods; certainly we have not recompensed my ransomer. (3) But I did expect that your affection, fired up by my absence, would scarcely be sated, that after that ill-omened journey you would have felt—as it were—reproved by such a dangerous outcome and would never again send me off, at least overseas. Hardly have I saluted the household gods when I am turned out—and most people might doubt if I had been let in. (4) Or are you trying to make it look as if my ransomer had done you no service? Doubtless,[50] I am so cruel, so undutiful, and (the best indicator of the presence of all vices) so ungrateful as not to value what I have received from a man who has been a father to me;[51] perhaps I don't know to whom I owe my life,[52] retain no memory of services rendered! (5) Ah me, that I cannot pay as much as I received!

(6) Yet my father goes back deeper into the causes for my disownment, taking his researches back past my foreign voyage—and that for two reasons: first, in order that, since the charges are not so enormous as to sink the defendant, their number may confound him; second, that a father's judgment may be thought more weighty, since he is condemning who normally forgives. 12. "Why," he says, "considering that I was the poor man's enemy, were you friends with his son?" I want, judges, to put all argument aside and, if I may, to proceed like this: I did wrong, I ask for forgiveness; it is for humans to err, and for fathers to forgive. (2) I was attracted by our similar ages, won over by his kindnesses, bound fast by his loyalty. He loved me, and I could not hate him. (3) All the same, I have been punished enough and more than enough: more, if I gauge

205

si pietatem tuam bene novi, plus quam velles, datum est.
Quantumlibet peccaverim, quid amplius iratissimus domi-
4 nus exigeret? Ludo tibi satisfeci. Nullumne cladibus meis
finem dari placet? Parum est quod insanos pertuli fluctus,
et saevis tempestatibus commissus arbitrio ventorum pe-
5 pendi? Parum est quod in nefarias latronum manus praeda
perveni—quae ultima malorum etiam servorum condicio
est—sine exceptione venalis? Inde me, si voluisset, emere
6 potuit inimicus. Parum est quod me diu piratae in carcere
retentum, quia redemptorem illis divitem promiseram patrem, in ludum vendiderunt tamquam decepti, quod cotidiana[47] pugnae meditatione tamdiu mori didici, quod
compositus armatus inductus perieram si melior amicus
fuissem, nisi me nova velut in portu adorta[48] tempestas
paternis laribus extorrem et necessarii quoque victus
7 inopem circum [ad][49] alienas mitteret domos?[50] Pudet
enumerare calamitatium mearum gradus: piratam, lanistam, patrem.

13. Atqui pars ista criminis, iudices, mei non defendi
meruit sed laudari. Neque enim reperio quid in rebus
humanis excogitarit natura praestantius amicitia, quid[51]

---

[47] -diana *Bur.*: -die β: -dianae *cett.*

[48] -orta ς: -opta A: -optata *cett.*   [49] *del. Sch.* (*frustra def.
Bur., Kr.*²)   [50] parum est quod me—domos *sic dist. Wint.
ap. Kr.*²   [51] quod *Obr.*

---

[53] Father, as in 9.10.2.   [54] Cf. 6.1.5.

[55] The contract for the sale of slaves might include restrictions
on their future use (cf. 3.16.5 with n. 77); and the law forbade the
sale of slaves—even bad ones—to a gladiatorial school as a means
of punishment without the approval of a judge (see Mod. *Dig.*

your affection for me correctly, than you would have wished. However much I sinned, what more could the most irate lord and master[53] demand? I gave you your requital in a gladiator school! (4) Are you determined that my run of disasters should have no end? Is it not enough that I endured the madness of the waves, that left to the mercy of wild storms I hung[54] at the whim of the winds? (5) Is it not enough that I passed as booty into the wicked hands of robbers, up for sale (the worst fate that could befall even bad slaves) with no restrictions?[55]—from them, if he had wished, an enemy might have bought me. (6) Is it not enough that the pirates, after keeping me for a long time in their prison because I had promised them a ransom from my wealthy father, sold me to the school on the grounds that they had been deceived; that in daily practice for combat I learned to die over such a long period; that paired off, armed, led into the arena, I should have died if I had been a better friend? Is all that not enough, without a new storm coming up—as it were—when I was back in port, to send me off around the homes of others, exiled from my father's house and lacking even the necessities of life? (7) I am ashamed to list the stages of my calamities: pirate, gladiator-manager, father.

13. But this part of my alleged crime, judges, deserved not defense but praise. Indeed I find that nature thought up no more excellent feature of human life than friendship,[56] or anything that could be a greater safeguard

---

48.8.11.1–2; Santorelli [2020a, 919–21]). None of these measures applied to the sale of the speaker, who was sold to a *lanista* without any protective restrictions.

56 Cf. 16.6.5.

2 concordia contra fortunam maius auxilium. Nam primum
praeter cetera animalia induit[52] nostris pectoribus quandam societatem, qua[53] mutuo gaudere congressu, con-
trahere populos, condere urbes edocuit, et, cum mentibus
nostris varios imposuerit motus, nullum profecto melio-
3 rem benivolentia tribuit affectum. Quid enim foret hu-
mano genere felicius, si omnes esse possent amici? Non
bella, seditiones, latrocinia, lites ceteraque mala, quae
4 hominibus ex se ipsis nata sunt, fortunae accessissent. Id
quidem[54] nimium deo visum est; at certe honestis conve-
nire mentibus, fidem colere, amoris gratiam referre, omnibus temporibus, omnibus gentibus praecipuum et quodammodo sacrum fuit. Neque enim nisi optimis mentibus
contingit ut aut sic amare sciant aut sic amari mereantur.
5 Hoc ego crimen expavescam? Scires quantopere gloriarer,
pater, si cum amico meo ego redissem.
6 Nisi forte similitudine flagitiorum ductus turpi me con-
iunxeram iuveni—quae vita[55] sine dubio nomen amicitiae
non accipit; ita[56] tamen, ad paria ducente natura, vitia
7 convenerant.[57] Obice mihi amicum, et habes maledicendi
materiam: "Gladiator fuit, quare amicus illius[58] fuisti?"
8 Ita, opinor, paenitet! Effers te longius, dolor, et, nimia

[52] indidit β, sed vd. Bur. et Håk.   [53] qua Gr.-Mer. (corrob. Håk.[2] 82): quae codd. (nequiquam def. Kr.[2])
[54] quidem Håk.: quia codd.   [55] vita ⟨ut⟩ . . . , ita Watt[3]
51–52, nescio an parum concinne
[56] del. Håk., sed cum convenerant iungendum
[57] -nerat Bur.: -niunt Watt[3] 51–52   [58] eius V

[57] I.e., added to what fortune brings (DAR).
[58] The "charge" of friendship.

against fortune than concord. (2) First, beyond all other living beings she put into our hearts a certain sociability, whereby she taught us to enjoy each others' company, to come together as peoples, to build cities; and though she implanted various emotions in our minds, for sure she gave no better feeling than benevolence. (3) For what would be happier than the human race if everyone could be friends? Wars, rebellions, brigandage, legal disputes and all the other evils that come naturally from within men themselves would not have been added to their lot.[57] (4) That, no doubt, seemed too much for god to give; but at least to be united in good intentions, to keep faith, to repay love with love, has been something special and in a way sacred for all nations at all times. For it is only given to the best natures to know how to love like this or to deserve to be loved like this. (5) Am I to fear this charge?[58] You would find out, father, how much I would be boasting if I had come back with my friend.

(6) Perhaps, though, it was because I was attracted by criminal qualities like my own that I had come to associate with a young man of ill repute. That sort of life, no doubt, is not called friendship;[59] but that was the way, as nature brings like minds together, to which our vices had come together. (7) If you want to cast my friend in my teeth, you have ample material for abuse: "He was a gladiator: why were you his friend?" That, I am sure, is cause for regret.[60] (8) You go too far, resentment, and stirred by excessive

[59] Friendship being possible only between good people (9.13.4; cf. Cic. *Lael.* 18).

[60] Sarcasm: he certainly cannot be ashamed of his friendship with a gladiator, because this is what saved his life.

concitatus ira, quo progrediare non respicis. 14. Non sen-
tis, pater, hoc te mihi obicere, quod vivam? Quisquam de
illa amicitia queri potest praeter pauperem?

2   "At ego inimicum habebam illius patrem." Decuerat
quidem simultates, quas maxime[59] omnium mortales[60]
esse voluere sapientes,[61] in his desinere, in quibus nasce-
3   rentur. Nam sic quoque immodicas serit discordiarum
fortuna causas, etiamsi non hereditaria subeamus odia, ac
4   diutius inimicitiae manent[62] quam inimici. Tamen, si quid
adversus te ipse commisit adulescens, sit hostis et meus.
Si innoxius et omni vacans culpa caritatem mereri cupit,
si nullius me amici filius validius amat, quid tandem vis,
5   pater?[63] Respuam et iratas obiciam manus? Tu quoque
non odisses pauperem, si te amaret. Inserit se et beneficiis
certat:[64] noras adulescentem omnia ultro praestantem, et
6   sic me amabat, quamvis tu esses inimicus patris. Adice, si
tanta in adolescente indoles fuit, quantam nulla umquam
cognovere saecula, si fides antiquissima et cum deorum
coetu permixtis inaudita temporibus, si me semper habuit
cariorem spiritu suo, etiamne despicienda mihi rarissimi
7   boni occasio fuit? At ego perpetuam quandam mihi glo-
riam reor, quod ille caelestis animus me potissimum,

---

[59] -me ς: -mi B Φ: *om.* V
[60] -les ς: -lium *codd.*: -lium ‹mortales› *Sh. B.*[2] *202*
[61] -ntis B V δ
[62] -ent *scripsi*: -eant (*sc. e super.* subea-) *codd.*
[63] *sic dist. Best 195–96*
[64] *sic dist. Str. ap. Kr.*[2]

---

[61] Cf. Cic. *Rab. Post.* 32; Livy 40.46.12; [Quint.] *Decl. min.*
257.9.

anger you do not see in what direction you are heading. 14. Don't you realize, father, that you are reproaching me with being alive? Can anyone complain of that friendship except the poor man?

(2) "But I regarded his father as an enemy." It would have been proper for quarrels, which the wise have recommended should most of all things be mortal,[61] not to go beyond the persons with whom they were born. (3) For even as it is[62] fortune sows a multitude of causes for discord, even if we do not enter upon hereditary hatreds, and enmities outlast the original enemies. (4) All the same, if the young man himself did anything to offend you, let him be my enemy too. But if he is blameless and quite without guilt, and longs to deserve affection, if no friend's son loves me more dearly, what do you want me to do, father? Reject him, and raise angry fists against him? (5) You too would not hate the poor man[63] if he loved you. His son[64] involves himself with us and competes in good services: you knew him as a youth who gave everything without being asked, and loved me as he did even though you were his father's enemy. (6) What is more, if[65] the young man was of a character such as no past ages have ever known, of an antique loyalty unheard of even in the days when gods and men lived side by side, if he always held me dearer than his own life, was I still to reject the opportunity of a blessing so rare? (7) No, I think it a perpetual source of glory for me that that heaven-sent soul chose me of all people

---

[61] I.e., without hereditary feuds.
[62] The father.
[64] Poor Man's son, back in the past.
[65] As was the case.

quem amaret, elegerit, ego sim probatus tanto iudice. Me quoque igitur feret fama per gentis, et amici laudibus inlustrior vivam. Credet aliquis idem me pro illo fuisse facturum.

15. "Cur, cum inimici nos essemus, vos amici fuistis?" Aliud hoc loco crimen agnosco: peccavimus enim, fateor, peccavimus, quod, cum amici essemus, vos inimici fuistis.

2 Haec, iudices, diutius exequerer, nisi absoluta essent ipso iudice patre. Longum iam istius criminis tempus est; num-

3 quam obiecit, numquam excanduit. Ecquid[65] hoc inter nos, pater, convenit, ne, si[66] longiores repetis offensas, apud malignos videaris me iratus non redemisse? Sed, si quid ante commisissem odio tuo dignum, potuisti me re-

4 demptum non recipere. Manifestum est ergo te patiente, id est te volente amicum mihi fuisse iuvenem, et sane non solus in hac fuisti sententia: idem filio permisit et pauper.

5 Atqui si pars haec causae, quae confessione longi silentii absoluta hodie in accessionem criminis alterius deducitur, potest apud vos impetrare veniam, facilior certe sequen-tium ratio est: ille enim sane fuerit inimici filius, hic iam est amici pater.

6 Nec ignoro, iudices, quam male ista defensio de hu-mano genere mereatur, si adeo nihil est per se misericor-

---

[65] ecquid *Obr.*: et (e V) quid *codd.*
[66] ne si V: nisi B Φ

---

[66] The implication being: "We were wrong not to try to win *your* friendship."
[67] Our friendship.
[68] The judges are addressed.
[69] Viz., that stated in 9.15.1.

to be the object of his love, that I was approved by so fine a judge. Because of this, fame will bear my name too throughout the world: I shall gain renown and live on through the praises that my friend will receive. Some will believe that *I* would have done the same for him.

15. "Why were you friends when we were enemies?" I acknowledge here another crime; we did wrong, I admit, we did wrong: though we were friends, you kept on being enemies.[66] (2) I should enlarge on this, judges, had not my father himself acquitted us. The offense[67] has been going on for a long time: he has never objected, has never lost his temper. (3) Surely we can agree on this point, father: for if you take up long-past offenses again, ill-wishers may think that it was because you were angry that you did not ransom me. Indeed, if I had done something earlier that merited your hatred, you could have refused to take me back *after* I was ransomed. (4) It is quite clear then that you tolerated the young man being my friend, that is, you wished it. And for sure you were not alone in taking this view: the poor man gave his son the same permission too. (5) Now if I can win your[68] forgiveness for this part of the case,[69] which is being brought up today to supplement another charge[70] even though long silence has already acquitted it,[71] that at any rate makes what follows easier to deal with: yes, he may have been the son of an enemy, but this man here is now the father of a friend.

(6) I am also aware, judges, how badly this defense deserves of the human race, if mercy is of so little intrinsic

---

[70] That of supporting my friend's father.

[71] Cf. 9.15.2. In fact, "silence means consent" (see Tosi [2017[2], 29–30]).

dia ut, nisi ulterior aliqua necessitas pudori vim fecerit,
pro summo crimine damnanda sit minus necessaria hu-
7 manitas. Ergo si alienum et ignotum, tamen, quae publica
omnium mortalium quippe sub uno parente naturae
cognatio est, hominem cibo forte iuvissem, poena dignum
videretur servasse perituram animam et ignovisse rebus
humanis et respectu communis omnium sortis velut ado-
8 rato numini[67] [et][68] stipem posuisse fortunae? Si[69] hoc crimen est, laudetur ergo crudelitas, nihil habeatur piratis
lanistisque prudentius! 16. Ferantur sane profutura hu-
mano generi duo exempla: intra tam breve tempus propter
misericordiam alter abdicatus, alter occisus est.

2 Quod crimen si fatendum sit, num animum mihi ipse
finxi aut mea potestate regitur affectus? An arbitrio for-
mantis mores[70] omnium naturae compositus cum crimine
3 meo natus sum? Nam sive caelestis providentia, sive inra-
tionabilis casus, sive assignata siderum cursu nascentibus
nobis necessitas, multa varietate pectora nostra distinxit
nec minus numerosas animorum quam corporum dedit
4 formas. Sunt quorum mentes etiam nocentium supplicia
confundant, qui ad omnium sanguinem pallescant, ignotorum quoque miseriis inlacriment. Sunt contra qui ne

[67] -ne ς
[68] del. Hdk.[2] 83
[69] est V: sed E β   [70] -res E: -re vel -rae cett.

[72] It would be inhuman to claim that kind behavior can be
accounted for only if accorded for the sake of superior (i.e., specific, personal) ties with the person to be aided (AS).

[73] The speaker and his friend, with a *hysteron proteron*.

value that, unless some superior tie overwhelms one's sense of shame, less than unavoidable humanity has to receive condemnation as a heinous crime.[72] (7) So, then, if I had given food to help a stranger, an unknown person, yet—for this is a relationship that binds everybody together as children of one parent, nature—a human being, it would seem to be a matter for punishment to have saved a life that would otherwise have been lost, to have made allowances for the vagaries of human life and, out of respect for the common lot of all, to (so to speak) have given alms to Fortune, as a deity we worship. (8) If this is a crime, then let cruelty merit praise, and let nothing be thought wiser than pirates and managers of gladiators! 16. Let two precedents be made known that will doubtless prove useful to humanity: within so short a time one man has been disowned, another killed—both for showing pity.[73]

(2) If I have to confess guilt on this count: did *I* shape my own mind, are my feelings under *my* control? Or was my makeup, rather, dictated by nature, which forms the character of us all, so that I was born along with my crime? (3) Whether it is divine providence, or blind chance, or a necessity assigned to us at our births by the movement of the stars—one of these has marked off our hearts with manifold differences, and given our minds shapes as various as those of our bodies. (4) There are men whose minds are distressed by the execution even of the guilty, who grow pale at the blood of any man and find tears for the misery even of persons they do not know. On the other hand, there are those who have no pity even for their own

5   suorum quidem misereantur.[71] Mihi mite pectus et mollis
affectus ad omnem calamitatium conspectum tremit. Noli
me aestimare mea fortuna, pater: non habeo gladiatoris
6   animum. Utinam quidem mihi[72] causa permitteret sic gloriari: iuvenis conceptus splendidis parentibus, cum solum
tam speciosae fortunae crederem fructum posse prodesse
et contra varios mortalium casus quasi portum benignitatis
aperire, concupivi quandam humanitatis civicam glo-
riam—periturum hominem, sive ille naufragio eiectus,
seu spoliatus incendio sive exutus latrocinio erat, naturae
patriaeque restitui. Ignotus sane sit et alienus, quid fuerit
7   ante non quaero: post hoc erit amicus.[73] Paria tecum facio,
res publica, quae propter me unum civem perdideras.
Haec me magis decet impensa quam vestis, argentum; ubi
pecunia melius poni potest quam ubi laus emitur,[74] ubi
faenus bonitatis extenditur? 17. Magna conscientia est
felicitatem meruisse.
2   At[75] hercule, quo quisque plus potest quoque[76] latius
patet ad incursus, hoc magis cogitare debet atque respi-
cere quantum in nos fortunae regnum sit, quam instabili

71 -ean- E: -en- *cett.*
72 quidem mihi V γ β (*cf. e.g. Sen. Ep. 19.5*): m. q. *cett.*
73 ignotus—amicus *huc transp. Håk. e 9.17.1 (post* meruisse)
74 quam—emitur *h.l. habet* A: *post* argentum *cett.*
75 at *scripsi:* et *codd.*   76 eoque *Russ.³*

74 This probably builds on the idea of the *corona civica*: a
crown of oak leaves "which one citizen gives to another who has
saved his life in battle, in recognition of the preservation of his
life and safety" (Gell. 5.6.11; trans. Rolfe).
75 This is the youth's fantasy.

family. (5) As for me, my gentle heart and tender feelings tremble at every sight of calamity. Do not judge me by what befell me, father: I do not have the mentality of a gladiator. (6) Would that circumstances allowed me to boast in the following terms: a youth born to noble parents, believing that the only benefit of so brilliant a fortune is to be able to help others and to open up, as it were, a harbor of kindness to the varying chances of mortal men, I aspired to a kind of citizen's prize[74] for humanity—a man who would have perished when shipwrecked or ruined by fire or stripped by a brigand, I have given back[75] to nature and homeland. He may be unknown and a stranger; I do not inquire what he was before: after this, he will be a friend. (7) I am getting level with you, my country: you had lost one citizen because of me.[76] Outlay on this is more appropriate to me than[77] clothes or silver. Where can money be better spent than where it is praise that is being bought, where you get an increased return in kindness?[78] 17. It is a great thing to be aware that you have deserved your own good fortune.[79]

(2) Indeed, the more power a man has, the wider open he is to injury, so much the more should he reflect and bear in mind how great a sway fortune exercises over us, how unstable is the foundation on which human affairs

[76] Saving one (Poor Father) would make up for the loss of one (Poor Son).

[77] = than on . . .

[78] I.e., kindness earns a better "rate of interest" (DAR).

[79] Helping people in need is "profitable," even though it costs us money (9.16.7), as it makes us feel that we have merited our own good fortune (AS).

sede humana consistant. Non me aurata laquearia nec
radiantes marmore columnae nec graves crustae fecerint
3 immemorem fragilitatis. Multa saepe et locupletibus acci-
dunt, saepe in imum summa decidunt. Ego vidi pauperem
4 auxilia diviti ferentem. Sed sane superbius aestimet miserias longa felicitas et alienum casum facile despiciat securus sui; ego quotiens auxilia calamitatis petere aliquem
video,[77] non possum non moveri fortuna mea. Succurrit
mihi continuo tempus illud, quo ipse clementiam opta-
5 bam. Ignosce, pater, si penitus animo meo hic insedit affectus; amare misericordiam miser coepi.
6   "Sed inimicus" inquit "meus est." Nam[78] quis nos tanto
7 opere laudaret, pater, si hoc amico praestaremus? Haec
est celebranda virtus, haec animi suspicienda[79] moderatio:
vincere iram et inter simultates quoque meminisse hominis. Ut Fabio Maximo immortalem attulit laudem ereptus
ex hostium manibus Minucius,[80] ut Tiberium Gracchum
admirata civitas est Scipione in carcerem duci prohibito,
8 te quoque similis animi magnitudo memoriae dabit. Tuis
enim opibus vivit inimicus; quicquid est istud, quod senex

[77] vidi V (prob. Håk. coll. 9.23.1)

[78] num Dess.[2]

[79] -spici- ⅽ (def. Håk.[2] 84): -scipi- codd

[80] Minucius Gron. ("inimicus Minutius" iam B. Asc.[1] lxiv v. in
paraphr.): mimicus O: inimicus O[2] cett.

---

[80] Echoing Dido's words in Verg. Aen. 1.630: see Pirovano
(2012, 547).

[81] The plural tries to bring the father into it: see 9.17.8.

[82] Q. Fabius Maximus Cunctator intervened to rescue M. Minucius Rufus, his political opponent, when the latter was surrounded by Hannibal at Gerontium (Livy 22.28.1–29.10).

rest. Gilded ceilings, columns shining with marble and deeply paneled walls shall not make me forget my vulnerability. (3) Many things often go wrong even for the rich, often what was highest falls most low: I have seen a poor man bringing aid to a rich man! (4) But, granting that a long period of success makes one look down arrogantly on wretchedness, and that one who is confident of his own position finds it easy to be contemptuous of the fortunes of others—whenever *I* see someone asking for help in disaster, I cannot help being moved as I think of my own good luck. I immediately recall the time when I myself had to ask for mercy. (5) Forgive me, father, if this feeling has sunk deep into my heart; I began to love pity when I needed pity myself.[80]

(6) "But," he says, "he is my enemy." Yes: who would praise us[81] so highly if we were doing this for a friend? (7) *This* is the virtue to be noised abroad, *this* the restraint to be looked up to: the ability to conquer anger and remember the human being even when you are at feud with him. As the rescue of Minucius from enemy hands brought immortal glory to Fabius Maximus,[82] as Tiberius Gracchus won the admiration of his fellow citizens when he stopped Scipio from being haled off to prison,[83] the like magnanimity will give *you* too a place in history. (8) For it is on your money that your enemy supports life. Whatever an

---

[83] L. Cornelius Scipio Asiaticus, brother of Scipio Africanus, charged with embezzlement and sentenced to imprisonment in 184 BC, was saved by the veto of the tribune Tiberius Gracchus the Elder (Val. Max. 4.1.8).

inops ex nostra domo accipit, si non irasceris, tu prae-
stitisti, tibi hoc pulchrum atque magnificum est. Nam ego,
si quid in patrem servatoris mei confero, non sum laudandus.

18. Neque expectaveris hoc loco, pater, ut illa dicam:
semper odiorum honestus occasus est, et, dum simultates
nihil aliud habent quam nocendi cupiditatem, speciosa in
melius animi mutatio est cum exempli honore, iunctaeque
2 ex hostili paene concursu in affinitatem manus. Unde tantum misero boni, ut inimicus sit? Aspice solum, egentem,
senem, omnibus praesidiis destitutum; nonne contumeliam fortunae tuae facis, si hunc odisti et adhuc putas tua
3 interesse ne vivat? Nulla tibi contingere maior ultio potest
quam si iam talis est, ut illius etiam nos misereamur.
Magna mehercule iam de vetere aemulo poena; superest
panem eripere mendico et gravissimae per se fortunae
4 manui[81] pondus imponere. Age, si perisset, cadaver cal-
casses? Ferae mehercules generosiores iacentes trans-
eunt, et, ‹ut›[82] reservati hostes restitutaeque urbes maiora
causa[83] exempla sint, quod scio, victis etiam gladiatores
5 parcunt. Post orbitatem, post egestatem quid amplius potest pati, nisi quod optat? Ulteriorne tibi aliqua ultio quae-
renda est, aut aliquid rerum natura peius capit? Quis non
te omnium mortalium inhumanissimum putet, si hoc ad-
6 versus inimicum tuum saltem optasti! Si mehercules inex-

[81] manui M AD β: magni E: manu cett.: maius Obr.
[82] ‹ut› (concess.) supplevi: ‹cum› Håk.² 84   [83] -a Sch.,
Obr. (cf. 13.15.3 maior . . . materiā adfectus): -ae codd.

[84] By condescending to regard him as a serious opponent
(DAR).   [85] His long-standing enemies.   [86] I.e., death.

old man without resources receives from our house, it is *you* (please don't be angry!) who provided it, *yours* is this fine and high-minded deed. As for me, if I do something to help the father of my preserver, *I* am not the one who deserves praise.

18. Do not expect me, father, to say at this point: the demise of hatreds is always honorable, and, while quarrels involve nothing but the desire to harm, a change of heart for the better is a splendid act, providing the respect due to a model to imitate, when hands are joined in friendship after it has almost come to a pitched battle in war. (2) How can a poor wretch like this have the good fortune to be an enemy? Look at him, alone, in need, an old man, bereft of all support; if you hate this man and still think it in your interest that he should not live, are you not insulting your own fortune?[84] (3) He is already in such a state that even *we*[85] pity him: you can get no greater revenge than that. Heavens, this is already a severe punishment to inflict on an old rival; all that remains now is to snatch bread from him as he begs, and to add new weight to the hand of fortune, heavy enough in itself. (4) Tell me: if he had died, would you have trampled on his body? Heavens, the nobler animals pass by those who are laid low, and—the saving of enemies and the restoration of cities being ‹admittedly› too grand examples for my case—even gladiators, so far as I know, spare the defeated. (5) After bereavement, after poverty, what more can he suffer except what he wishes for?[86] Do you have to look for a revenge that goes further than this? Does the whole world hold anything worse? Who would not think you the least humane of all mortals if you had even *wished* for such a thing to afflict your enemy? (6) Now really, if the causes of your

221

piabiles odiorum causae et compositis quoque fabulis ul-
teriores inimicitiae fuissent, ausim dicere, si propter illum
liberos perdidisses, accipienda tamen erat a fortuna tali[84]
satisfactio, certe ad vitandam insolentiae opinionem, quae
fere immeritam quoque potentiam carpit, ne vagaretur
per urbem invidiosus mendicus et calamitatis auctori cri-
minosus[85] causas vulgo suggereret[86] odiorum. 19. Nescio
quomodo omnis pro laborante favor est, nec ulla[87] perpetuam gratiam servat nisi modesta victoria. Nostra potissimum clementia sustineatur, ne illius alii misereantur.

2   Facilis, ut animadvertere vos spero, iudices, defensionis meae cursus est. Antequam incipiam habere causam
nimium bonam, hic iam conscientia trepidat oratio, et
velut inter binos deprehensa scopulos, cum aliud obiciatur, aliud defendendum sit, haeret in dubio; cum benefi-
3   ciis meis computare non audeo. Cognovistis expositionem
causae, quanta quamque excedentia fidem adulescentis
4   optimi merita narraverim. "Haec mihi omnia sine dubio[88]
ille praestitit, sed quid interest? Debitor delicatus sum."[89]

---

84 -i *Håk.*² 85: -is *codd.*

85 -nosus *Håk.*² 85: -nis *codd.*: -nans *Sch.*

86 -go sugge- *Håk.*² 85: -gus ege- *codd.*

87 -a ⌠: -am *codd.*

88 dubio ⟨ultro⟩ *Håk., sed vd. Sant.*² 547–48

89 *verba personata significavi*

---

87 Instead, Poor Man *has* lost a child because of you.

88 As mirrored in 9.19.4–7 (cf. Dessauer [1898, 76–77]): *Sic
. . . agam . . . ? Dicam . . . ? Itane . . . ? An . . . ? Dicam . . . ?
Utro . . . ? Tamquam . . . ?*

hatred had been incurable and your enmity had gone beyond what myth invents, if (I venture to say) you had lost children because of him,[87] yet even then you would have to agree to reparation from a man so unfortunate—if only to avoid a reputation for insolence, which often snipes at powerful men even when they do not deserve it, to prevent him shaming you by roaming the city as a beggar and supplying ordinary people with reasons to hate you by his reproaches to the author of his calamity. 19. I don't know how it is, but everyone favors a man in trouble, and only a modest mien in victory ensures lasting popularity. Let him be maintained by *our* clemency, lest others pity him.

(2) As I hope you notice, judges, the course of my defense is proving easy enough. But before my case begins to be *too* good, my speech now falters[88] from a sense of guilt, and as though caught between two rocks[89] it finds itself in a fix: for I am being accused on one charge, but need to defend myself on another;[90] and I dare not draw up a balance sheet of the good I have done and the good I have received.[91] (3) You are aware of the way the case was narrated, how great and indeed beyond belief were the merits of the excellent young man that I described. (4) "True, all these things he did for me, but what does that

[89] This is like saying: between Scylla and Charybdis, or a rock and a hard place.

[90] He is accused of (a) helping an enemy; but he is aware that he should defend himself for (b) not helping him enough (see already 9.10.1).

[91] Because I know that I received more than I gave.

5 Sic[90] in hac parte defensionis agam, iudices? Dicam: "Referre gratiam beneficiis volui"? Itane tandem aliqui[91] mendicare amici patrem aequo animo visurus fuit? An[92] ille

6 me redemit, cui nihil debui[93]?[94] Dicam moveri me supremis amici mei precibus? [Egregia vero comparatio.][95] At

7 ille mihi praestitit quod non rogavi. Utro me vertam? Tamquam honestum defendam factum an tamquam necessa-

8 rium? Alterum absolvi facilius potest, alterum laudari. Rectissimum, opinor, veritatis iter est.[96]

20. Audi, pater, alimenta ista, quae donata egenti putas, quanti illi constent. Si accepto captivitatis meae nuntio nullis precibus adductus, nullis epistolis vocatus adolescens ad liberandum me vinculis piratarum profectus esset, quibus tamen meritis pensarem, cum id mihi praestitisset,

90 *scripsi* (*cf. 9.12.1 et i.a. 1.6.1, 5.12.4, 18.8.2*): quid *codd.*

91 -qui (*vel* -quis) ⊊: -quem *codd.*

92 *an scripsi*: at *codd.*

93 (at . . .) debuit *Dess.*[2] (*prob. Sant.*[2] *549*)

94 *interrog. distinxi*

95 *del. Håk.*, nempe (*Str. ap. Kr.*[2]) *marginalia fuerunt ad* §2 velut—scopulos *spectantia*

96 iter est *Håk.*[3] *131* (*qui* laudari—est *sic dist.*): interest *codd.*

---

92 Poor Son has done a great deal for Rich Son: but the latter envisages doing no more than strictly repaying the debt he negotiated with his friend (cf. 9.9.2), giving just basic support to his destitute father. See Santorelli (2018b, 547–48).

93 Of course not: this would exempt Rich Son from the charge of not doing *enough* for the old Poor Man (see n. 90, b), but would deprive him of all sympathy. The speaker proceeds to air a number of (in)expedient moves he might possibly make (9.19.4–8) (AS).

matter? I am a fussy debtor."[92] Shall I plead like *this*,[93] judges, in this part of my defense? (5) Or shall I say: "I wanted to repay a good deed"? Was *anyone* then really going to fail to be moved by seeing his friend's father begging?[94] Did I owe *nothing* to my ransomer?[95] (6) Or else shall I say I was moved by the last requests of my friend? [An excellent comparison indeed!][96] Yet he did for me something I did *not* request of him.[97] (7) Which way shall I turn? Shall I defend the act as honorable or as necessary? (8) The one is easier to absolve of guilt, the other to be praised.[98] The most direct course, I think, is to tell the truth.

20. Let me tell you, father, how much these living expenses, which you think were just a gift to a needy man, are in fact costing him. If the young man, on receiving the news of my imprisonment, had set off to free me from the pirates' chains with no prayers to prompt him, no letter to summon him, by what services could I even then[99] have recompensed his, seeing that he would have done

---

[94] Sc., no: anyone would have helped a friend's father in need, even if there were no debt to be repaid.

[95] = Wasn't I morally obliged to give some help to my ransomer's impoverished father? (AS).

[96] A gloss on 9.19.2, "as though caught between two rocks."

[97] So, in principle, I owed him nothing in return.

[98] If I maintain that I was bound to support Poor Man, I can be easily absolved (as I did not in fact have a choice); if I maintain that I did this because I considered it an honorable action, I can more easily earn praise.

[99] Sc., even "only" for all that—and not also for the fact that, in order to rescue me without delay, he was dooming his father to beggary (9.20.3).

2 quod ego tantum a patre speravi? Intrare maria, praesertim tam recenti documento timenda, et latrones ultro quaerere et, cum praeter vicarias manus nihil esset, navigare voto captivitatis, quis posset alius quam qui paratus

3 esset pro amico mori? Magnum hoc per se ac saeculo nostro vix credibile, iudices; illud vero omni praedicatione maius: ad redimendum me profectus est, cum mendicatu-

4 rum patrem suum sciret. Atquin sperare poterat futurum ut sine periculo suo redimeretur nihilominus amicus, cum haberem divitem patrem; sed noluit ipsum itineris apparatum et,[97] ne qua periret redemptionis[98] hora, praeceps

5 cucurrit. Pro fidem deum hominumque, quemadmodum ad redemptionem amici festinat, etiam cuius[99] pater lentus est!

6 Terentium, quem inter ceteros captivos secundo Punico bello Scipio Africanus vinculis exsolverat, memoriae tradidere maiores insigni receptae libertatis pilleo ⟨grates⟩[100] testantem[101] in triumpho ducis esse conspectum. Et ille quidem maioris momenti accessio[102] publicam senserat felicitatem, privatim tamen debere se putavit vic-

---

97 ⟨expectare⟩ et *Wint. ap. Kr.*[2]
98 -ni *Bur.*
99 etiam cui *Franc., sed vd. Kr.*[2]: cuius etiam *Reitz.*[2] 77
100 *supplevi:* ⟨gratiam⟩ *Håk.*
101 -te π ψ: (insigne . . . pilleum) gestantem *Bur.*
102 -io B AD δ (*def. Bur. et Kr.*[2], *cf. vMor.* 5): -ione *cett.*

something that I looked for only from my father? (2) To embark on the seas, especially when such recent experience showed how perilous they were, to go out of his way to look for the robbers, and, taking with him nothing except his hands as substitutes for mine, to sail with the explicit intention of being imprisoned himself—who could have acted like this except someone ready to die for his friend?[100] (3) This is a great deed in itself, judges, and one hardly credible in our day;[101] but what is beyond all praise is that he set out to ransom me even though he knew his father would be beggared as a result. (4) Yet he might have hoped that his friend would be ransomed in any case without himself running any risk, for I had a rich father; but, refusing even to make any preparations for the journey, he rushed off full tilt so as not to waste a moment that could be devoted to my ransoming. (5) Believe me, gods and men: how he hurries to ransom his friend, even one whose father is taking his time!

(6) Our ancestors have told the story of how Terentius,[102] whom Scipio Africanus had along with the other prisoners freed from captivity in the second Punic war, was seen in the general's triumph expressing ⟨his thanks⟩ by wearing the cap[103] in token of the freedom he had been given back. He, a mere appendage in matters of greater moment,[104] had rejoiced at the public good fortune like everyone else; but he thought he had a private debt to pay

---

[100] Cf. 6.5.3.   [101] Cf. 6.7.5.

[102] Q. Terentius Culleo, a senator taken prisoner by the Carthaginians and freed by Scipio (Livy 30.43.11; Val. Max. 5.2.5).

[103] A soft conical cap, normally worn by freedmen.

[104] I.e., one among many more important people.

7 toriae[103] beneficium. Quid me facere convenit, qui per maria latrociniis infesta solus petitus sum, qui lucem, libertatem, denique quicquid patri debeo, non ignarus, ut primo natalis horae tempore, sed videns sentiensque acceperim, nec solum donatus his bonis sed summis periculis liberatus sum? 21. Nonne me ex amici fide natum et tenacioribus beneficiorum vinculis fatear esse constrictum? Miserum me![104] Amice fidelissime, ingratum me moriendo fecisti.

2 Et quantulum est quod adhuc loquor de mea infelicitate, de piratis! Levis [est][105] ista fortuna, quae[106] etiam nunc recepit[107] moram: solent expectare latrones redemp-
3 torem. In ludo fui, qua poena nullam ulteriorem scelera noverunt, cuius ad comparationem ergastulum leve est. Hoc si scisses, pater, affirmo, promitto: cuius pietatis es,
4 nemo te antecessisset. Illa, certum habeo, expectas, ut dicam: morabar inter sacrilegos, incendiarios et—quae gladiatoribus una laus est—homicidas, inclusus[108] turpiore[109] custodia et sordido cellarum situ, iamque in eam veneram fortunam ut me victum recipere non posses, vic-

---

103 -ori ς, sed vd. Kr.²   104 -rum me Dess.²: -rrime codd.
105 del. Håk. (et vd. Kr.²)
106 quae Håk.: haec codd.: hanc (. . . recipit) Watt² 26
107 -cip- π E S, sed vd. Håk.² 86
108 -sus π: -sos cett.
109 tam turpiore V, unde etiam tur- Sch.

---

105 Not only did he rejoice at Scipio's victory, like every Roman citizen, he also acknowledged his *personal* debt to the victor and showed his gratitude by declaring himself his freedman.

106 Contrasted with Terentius, rescued among many others

to the victor.[105] (7) What is it fitting for *me* to do? Only I[106] was searched for, through seas infested by pirates; I received life, liberty, everything I owe to a father—yet not unknowingly, as in the moment of my birth, but seeing and feeling everything;[107] and I was not just granted these boons: I was freed from the most pressing dangers. 21. Shall I not confess that the loyalty of my friend gave me birth, and that I am bound to him by the stronger[108] ties of what he did for me? Ah me! My most faithful friend, you made me ungrateful by dying!

(2) And how trivial is what I have hitherto been saying about my ill luck, about the pirates! Petty was the misfortune that still allowed a delay: kidnappers normally wait for someone to bring a ransom. (3) I was by now in a school for gladiators, a punishment more extreme than any known to criminals, in comparison with which a slaves' prison is nothing. If you had known this, father, I affirm, I guarantee that you have such a strong sense of duty that no one would have got there before you. (4) You expect me, I am sure, to say: I was housed among men who had committed sacrilege, arson, and—the one thing that brings fame to gladiators—murder, confined in more[109] shameful constraint and dirty moldering cells, and I had by now come to the point where you would not have been able to take me back if I were defeated, and would not

(9.20.6). It follows that my debt to my liberator is even greater, since he did all this *only* for me.

107 Cf. 9.11.4. On the pleonastic *primo* natalis horae tempore (cf. 4.12.7), see Traina (1966–86², 283n1) (AS).

108 I.e., than those binding him to his natural father.

109 Than with the pirates.

5   torem nolles. Aderat hora supplicii mei, qua nusquam
morandum: iam praebendus erat iugulus et fundenda vita
cum sanguine. Neque enim dubitare de eventu licet;
6   exemplar fati mei vidi. Si me ab his imminentibus malis
pecunia redemisset, beneficium tamen potius dicerem[110]
magis aestimandum esse quam pretium; sed apud malignos interpretes posset videri vel spem secutus aliquam
7   venturi temporis vel praesentis voluptatem. Hoc admirabile et uni tantum pietati referendum est: dedit beneficium quod numquam reciperet, et, cum amicum quem
redimebat habiturus non esset, nihil aliud emit quam
honestae[111] mortis conscientiam. Transtulit ergo in se fortunam meam subiitque non solum fortiter, sed etiam libenter, id quod mihi miserum putabat.

    22. Res dictu incredibilis: gladiator dimissus, redemp-
tor occisus est! Recepit pectore adverso ferrum et[112] quasi,
quam emittebat animam, in meum pectus transfunderet,
et hoc uno tristis occiditur, quod amplius amicum visurus
2   non erat. Eant nunc antiquarum conditores fabularum
poetae et se ad exhortandam amicitiae fidem magna quaedam composuisse carminibus putent, si dixerint aliquos

---

[110] p. d. ⟨et⟩ *Dess.*[2], *sed vd. Håk.*[2] 86
[111] -tae *Håk.*[2] 86: -tam (-tum E) *codd.*
[112] ut ⟵, *sed cf.* 19.3.2

---

[110] I would be dead in the first case; I would have become a
murderer in the second. Cf. 9.22.6.

[111] A prisoner of pirates may have his sentence delayed, if
there is the prospect of a ransom (9.21.2); no delay is possible for
a gladiator—awaiting combat in the arena.

have wished to if I were victorious.[110] (5) The hour of my execution, allowing for absolutely no delay,[111] was upon me: now I had to offer my throat, and pour out my life with my blood. There is no question about the outcome: I had seen my fate prefigured.[112] (6) If it had been money that redeemed me from these evils hanging over me, I should still rather say that the good deed was of higher value than the price; yet anyone judging the case in an unfriendly spirit might have thought that he[113] pursued some hope for the future or satisfaction for the present.[114] (7) But here is something to be judged astonishing, and attributable to affection and nothing else: he did a good deed that would never be returned, and, since he was going to lose the friend he was ransoming, all he bought was death with a good conscience. So he transferred my fortune to himself, and underwent, not only bravely but with positive gladness, what he imagined caused me distress.

22. Here is something no one will credit: the gladiator was set free, the ransomer killed. He took the sword full in the breast, and as though he were pouring across into *my* breast the life he was breathing away. He died a sad man only because he would not see his friend again. (2) Away with them now, the poets who construct fables about the distant past, and think their verses have done some great service in encouraging true friendship if they

[112] In previous fights of other gladiators.

[113] My friend.

[114] I.e., that my friend ransomed me in hope of a return, or for the mere pleasure of a dramatic beau geste (AS).

per maria terrasque asperiorem fortunam amicorum tantum secutos, aut principem Graeciae virum in ultionem interfecti amici inauspicata bella gessisse. Nam inter fratres quoque illa maxime admirabilis, tamen alterna
3 mors est. Una fingitur coniunx, quae[113] iam perituri vitam mariti vicaria morte sua redemerit, adiciturque miraculo fabulae fecisse hoc eam, quod non praestitisset pater. En indubitabile saeculi decus et fictis maius: ut moreretur pro
4 me amicus, suum reliquit patrem, meum vicit. Et sane quid profuisset festinatio patris, etiamsi ad redimendum me prior forte venisset? Hoc me pretio nemo alius rede-
5 misset. Neque vero plurimum fuit praestitisse mortem; namque interim specioso titulo bene vita pensatur. Illud honesto amico[114] gravius: nomen gladiatoris accipere,
6 subire dominum lanistam. Minus te, amice, laudarem, si vicisses. An ille animus rediret in cellulam, ferret sagi-
7 nam, magistrum,[115] personam denique sceleris? Mea depugnasti causa, tua peristi. Haec tamen omnia ultimae[116]

[113] quae M: quod *codd.*
[114] honesto amico ς: non aestimo O: non est (esto B H) amico *cett.*   [115] magistrum ς: -ram B V γ β: ministram δ
[116] -ae S (*cf. e.g. Sen.* Ben. 6.33.2): -a *cett.*

[115] Sc., than theirs: a comparison with such mythical friends as Orestes and Pylades (expressly mentioned for the same purpose in, e.g., Favorin. *Exil.* 16.4). The latter accompanied his friend in hardship, but he did not have to sacrifice his life—as Poor Man's son did.

[116] Achilles, who went back into battle to avenge Patroclus' death, despite the omens predicting his own death (cf. Hom. *Il.* 19.404–23).

say that men have done no more than follow over sea and land friends suffering a harder lot,[115] or that a leading Greek fought ill-omened wars to avenge a slaughtered friend.[116] In the case of brothers, too, that kind of death is highly admirable—but it is taken in turns.[117] (3) A single wife is told of in fable who bought back the life of a husband at death's door by dying in his stead, and the tale is made more astonishing by the fact that she did something his own father had declined.[118] *Here*, behold a glory of the age, who performed a deed beyond all doubt[119] and greater than anything in poetry: to die for me, my friend abandoned his own father and outdid mine. (4) And indeed what would it have availed if my father had hurried, even if by some chance he had been first to come to ransom me? At *that* price[120] no one else would have ransomed me. (5) But it was not the greatest sacrifice to have offered to die; for sometimes a life lost is amply compensated by the brilliant reputation that is won. *That* was harder for my noble friend: to be called gladiator, to endure a manager of gladiators as his master. (6) I should praise you less, friend, if you had been victorious.[121] Was a man of such spirit to go back to his tiny cell, to put with the fattening diet,[122] the trainer, the very role of criminal? (7) You fought to the end for my sake; you died for your own. All

---

[117] Castor and Pollux.

[118] Alcestis, who died instead of her husband, Admetus, after his parents refused to take his place.

[119] Unlike the mythical personages.

[120] Sc., dying in my stead.

[121] Cf. 9.21.4.

[122] Cf. 9.5.6.

8 fortunae nomina, ut mihi detraheret, induit sibi. Venit in harenam homo nec sceleratus nec infelix. Ecquando,[117] iudices, hoc audistis? Bonitate sua gladiator factus est!

23. Utinam, iudices, haec, quae illi speciosa sunt, tam honesta essent et mihi! Quotiens ad infelicissimum respexi senem, cuius orbitate vivo, cum confectum cladibus et tantum poenae suae residuum considero, verum faten-

2 dum est: pudet me pretii mei. Video senem meliore sui parte praesepultum, omnis etiam spei superstitem, or- bum, destitutum. Illud tamen solacium est, quod, nisi ta-

3 lem amicum habuissem, haec de te dicerentur. Huic patri invidiosa quaedam,[118] opinor, et, quae bene filii[119] morte pensetur, criminosa liberalitas contigerit egenti. Alioquin duo egentes, et[120] circa omnium vel ignotorum domus sti-

4 pem rogabimus pariter. Si quis grandis natu parens est, miserebitur senis; si quis iuvenis filius, miserebitur adoles- centis. Fortasse proderit mendicaturo mihi quod ipse ali-

5 quando egentem pauperem alui. Accipe satisfactionem, in quacumque parte rerum naturae es, amice carissime. Non

---

117 ecqu- 5: necqu- B: nec qu- V: et qu- Φ

118 quidem *Str. ap. Kr.*[2]

119 bene filii *Wint.*[9] ([bene] filii *Håk.*): beneficii *codd.*: -ficio (mortis) 5: -fici (*e* -ficus, *subst.*) *Str. ap. Kr.*[2]

120 *del. Wint.*[9], *sed cf. e.g.* 9.23.6

---

123 The name of "gladiator," and in general the name of a person forced to obey his master and his trainer, to live in a cell and eat the food of a gladiatorial school, and to kill (9.22.5).

124 Not because of his vices or crimes, as would be normal for gladiators.   125 Cf. 9.1.4 and 9.18.3.   126 I.e., his son.

127 Sc., my father.   128 Poor Man.

these names,[123] though marks of extreme misfortune, he took upon himself so as to strip me of them. (8) Out into the arena came a man neither wicked nor unlucky. Have you heard ever such a thing, judges? He became a gladiator because of his *virtue*![124]

23. If only, judges, these things, which reflect so well on him, were bringing as much credit to me also! Whenever I look at this most unfortunate old man, to whose bereavement I owe my life, when I see him overborne by calamities, surviving only to suffer,[125] I have to confess the truth: I am ashamed of what I cost. (2) I see an old man, buried before his time in the better part of himself,[126] outliving all his hopes, bereft, destitute. But there is a consolation: if I had not had the kind of friend I did, these same things would now be said of you.[127] (3) The lot of *this* father[128] in his need will be, I think, a kind of liberality accompanied by ill will and—though it is amply made up for by the death of his son—reproach.[129] Otherwise,[130] we shall both be in want, begging together for alms round the homes of all, even people we do not know. (4) If anyone is aged and a father, he will pity this old man; if a youth and a son, he will pity this young man. Perhaps it will help me as I go a-begging that I myself at one time fed a poor man when he was in need. (5) Take this reparation, my dearest friend, in whatever part of the universe you are. It

[129] Rich Man might well be generous and agree to give alms to his enemy, though unwillingly and keeping his grudge against him; such reluctance, after all, would be unjustified: Poor Man has lost his own son to save the son of Rich Man, so the latter would just be compensating his enemy for the loss (AS).

[130] I.e., if you persist in disowning me (AS).

excidere mihi tua mandata: fortuna defecit, opes auferun-
tur; quod unum mihi relictum est, en polliceor patri tuo
6 vicarias manus. Quid vis porro faciam? Agrestia opera?
Delicatior, quod a fortuna non didici; et cotidiani quaestus
7 operis duobus egentibus non sufficit. Miserum me! Si
exsolvere fidem voluero, fortasse mihi in ludum rever-
tendum est.

is not that I have forgotten your instructions:[131] my fortune is spent, my wealth taken away; the only thing left to me is here, see: the hands I promise your father to take the place of yours. (6) What else do you want me to do? Farm labor? I am too soft: wealth did not teach me how; and the wages of everyday work do not suffice for two destitute men. (7) Ah me! If I want to keep my promise, perhaps I must return to the gladiator school.

[131] Stated at 9.9.2.

DECLAMATION 10

INTRODUCTION

In a trial for ill-treatment, a woman levels an unusual complaint against her husband: after the death and burial of their son, she had started to see him at night; when she revealed this to her husband, he called in a sorcerer to cast a spell on the tomb and make the visions end.

In *DM* 10 we have the speech of the wife's advocate: he presents himself as sharing the woman's sufferings (4.5, 17.6–7), makes it clear that the present case does not arise from ordinary marital quarrels (9.2–5), and purports to let the voice of the mother herself utter the most emotional passages of the speech (11.6–12.2, 13.4–14.8, 16.5–6, 18.5–8, 19.5).

Son's shade is the focus of the whole speech. The advocate and Mother herself describe in detail the visions the woman received (5.2–6.4, 13.6–14.8), as well as the nights in which the shade did not visit her (7.6–8). The speaker exploits to the full the traditional classification of revenants, to determine whether or not the visions were "real."[1] According to Mother, her visions were not deceptive dreams or hallucinations, nor was what she saw a malevolent ghost sentenced to eternal restlessness (16.1–6); indeed, the woman insists on the bodily nature of the vi-

[1] Cf. Schneider (2013, 31–46) for a survey of the ancient sources.

sions: Son's presence was so real that she no longer felt bereaved, and Son's ability to visit his mother was a sign of the divine nature of his soul (e.g., 14.6–8). Father, however, maintains that the woman did not actually see her son: she just conceived an empty consolation for her grief (11.4–12.3), and, in any case, a vision can never be real, because spirits of the dead simply do not exist (16.8).

Most of the speech exploits pathetic arguments, emphasizing, for example, that Mother was emotionally closer to Son than Father (3.1–4.3), or that a woman is naturally inclined to suffer more deeply than a man (10.3–6); the culmination of both parties' argumentations, however, rises to philosophical heights. Father stands by the Epicurean doctrines on death:[2] "like a man who feels no pain" (16.8), he believes that everything perishes with the body and that ghosts are products of the mind rather than objects of the sight; he did call up the sorcerer, but only to grant Mother a peaceful night's rest (17.5)—an intention consistent with the Epicurean pursuit of ataraxia. Mother, however, maintains that the human soul takes its origin from the heavenly fire, and as such is immortal and cannot be dissolved with the body at death (17.2–4); she thereby follows a doctrine first enunciated by Heraclitus, then developed by the Platonic tradition, and adopted by the Stoics.[3]

---

[2] Cf. Schneider (2013, 286–87n442).

[3] See Schneider (2013, 280–81nn429–30). The account of the origin of the soul given by Mother in 17.1–4 was probably inspired by Anchises' speech in Verg. *Aen.* 6.724–51. The opinion that the shades of the dead could visit the living in their dreams will be refuted on different grounds by Augustine: cf. *De cura pro mortuis gerenda* (esp. 13.16).

Substantial attention is devoted to the character of the sorcerer and to the spell he cast on the youth's tomb. Throughout the speech, he is portrayed as cruel and inhuman (9.1), a practitioner of black magic who exploits the powers of darkness (15.2–3).[4] Nevertheless, the speaker does not disdain to appeal to his pity in the final peroration (19.1–4). The spell that prevented Son from visiting Mother is alluded to obliquely for most of the speech: right from the beginning we are told that the reciting of magic formulae ("barbarous": 2.4 and 15.2; "fearful . . . and imperious": 7.1; "baleful": 7.4) was involved, as well as the use of something made of iron (2.2, 2.5)—apparently a number of iron bars stuck in the ground and chained together,[5] intended to lock the soul inside the cinerary urn (8.2–7). Then in the second narration the advocate offers an account (as vivid as it is conjectural) of the whole performance: after casting his spell around the tomb (15.2), the necromancer invokes dark supernatural powers to his aid (15.3–5), then lies flat on the urn and utters magical words directly over the ashes (15.6). Son's soul tries to fight against the spell, but this only prompts the sorcerer to surround the mound with iron bars and chains (15.6), so that the shadow can no longer leave the tomb (see already 2.4–5).

The structure of the speech may be analyzed as follows:[6]

---

[4] The speaker seems to echo the language of technical handbooks on magic, best seen in papyri: cf. Schneider (2013, 146–47nn129–30, 170–71n183, 256n372).

[5] Cf. Stramaglia (1999a, 322n22); Braccini (2011, 211–13).

[6] Cf. Schneider (2013, 16–18). *DM* 10 was long thought (since

In view of its fanciful theme, and also of several technical features,[7] this speech is the least "Quintilianic" of the whole collection; its dating has long been debated, but it should probably be located around the middle of the second century AD.[8] The author of *DM* 8 seems to have imitated it in several passages;[9] Jerome might have alluded to 10.2.8 in one of his letters.[10] A modern reply to the *Sepulcrum incantatum* is included in Patarol's *Antilogies*.[11]

Reitzenstein [1909, 4–6, 19–24]) to be the conflation of two distinct developments of the same theme: but the unity of the speech, and the presence of a second narration in it (*epidiegesis*: see Introduction to *DM* 5, n. 4), has been recognized by Hömke (2002, 106–12) and further explained by van Mal-Maeder (2007, 102–3) and Schneider (2013, 19–20).

[7] See in detail General Introduction, nn. 28 and 83.

[8] Cf. General Introduction, §4.

[9] Cf. Santorelli (2021a); General Introduction, §4.

[10] Jer. *Ep.* 14.3.2: see Stramaglia (2006, 557); Schneider (2013, 126–27n88); Santorelli (2017a, 325–26).

[11] (1743, 291–309).

10

Sepulcrum incantatum

MALAE TRACTATIONIS SIT ACTIO. Quae amissum filium nocte videbat in somnis, indicavit marito. Ille adhibito mago incantavit sepulcrum. Mater desiit videre filium. Accusat maritum malae tractationis.

1. Quamvis, iudices, inter eos, qui liberorum mortibus destituti cuncta vota et praeparatas spes in senectutem ante se egerunt, id fere acerbissimum certamen conflictationis oriatur, ut unusquisque luctibus ac lacrimis suis credat accedere quandam dignitatem, si miserrimus esse vi
2 deatur, haec tamen femina, neque noto neque publico genere miserabilis, non impudenter inter ceteras matres, quae aut unicos aut iuvenes ‹aut›[1] pios filios perdiderunt, eminere et occupare quendam maerentium principatum differentia novae calamitatis affectat, quae sola omnium, supra fidem infelix, in uno filio iam alteram patitur orbita
3 tem. Priorem quidem illam, ut communem ceteris et fato

[1] *add. Leh. (firm. Wint.[7] 151)*

10

The spell on the tomb

ILL-TREATMENT IS TO BE ACTIONABLE. A woman who had lost her son started to see him in her dreams at night, and told her husband. He called in a sorcerer and put a spell on the tomb. The mother ceased to see her son. She accuses her husband of ill-treatment.

(Speech of the woman's advocate)

1. Admittedly, judges, among those who, bereft by the death of their children, bear to the grave in advance of themselves all the prayers and the hopes they had stored up for their old age, there often arises a most bitter rivalry, each believing some dignity accrues to his own laments and tears if he is thought to be the most wretched of all; (2) this woman, nevertheless, who claims pity in no familiar or common manner, does not show undue presumption in claiming to stand out among all the mothers who have lost only sons, or youthful sons, <or> dutiful sons, and to occupy a position of preeminence among grievers because her calamity is novel and unparalleled: unhappy beyond belief, alone of all women she is now suffering a second bereavement of one and the same son. (3) The first, as an event shared with others and the outcome of fate, she bore

accidentem, fortius utcumque tolerabat. Nam et de filio nihil aliud perdiderat misera nisi dies, nec iam timebat ne ille, quo fruebatur, mori posset; planctibus lacrimisque— paene improbe dixerim—parcius utebatur, nec sibi per-
4 mittebat dolor lugere venientem.[2] Nunc destituta solacio, persuasione fraudata est.[3] Dum non putabat perire posse[4] quem poterat videre, eripuit ingrata[5] filio alterum titu- lum:[6] miser ille, nisi teneretur, iam et ad patrem veniret.

5   Tantum misera petit, ne minus perdidisse videatur
6 quam ipsa desiderat. Non inani persuasione nec cogitatio- nibus ficta lugentis umbra veniebat, nec agitabat incertos levis imago somnos, ac[7] ne confusi quidem tristi cinere vultus et inspersum[8] favilla caput noctibus suis obibat, sed filius erat qualis aliquando, et iuvenis et pulcher habitu, nec aspici tantum viderique contentus, verum—si quid desiderio creditis miserae, quae sola vidit—amplexus et oscula dabat et tota nocte vivebat. 2. Multum perdidit mater, si contingebat hoc illi, non minus, si videbatur.
2 Nunc tenebras inanis et longas oculis flentibus noctes iuxta somnum mariti pervigil et tandem[9] deserta metitur;

---

   [2] vive- *Sch., sed vd. Håk.*   [3] *gravius dist. Leh.*
   [4] -ire posse *Sch. coll. 10.1.3:* -isse *codd.*   [5] -tus *Helm*[1]
339–40 (*et vd. Sh. B.*[4] 200), *sed cf. Wint.*[7] 151
   [6] *sic dist. Sh. B.*[4] 200
   [7] [ac] *vel* at *Sh. B.*[2] 203, *sed cf.* 10.9.3, 12.6.3, *al.*
   [8] inspersum *Bur.* (*firm. Håk.*): infernum *codd.*: informe *Gron.*
   [9] -dem *Håk.*[2] 16.12, *cf. Håk.:* -tum *codd.*

---

   [1] Mother had not imagined that telling Father about Son's appearances might result in her being deprived of them; but nor could Son now appear to Father either (though in fact the youth

somehow, as bravely as she could. Indeed, the poor woman had lost of her son only the daytime hours, and she did not now fear that the son whom she was still able to enjoy could die. Of her laments and tears—to put it almost shamelessly—she was all too sparing: grief did not allow itself to bewail one who was still coming to her. (4) But now she has been deprived of all comfort, cheated of her set belief. Thinking that one whom she could see could not die, she ungratefully deprived her son of a second claim to merit: that poor boy would now be coming to his father as well as to her, if he were not being held back.[1]

(5) The poor woman asks only that she may not be thought to have lost less than she herself feels to be lacking to her. (6) The shade that used to come was not the product of unfounded fancy or the invention of the griever's mind, nor was it a fleeting phantom that kept disturbing her broken sleep. It was not, either, a face disfigured by gloomy ash or a head sprinkled with embers that kept appearing on the nights that belonged to him:[2] it was her son as he once was, looking young and handsome. And he was not content just to be seen and gazed at, but—if you give any credit to the longings of the poor woman, who after all was the only one to see him—he would give embraces and kisses, and *live* all night long. 2. The mother's loss is great if this really happened to her, and not less if she *thought* it did. (2) *Now*, alongside her sleeping husband, wakeful herself and finally abandoned, she measures out with weeping eyes the empty darkness and the long nights;

had not done so even before the spell, for reasons explained in 10.2.7–8).

[2] I.e., those on which he chose (or was allowed) to appear.

[Non desiderio fictum aut fucatum[10] habitu,[11] nec ut som-
niorum vanitate conspicitur, sed experta non totum mori
hominem, illud, quod nec flammis uritur nec cineribus
extinguitur nec urnis sepulcrisque satis premitur, expectat.][12] nunc ista[13] carcere obseratam animam et repugnan-
tem magico iuvenem cogitat ferro. Infelicissima omnium

3   mater plus aliquid esse quam umbram filium putat, postquam potuit includi, nec sua tantummodo poena pro-
prioque supplicio deserta consumitur;[14] rescissa orbitate
vel magis cruciatur, quod non licet filio venire cupienti:

4   "Nunc barbaro carmine gravem terram totis noctibus pul-
sat, et impositum sibi sepulcrum, quod non possit evol-
vere, quae solebat ipsos discutere inferos, umbra miratur.

5   Miser, quem non tantum verba clauserunt (nam forsitan
per illa transisset), sed vincula ferrea solidique nexus ad
mortem reduxerunt! Quomodo tenetur infelix, qui ne
propter hoc quidem venit, ut queratur!"

6   Misereor feminae, cuius invidiae totum facinus ascri-
7   bitur. Maritus sic filium inclusit, tamquam se inquietari
mater ista quereretur. Igitur, iudices, nemo miretur si ad

---

[10] fictum aut fucatum *B. Asc.[1] lxviii r.*: -us aut -us (fug- B V E
S, fusc- π) *codd.*

[11] ambitu *Russ.[3] (cf. e.g. 1.1.1, 5.19.6)*

[12] *secl. Håk.[2] 16.12 post Reitz.[2] 5, utpote versionem alteram
verborum (10.1.6) non inani—habitu*

[13] -am M[2], *sed cf. e.g. 10.7.5*

[14] *dist. Cal. (firm. Reitz.[2] 5.7)*

---

3 The iron objects used by the sorcerer to seal the tomb. See
Introduction to the present declamation.

4 She is thinking of her son's torments too.

[She is not expecting something invented by her sense of loss or counterfeited in appearance, nor such as vain dreams present to the eyes, but, having learned by experience that a person does not wholly die, she awaits that which is not burned by flames or reduced to ashes or sufficiently kept down by urns and gravestones.]; *now* she dwells on the thought of a soul locked up in prison and a youth fighting back against enchanted iron.[3] (3) Most unfortunate of all mothers, she thinks her son is something more than a shadow, now that he has been found capable of being confined; she is all alone, and it is not only her own punishment, a torture unique to herself, that consumes her[4]—no, the scar of her bereavement has been torn open again, and she is even more tormented because her son is not allowed to come even though he wishes to: (4) "Now all night and every night he batters at the earth that lies heavy on him thanks to barbarous spells: a shadow that used to be able to scatter the denizens of hell itself[5] is trapped, to its amazement, beneath a tomb it cannot roll away. (5) Poor boy, not just shut in by words (maybe he could have found a way through *them*) but taken back to death by chains of iron and bonds that do not yield![6] How fast must the unfortunate boy be being held, if he cannot come even to complain!"

(6) I pity this woman, for it is to jealousy of her that this outrage is entirely due. (7) Her husband has confined their son, as though his mother here were complaining about being *disturbed*![7] So, judges, let no one be surprised if the

---

[5] I.e., by passing through them to visit his mother.

[6] Cf. Introduction to the present declamation.

[7] Cf. 10.7.2, 10.17.5.

tam crudelem, ad tam immitem patrem umbra non venit.
8 Sciebat ubi lacrimas, ubi posset invenire singultus, a quo
magis desideraretur. Namque isti ferreum pectus et dura
praecordia, nec sunt de orbitate sensus.

3. Quid enim inhumanius patre, quid inveniri truculen-
tius potest? Invidit matri ne filio frueretur, nec hoc ideo
fecit, quia videre ipse malebat; ne viventem quidem adhuc
et incolumem tam blanda tamque debita pietate prose-
quebatur, ut defuncto servaturus affectum etiam sepulti
2 pater videretur. Tanto magis effusa mater et suis ac paternis vicibus occurrens: haec pallidior ad metus, ad vota
pronior, non diebus secura, non noctibus. Et ille miser
intellegebat utri promptior ex parentibus et facilior esset
3 affectus. Itaque ab huius osculis, ab huius feminae cervice
pendebat. Et, quia longum est officia praeterita debitae
pietatis agitare: illo ipso languore, quo filius caducum illud
et fragile corpus amisit, quam perdite mulier et usque in
exemplum modo super ora pallentis infelices[15] lacerabat
oculos, nunc siccata frustra ubera querebatur, nunc super-
4 stitem caedebat uterum! Notabat haec ille deficiens
mandabatque morti suae, cui periret. Ubi sunt, qui cito

---

15 -cis B V

---

8 As such, Father was unable to understand that Mother was
not at all disquieted by her son's appearances: it was no surprise,
then, if Son refused to appear to him too.

9 Cf. 6.19.6. This sentence seems to be echoed in Jer. *Ep.*
14.3.2.

10 I.e., arrange for the spell.

11 Implied: I say merely what follows.

12 Of grieving love.

shade did not visit a father so cruel, so brutal.[8] (8) It knew where it could meet with tears, with sighs; it knew by whom it was more sorely missed. For this man has a breast clad in iron and a heart of flint:[9] he does not feel his bereavement.

3. What, in fact, can be found more inhuman, more callous than this father? Out of envy he prevented the mother enjoying her son—and he did not do this[10] because *he* wanted to see him more; indeed, even when his son was still alive and well, he did not give him such kind and natural affection that he looked likely to preserve his love for him after death, and in that way seem to be his father even when he was in his grave. (2) So much the greater *her* emotion—she played the father's part as well as her own: more pale at her son's moments of fear, more attentive to his requests, careworn by day and by night alike. The poor boy too knew which of his parents had the closer and readier feeling for him. (3) So it was that he hung on *her* kisses, on *her* neck. And, because it would take too long to dwell on the earlier duties she performed out of the affection she owed him:[11] during the very illness in which the son lost that fleeting and fragile body, how desperately his mother—as though to provide a paradigm[12]—at one moment hung over the face of the pale boy and tore at her unfortunate eyes, at another complained that her breast had been sucked dry in vain, at the next beat upon the womb that would outlive her son! (4) All this the sinking man observed, and told his dead self to which of the two he was lost.[13] Where are they, the people

---

[13] I.e., he would come back to *her*, because (only) in *her* was he really leaving a void.

iubent stare lacrimas, quibus non placet longum agere
5 maerorem? Retulit umbra gratiam matri. Scio et intellego:
cum inter gementis iacet medium cadaver, et cum omnis
videtur remisisse curas, tunc sentit aliquid et intellegit
6 et inter suos iudicat. Moneo te, orbitas, moneo: effusius
fleas, effusius ⟨te⟩[16] efferas, numquam perisse ⟨lacri-
mas⟩[17] credas. Filii sui umbra cui non apparet, irascitur.

4. Iam gelidi piger corporis sanguis omnis in mortem
strinxerat venas et nutantium[18] fulgor extremus vanescebat oculorum, et iam desperantibus medicis crediderat
pater. Adhuc tamen spirare[19] matri videbatur, et quam-
cumque corporis partem osculis misera tepefecerat, illo
2 vitae calorem redisse clamabat. Oderat ignes, oderat rogos; reponi corpus et servari membra cupiebat. Et nunc
infelicem magis matrem paenitet quod sepultus est qui
3 poterat reverti. Scitis ipsi quo exequiarum dies[20] labore
extracta sit, quamdiu filium tenuerit a lambentibus[21] flammis. Unde enim speraret ut postea videre contingeret, ut
extra orbitatem haberet oculos? Iam magum misera quae-
rebat, ut umbra evocaretur.

---

[16] add. Wag. 435 coll. 9.13.8   [17] add. Håk.[3] 132 coll.
10.16.9   [18] nat- Gron, sed cf. Beck.[2] 32 et Sen. Ag. 714
[19] spirare M β (def. Håk.[2] 88): sperare vel spare cett.
[20] -es Gron. (cf. ThlL V.2.2069.19–23): -e codd.
[21] a lamb- B P (def. Ritt. 9.**, Håk.[2] 88): a lab- V ψ δ S: ab
alb- A: allamb- ⌐

---

[14] For her show of grief, by coming back only to her.
[15] Cf. 8.9.3, 8.11.6.
[16] Cf. 8.5.3.
[17] By the genre's conventions, bereaved mothers lose their
eyesight through prolonged weeping (cf. Introduction to DM 6,

who order tears to come to a prompt halt, who disapprove of a long period of mourning? The shade expressed his gratitude to his mother.[14] (5) I know and I understand: even when a dying man lies amid those who mourn him, when he appears to be freed of all his cares, he retains some feeling and understanding—and he judges between his kin. (6) I advise you, bereaved ones, I advise you: weep more effusively, be more emotional, do not imagine that ⟨tears⟩ have ever gone to waste. If the ghost of your son does not appear to you, it is because he is angry with you.

4. Now the blood flowing sluggishly through the cold body had contracted all the veins to bring on death and the last gleam in his fading eyes was vanishing—and now the father had come to believe the despairing doctors.[15] But his mother thought he still breathed, and to any part of his body that she had warmed with her kisses, the poor woman cried that the warmth of life had returned.[16] (2) She loathed the funeral fires, she loathed the pyre; she wanted the body to be put to one side and the limbs preserved. And *now* the unfortunate mother regrets all the more that he was buried—for he has proved capable of returning. (3) You yourselves know how painstakingly the day of the funeral was protracted, how long she went on holding her son back from the flames licking at his body. How indeed was she to hope that later on it would fall to her to keep her sight, that she would have eyes beyond bereavement? The poor woman was already looking for a sorcerer to summon up the shade.[17]

n. 2); but this woman somehow kept her sight in the hope of seeing the shade of her son—the reason for her looking for a necromancer.

4   Reliqua, mater infelix, tu ad iudices referre debebas,
et nisi orbitate, nisi lacrimis vox mutaretur in gemitus,
noctes tuas quanto melius tuo ore lugeres! Ego, utcumque
5 potero, perferam. Satiare, misera, satiare saltem memoria
diei illius, quo exequias unici duximus. "Iam planctus"
inquit "lacrimasque consumpseram et tenebras veluti per-
petuas venire gaudebam, iam fatigata propinquorum officia defecerant, iam plangorem familiae altus sopor vicerat." 5. Rogo, ne quis tam contumeliosus sit in matrem, ut
per quietem contigisse filium dicat; unde miserae tunc,
2 unde somnus?[22] "Nihil de te, marite, nihil queror; satis
magnas dedisti[23] poenas. Si totis noctibus mecum flere
voluisses, vidisses utique, non quemadmodum tenues rerum imagines solent cogitationibus accipere corpus, cum
vana[24] absenti animo [cogitationes][25] finguntur, sed ipsum
filium, qualis blandissimus erat—et, si dimittatur, vide-
3 bis.[26] Subito ante me diductis[27] constitit tenebris, non ille
pallens nec acerbo languore consumptus, nec qualis super
rogos videbatur et flammas, sed viridis et sane pulcher
habitu;[28] nescio ubi totam reliquerat mortem: non igne

<hr/>

[22] rogo—somnus *advocato vindicavit Schn.*[2]

[23] -isti (*et usque ad* vidisses *sic dist.*) *Reitz.*[2] 20: -isse B D P:
-isses (dixit O) *cett.*   [24] -a *Wint.*[7] 152: -ae *codd.* (*sc.* imagines
Russ.[2] 152, *vocabulo* cogitationes *mox deleto*)

[25] del. *Sch.*: persuasiones *Håk.*

[26] -bis *Gron.*: -bo *codd.*

[27] did- π: ded- *cett.*

[28] *dist. vulg.*: nihil *Håk.*

<hr/>

[18] Mother and her advocate, who portrays himself at the
woman's side to emphasize his empathy (cf. 1.1.3 with n. 6).

(4) It is you, unfortunate mother, who should be telling the judges the rest of the story, and if bereavement, if tears, were not turning your voice to groans, how much better you would lament by words from your own mouth the nights allotted to you! I shall take up the story, as well as I can. (5) Take your fill, poor woman, yes, your fill, at least of the memory of the day when we[18] conducted the funeral of your only son. "Now," she says, "I had used up my laments and tears, and was glad at the coming of darkness that I hoped would last for ever,[19] now the weary relatives had ceased paying their dutiful respects, now profound sleep had conquered the mourning of the household." 5. I ask that no one should so insult the mother as to say that she saw her son by chance, in a dream. How, yes how could the poor creature have slept *then*?[20] (2) "I make no complaint of you, husband, none at all: you have been punished quite enough.[21] If you had been willing to weep the nights through with me, you would certainly have seen him—not as insubstantial images of things commonly materialize in one's thoughts, when illusions are conjured up by the absent mind, but our son in person, such as he was at his most engaging; and, if he is released, you *will* see him! (3) Suddenly in front of me the darkness parted, and he stood there, not pale as he had been, or wasted away by his grievous illness, or as he looked when he lay on the flaming pyre, but fresh and handsome to behold; he had (who knows where?) left death entirely behind him: his

---

[19] Now that she could no longer see her son, darkness came as a relief, as it prevented her from seeing at all.

[20] In the emotional state she must have been in, the night after the burial.　　[21] By not seeing Son.

torridae comae nec favilla funebri nigra facies nec vix
bene[29] cinere composito umbrae recentis igneus squalor."

4 Proclamaret mater infelix, etiamsi talem videre desisset.[30]

5 "Primo tantum stetit et se permisit agnosci. Ego tunc
plurimum stupui; non ausa oscula dare, non iungere amplexus; infelix primam perdidi noctem, dum timeo ne fu-

6 geret."[31] Hanc tu, marite, persuasionem putas et vanum
animi [mei][32] lugentis errorem? Quicquid est in filio,

7 plus[33] apud matrem fit, cum desinit.[34] Vis denique scire
quid uxori tuae detraxeris? Ex defuncto filio non habet
aliud quod speret.

6. Iam nox altera aderat, et primis statim tenebris
praesto filius erat, non ille, ut pridie, procul et tantum
videndus, sed audacius et propius [et][35] ad matris manus
tamquam corpus accedens. Nec iam nisi cum luce certa
fugatisque sideribus invitus ille vanescebat[36] ex oculis,
multum resistens, saepe respiciens et[37] qui se promitteret

2 etiam proxima nocte venturum. Iam maerori locus non
erat: mulier filium nocte videbat, die sperabat. Quid at-

3 tinet singula referre? "Nullis" inquit "destituta sum tenebris, donec scelerata tacui; satiabar osculis, satiabar amplexibus et colloquebar et audiebam. Misera plus perdidi,

---

[29] paene *Håk., sed vd. Schn.*[2]

[30] proclamaret—desisset *advocato tribuit Str. ap. Schn.*[2] (*post
Wag. 437*)   [31] *verba personata hic finit Wint.*[9]

[32] *del. Reitz.*[2] 20

[33] pluris *Sch.*

[34] -iit *Russ.*[3]

[35] *delevi*

[36] eva- V, *sed vd. Schn.*[2]

[37] ut *Russ.*[3], *sed cf. Breij*[1] 181.95

hair was not scorched by the fire, his face not black from the funeral embers; there was none of the soot that disfigures a new shade when the ashes have only just been duly disposed of." (4) The unlucky mother might well have raised a cry of joy even if she had never seen him in such a state again. (5) "The first time, he just stood there and let himself be recognized. I was completely dumbfounded then. I did not venture to kiss him, venture to embrace him. Unlucky woman, I wasted the first night fearing he might go away." (6) Husband, do you think this mere hallucination, the empty delusion of a grieving mind?[22] Whatever there is in a son[23] becomes something more for a mother, when it ceases to exist. (7) Do you want to be told what you have robbed your wife of? She now has nothing else of her departed son to hope for.

6. Now the second night had come, and the moment darkness fell the son was there at hand, not as on the previous day, just visible from a distance, but coming to his mother's arms more boldly and closely, like a body. This time he only began to vanish from sight at dawn, in full daylight when the stars had been put to flight, and that not willingly: with much faltering, often looking back, and like one promising to come the next night too. (2) No need now for mourning: the mother saw her son at night, and looked forward to him during the day. Why go into details? (3) "I was not left alone," she says, "at any time of darkness, so long—wicked woman!—as I said nothing. I took my fill of kisses, of embraces; I conversed with him and heard him speak. Ah me, my loss is all the greater if no one be-

[22] Picking up 10.5.2.
[23] I.e., all the joys of having a son.

4   si nemo credit. Iam coeperam tuam quoque, marite cru-
     delis, agere causam rogabamque iuvenem ut paternis ocu-
     lis quoque laetus occurreret, et tibi, ingrate, dimidia nocte
     cedebam. Iam miser et ille pollicebatur. Haec me fiducia
5   perdidit, ut confiterer." Rogo, quid tam muliebre, quid
6   tam maternum fieri potest? "Gaude," inquit, "marite,
     gaude; filium fortasse nocte proxima videbis, illum, quem
     crudelibus flammis exussisti, ex quo cineres et ossa super-
     sunt, iuvenem videbis et forte etiam ‹quam›diu[38] speres.
     Ego certe totis noctibus mater sum, video, fruor, iam et
7   narro." Exitum paterni affectus quaeritis? Filium videre
     timuit.

     7. Sic magum protinus nescia matre, cuius horrido
     murmure imperiosisque verbis dii superi manesque tor-
     quentur, excogitator iste mortis alterius advocat, non ut
     exorati manes deducerentur, nec ut evocata nocturnis ulu-
     latibus undecumque umbra properaret, sed tamquam
     parum sepulcra premerent et tumulorum leve pondus es-
2   set.[39] "Filius" inquit "meus non satis periit; adhuc fulgore
     siderum fruitur et nocte nostra. Nam, cum dies occidit,

---

[38] ‹quam›diu *Wint.*[6] 260 (*cf. 10.10.6, Liv. 24.14.6;* diu *Reitz.*[2]
20.9): die *codd.* (*tradita def. Hömke* 291.724): fortem, ut iam die
Str.[1] 278–79 (*cf. 10.6.2, 10.12.5*)   [39] *gravius dist. Obr.*

---

[24] If I am not believed, there will be no chance for me to have
the spell removed, so I will be unable to see my son again—for-
ever, this time. My loss will thus be even greater than when the
boy died (cf. 10.12.1).

[25] She now thought her son, although already dead, could not
be lost to her whatever she did; relying on this confidence, she
was not afraid to tell her husband about her visions.

lieves me![24] (4) I had by now started to plead your cause too, cruel husband, and was asking the young man to come joyfully to be seen by his father too; indeed—you ingrate!— I was ready to let you have half of each night. The poor boy was now giving his promise too. Hence the confidence[25] that was my undoing, for it made me speak out." (5) What, I ask you, can be so typical of a woman or a mother? (6) "Rejoice, husband," she said to him, "rejoice! Perhaps you will see your son tonight,[26] you will see the young man whom you burned up in cruel flames, of whom only ashes and bones remain—and perhaps even for ‹as› long as you hope. *I* at least am a mother all night and every night; I see him, I enjoy his company—now I am even giving a narration of all this!"[27] (7) Do you ask the outcome of his paternal feelings? He was afraid to see his son!

7. So it was that straightaway, without the mother knowing, this deviser of a second death called in a sorcerer, by whose fearful incantations and imperious formulae the gods above and the spirits of the dead are tormented, not asking that his son's spirit should be won over and brought forth, or that his shade, summoned by nocturnal shrieks, should hasten from wherever it dwelt, but on the plea that the pressure of the tomb was too slight and the weight of the mound not heavy enough.[28] (2) "My son," he said, "has not died sufficiently; he still enjoys the starlight and *our* night.[29] For when the day goes down, he

[26] Cf. 10.15.7. She is represented as speaking in the daytime.
[27] Metarhetoric: this is the *narratio*. [28] Necromancers were usually asked to summon the souls of the dead, not to prevent them from appearing. Cf. 10.15.5; Stramaglia (1999a, 319n14). [29] I.e., the night we living persons enjoy (DAR).

imponit morti suae finem, domum repetit et maternos ter-
3 ritat somnos. Inveni aliqua, inveni vincla verborum, sed
arte tota, sed labore toto. Magna tua gloria est, si retines
4 filium qui redit etiam a morte ad matrem." Noxium sepulcro circumdatur carmen. Tunc horrentibus verbis urna
praecluditur, tunc primum miser filius mors et umbra fit.
5 Ite nunc et putate vana fuisse matris solacia; filium ista si
cogitationibus et inani persuasione vidisset, adhuc videret.
6   At quae supplicia sustinuit infelix illa statim nocte! Iam
totam domum ac familiam quies prima sopiverat, et tacen-
7 tibus tenebris venerat tempus dulcissimum matri. Iacebat
haec insomnis, inquieta, cum diceret: "Iam statim appare-
bit, iam statim veniet. Numquam tamen tardius venit.
8 Miseram me, fili, proxima nocte iam veneras. Ecce iam
medios sidera tenent cursus: indignor, irascor; ita demum
mihi satisfacies, si apud patrem fuisti. Miseram me, iam
maligna mundus luce clarescit: quando venies? Iam redire
debebas." 8. Ac[40] postquam alteram tertiamque noctem
deserta vanis questibus duxit, tum tristiora lugubria, tum
squalidae magis placuere vestes, tum repetitis sanguina-
vere planctibus iam convalescentes lacerti. Nihil est infelicius matre, quae perdidit aliquid in filio postquam ex-
tulit.
2   Cum vero comperit noctes suas iuveni[41] necessitatibus
magicis et[42] cantato perisse ferro, quam tum[43] illa prae-

---

40 at Φ
41 -i *Sch.*: -is *codd.*
42 et *Dess.*[2]: ex *codd.*: ‹et› (*Sch.*) excan- (ς) *malit Wint.*[9]
43 quam tum *Gron.*: quantum *codd.*

---

30 Cf. 10.2.7, 10.17.5.   31 Contrast 10.6.2.

puts an end to his own death, returns home and frightens his mother in her sleep.[30] (3) Find something, find words to bind him, but using your whole art, all your effort. Great will be your reputation if you can hold back a son who comes to his mother even from death." (4) The baleful spell is recited all round the tomb. It is then that the urn is barred off with fearful words, then that the poor son becomes a dead man and a shade for the first time. (5) *Now* believe that the mother's consolations were empty; if she had seen her son only in fancy and vain imagination, she would be seeing him still.

(6) But what torment did the unlucky woman endure from that night on! By now the whole house and house-hold were sunk in their first sleep. It was pitch dark and silent: the time most sweet to the mother had come. (7) She lay wide awake, uneasy, saying to herself: "He will be here presently, he will come presently. Yet he has never been so late. Ah me, son, last night you had come by this time! (8) Look, the stars are already in midcourse. I am indignant, angry; you will only make me amends if you have been with your father. How wretched I am! Now the sky is brightening—to spite me with its light. When will you come? You should have been going back by now!" 8. Forlorn now, she spent the second and third nights in fruitless complaints; it was then that she came to choose to be in deeper mourning,[31] to wear shabbier clothes, then that her arms, that had been recovering, grew red with renewed blows. There is nothing more unfortunate than a mother who has lost something of her son—after she has buried him.

(2) But when she realized that the young man's nights had been lost to him through inescapable magic and iron

fixum clausumque tumulum nudis cecidit uberibus, quo
fletu sepulcra perfudit, quo gemitu audientem forsitan et
3 exire cupientem frustra vocavit animam! O natura crudelis, plus magum posse quam matrem! Ubi sunt, qui acer-
bas mortium necessitates et ferrea iura fatorum et invictas
nec ullo maerore mutabiles inanium leges querebantur
4 umbrarum? Filium tuum, mulier infelix, non impositae
inferis clusere terrae nec spissa perpetuae noctis caligo
compescuit, non fabulosa vatibus palus multumque cele-
brati curvato igne torrentes. Haec permeabat, haec omnia
nocte transibat levioremque mortem suam fecerat, quam
5 si peregrinaretur et abesset. Et nunc minus mali pateretur,
si non sentiret: ille qui non venit,[44] in quendam carcerem
6 translatus a tumulo,[45] patitur veneficia[46] vitae. Magnae
sunt ergo umbrarum catenae et, quamquam volatilem
vagamque imaginem, morti stringunt atque alligant tamquam reum corpus animam. Ferro vero ac lapidibus artare
et, ut solent bellicae robur accipere portae, ipsam umbram
iam catenis alligare, iam claustris, non dico crudele,[47] est
portentosum, nefarium: utique si hoc faciat qui sensurum

[44] *an* venit, ⟨velut⟩?
[45] *dist. Tos. 144*
[46] be- B ψ, *sed vd. Håk.*
[47] *dist. Bur.*

[32] A jibe at the recurring topics of consolations, which repre-
sent the laws of fate as relentless and not influenced by human
despair (cf. Sen. *Pol.* 4.1). If that were so, how could a sorcerer
interfere with them?
[33] Two familiar features of the classic underworld: the Stygian

placed under a spell, how then did she beat the closed and
barricaded tomb with her bare breasts, with what tears did
she drench the grave, with what groans did she summon
a soul that was perhaps listening and wanting to come
forth!—all in vain. (3) O the cruelty of nature, that a sorcerer should be more powerful than a mother! Where are
they who complained of the bitter imperatives of death,
the iron dictates of the fates, and the laws of the insubstantial shades that are unconquerable and not to be
changed by any grieving?[32] (4) Your son, unhappy woman,
was not shut in by the earth laid on the dead, not restrained by the thick darkness of everlasting night, or by
the swamp fabled by poets and the oft sung torrents with
their overarching fires.[33] Through all of these he *used* to
come, all of these he *used* to pass by night: he had made
his own death less hard to bear than if he were merely
away on his travels. (5) And now he would suffer less evil
if he had no feeling; but in fact he who comes no more has
been transferred from the burial mound to some prison
cell and is suffering spells that a *living* man might suffer.[34]
(6) Great then are the bonds holding down the shades:
they constrain and tie down the soul to death, however
winged and wandering a specter it is, like the body of a
guilty man. But to constrict a shade itself with iron and
stones, in the way that gates are strengthened in time of
war, to load it now with chains, now with bars, is—I will
not say cruel, it is monstrous and wicked: especially if this
is the work of someone who believes his son will feel it.

swamp (cf., e.g., Verg. *Aen.* 6.323) and the flaming stream of the
river Phlegethon (cf., e.g., Verg. *Aen.* 6.550–51).

[34] I.e., he does have feeling.

7   filium credat. Et nunc illos miserrima mater in corpus
putat et in membra descendisse mucrones.

9. O mage saeve, crudelis, o in lacrimas artifex nostras,
vellem non dedisses tam magnum experimentum! Irasci-
mur tibi, et blandiri necesse est: dum cludis umbram, in-
telleximus solum te esse, qui possis evocare.

2   Videtur itaque mulier infelix a dignitatis dolore[48] se-
cedere, quod tam‹quam›[49] uxorias in forum querelas et
tamquam delicata matronae desideria pertulerit? Non
enim vestes nec aurum nec ambitiosos quaerit ornatus;
3   contenta est orbitas sordibus suis. Ac ne pelicis quidem
dolore compellitur, nec tacita gaudia mariti impatientia et
muliebri vanitate complorat. Sed nec relictum torum de-
sertumque genialem velut contempta vilitas uxoris ulcis-
4   citur: alia longe, alia de noctibus cura est. Ne timueris,
quaecumque dignitas es[50] magni doloris: nihil queritur
misera nisi par orbitati, nisi matri dignum, quod publicos
consumat oculos, quod ignotas quoque exigat lacrimas.
5   Quantam enim a marito acceperit iniuriam, scire vultis?
Sola mater filium perdidit nec potest invidiam facere
morti.

[48] -tate -oris *Scheff. 450*
[49] tam‹quam›> ꙅ (*def. Wint. ap. Schn.²*): tam *codd.*
[50] es V: est B Φ

[35] I.e., that Son is body enough to suffer physically (cf. 10.8.6).
[36] The sort of thing that wives usually bring up against their
husbands in trials for ill-treatment: cf. 8.6.1–4.
[37] Amounting to: Do not fear, judges, that the dignity appropriate to a great cause for resentment is lacking in this case (cf.
10.9.2).

(7) And indeed the all-wretched mother thinks that those sword edges have now been brought down into a body and into limbs.[35]

9. O barbarous and cruel sorcerer, so skilled in arousing our tears, I should rather you had not given so signal an instance of your art. We are angry with you—and yet flattery is called for: when you shut the ghost up, we realized that there is no one except you who can call it back.

(2) Does then the unhappy woman seem to be departing from the grief appropriate to a respectable lady, having supposedly brought to the forum conjugal complaints[36] and the frivolous wish-list of a married woman? No, she is not asking for dresses or gold or showy finery: bereavement is content with the shabby clothes that suit it. (3) Nor is she impelled by resentment at a mistress either: she is not complaining, with a woman's silly intolerance, of her husband's secret pleasures. But neither is a wife who feels she is despised as worthless seeking to avenge a marriage bed left deserted: *her* concern for what goes on at night is completely different. (4) Fear not, dignity—whatever your demands—appropriate to a great grief:[37] the poor woman is complaining of nothing that is not commensurate with bereavement, nothing that is unworthy of a mother, but of something fit to wear away the eyes[38] of the public, to call forth the tears even of strangers. (5) Do you want to know how much she has been injured by her husband? She is the only mother who has lost a son without being able to reproach death for her loss.

---

[38] They will be blinded by excessive weeping; cf. n. 17.

6   Ante itaque quam sciatis, iudices, quis dolor quisve
maeror, quae tanta impatientia eruperit, ut mulier aliquando dulcium oblita tenebrarum clarum nitorem publicae lucis et diem etiam domi invisum in foro interque leges notabilis et sepulcris abstracta pateretur, certum
profecto habetis non audaciam neque impudentiam nec
7   vanitatem umquam querelas habuisse miserorum. Quam
verum est quicquid exclamat calamitas, nec ab infelicibus
8   ficti temere exeunt gemitus! Mulier, quae sanguinantes ad
iudicem[51] porrigit lacertos, quae scisso laniatoque vultu,
quae lividis profertur uberibus, magno dolore cogitur ut
hoc potius agat quam cineres osculetur, quam complec-
tatur urnam. Gravis testis querelae suae orbitas est.

10. Et antequam ad genus illatae inique ei iniuriae
venio: cur, marite, quae ex te filium perdidit, quicquam
2   potest queri? Crudelis orbitatem feris adhuc alio dolore,
tamquam parum desideria conficiant quae de unico gerit;
non pateris animam vacare lacrimis suis tu, qui sinum
debes, qui colloquia et amplexus. Quam misera est, quae
3   queritur et de solacio suo! Nunc[52] coniugis desideriis large
indulge:[53] nihil aspere, nihil contra voluntatem! Habet pri-
4   vilegium suum mater infelix. Molles manus et mitia fomenta magnis vulneribus admoveas. Quae se adhuc secari

[51] -ces B[ac] ς (*sed* sanguinantes ad iudices *ambigue dictum sit*)
[52] nunc *Håk.*[2] *90–91*: non *codd.*
[53] -e *Gron.*: -et *codd.*

(6) So before you learn, judges, what is the pain, what the grief, what the intolerable distress that has burst forth so strongly that a woman, forgetting for once her beloved darkness, is ready to endure the glare of publicity and the daylight that she loathes even at home, torn away from the grave to be pointed at in the courts of law, you must surely be well aware that audacity, impudence and folly have never played a part in the complaints of the wretched. (7) How true is everything that calamity cries aloud!—for from the unfortunate come forth no random or feigned groans. (8) A woman who holds out bleeding arms to the judge, who appears in court with scratched and lacerated face, her breasts livid with bruises, is forced by no trivial grief to act like this instead of kissing the ashes and embracing the urn. Bereavement acts as a weighty witness in support of its own accusation.

10. Now, before I come to the type of injury unjustly inflicted upon her, I ask: Why, husband, if she has lost a son who is yours also, does she have any reason for complaint? (2) Well, you are cruel enough to strike her in her bereavement with a further source of pain, as if the longing she feels for her only son did not overwhelm her enough. You are not letting her soul have time for its tears, yes you, who ought to be pressing her to your breast, talking to her, embracing her. How wretched a woman must be, when she has into the bargain to complain about the one who should be comforting her! (3) Now you must be generous in letting your wife have her way: nothing harshly, nothing against her will! An unfortunate mother has her own special rights. (4) A wide-open gash should be treated with gentle hands and soft poultices; when a

5   plaga permittit, in summo est. Viri forsitan, quomodo fortior sexus, sic[54] et contra dolorem quam imbecillis animus
magis pugnat; itaque totum istud lugere femineum est, et
simul orbitas imbelle pectus invadit, animus ille, qui luctus
suos sequitur, incipit indulgentiam sentire lacrimarum.

6   Fidem tuam, marite, coniugi flere liceat; satiare gemitu
orbitatem permitte, quamdiu velit, flere. Odi patrem qui,
cum filium et ipse perdiderit, putat nimis lugere matrem.

    11. "Quid ergo queritur?" inquit. Hoc primum: filium
⟨non⟩,[55] quomodo debes, scelerate, desideras; magno
animo orbus es, loqueris fuisse mortalem et interpretaris

2   nihil superesse post flammas. Flet iuxta latus et plangit
uxor, tu siccos oculos habes. Illa totis noctibus funebres
exercet ululatus, tu graves somnos ac placidam quietem.

3   Pater crudelis, pater immemor, quid vis tibi amplius obi-
ciamus? Ex quo perdidisti filium, numquam sic deside-
rasti, ut videres.

4   Quid, quod eripuisti matri solacium, puta vanum et
supervacuum? Nolo iudices, nolo corripias; scires quantum esset hoc, si tantundem doleres. Res indignior non
est, quam quod tibi de eo postulas credi, quod non vidisti.

5   Indulge sane vanae rei, ignosce: libenter se orbitas decipit.
Magnas calamitates una[56] ratio sustentat, quod indulgent

---

54 sic *Gron.*: sit *codd.*   55 add. ⟨
56 una *Obr.*: vana *codd.*

---

39 I.e., only those who experience a superficial sorrow may be
treated roughly; this woman is suffering deeply, and so should be
comforted gently.   40 You claim that seeing Son was only an
empty consolation, but you did not experience the visions as she
did: so you cannot ask to be believed rather than her.

wound admits of a further cut, it is only superficial.[39] (5)
A man, belonging as he does to the stronger sex, perhaps
fights pain too better than the weaker; all that lamenting
is in fact a hallmark of a *woman*: as soon as bereavement
invades her unwarlike heart, her mind, at the beck and call
of her grief, starts to find comfort in tears. (6) Trust me,
husband, you should allow your wife to weep; let her do
justice to her loss by her groans, and weep for as long as
she likes. I cannot endure a father who has himself lost a
son, but thinks the mother's mourning excessive.

11. "What is she complaining about, then?" he says.
This to start with: you ⟨do not⟩ miss your son as you
should, wicked man. You are taking your loss bravely, you
say he was mortal, and according to you there is nothing
left after the flames. (2) While your wife weeps and wails
at your side, your eyes remain dry. She continues her funeral shrieks all night, you enjoy deep sleep and tranquil
repose. (3) Cruel father, forgetful father, what more do
you want me to reproach you with? Since you lost your
son, you have never missed him enough to be able to see
him.

(4) What then of the fact that you have robbed his
mother of her solace, empty and superfluous though it
may have been? I do not wish you to judge her, to upbraid
her; you would know how much this meant to her, if you
felt the pain she feels. There is nothing more shocking
than to demand to be believed about something *you* did
not see.[40] (5) Indulge her in what may indeed be without
foundation, forgive it: a woman who has lost her son is
happy to deceive herself. One thing keeps people going
amid great disasters: those in evil fortune look complai-

269

mala persuasionibus suis. Quicquid ad miseros pertinet,
6 crudelius[57] eripitur quo minus est. Clamat itaque, clamat
mater infelix: "Si mihi aliquam imaginem filii mei vel parvuli vel iam adulti vel novissimam iuvenis auferres, inice-
rem tamen misera tamquam corpori manum, illam simili-
tudinem flens tenerem, illos oculos, illam gratissimam
faciem et risus[58] oris, expressos et adumbratos artificis
7 manu vultus. Sed illum perdidi, unde imago, unde similitudo, unde solacium. 12. Fili, plus hodie amisi, quam cum
2 elatus es: post mortem te tuam vidi. Si mehercules notas
in corpore unici vestes subtrahere temptares, dicerem:
succurre solacio meo. Haec omnia apud me filii mei mem-
3 bra[59] sunt; ego osculabor, amplectar, flebo supra."[60] Non
est ratio fortasse; adeo[61] quicquid rationem vincit,[62] affectus est. Nihil est sceleratius prudenti orbitate.

4   "Levia," inquit, "levia loquor; ego filium meum videbam." Quaenam istum[63] fortuna, quae indulserat condicio
5 naturae? Non excludebat orbitas oculos tuos, eras iam
consecuta, mater, ut iuvenem die absentem putares. Maxi-

---

57 *expectes* ⟨eo⟩ cr-, *sed cf. Vitr. 1.4.7, Cels. 5.26.20f*
58 risus A: rictus *cett.*   59 umbra V (*vind. Wint.*[7] *152*)
60 semper *Håk.; verba personata hic finit Schn.*[2]
61 ad- *Håk.*: id- *codd.*   62 vinc- V: vic- B Φ
63 *an* -ud?

---

41 Here and in 10.12.2: husband (or generic?).
42 In his most recent portrait: perhaps a reference to the funerary wax mask customarily made from the face of the deceased
before the burial.
43 *Hysteron proteron.*
44 Now that I see you no more, my loss is heavier still. Cf.
10.6.3.

santly on their own convictions. The more trivial anything the wretched possess, the crueler it is to take it away. (6) So she cries, the unhappy mother cries: "If you[41] took from me some picture of my son, when he was young or just grown up or—lastly[42]—as a young man, I should in my distress lay hands on it as if it were his body, I should weep as I held that likeness, those eyes, that lovely face, the smiling lips, the features represented and sketched[43] by the artist's hand. (7) But in fact I have lost *him*—the original from which the picture, the likeness, the consolation, were all drawn. 12. Son, I feel my loss more today than on the day of your funeral: after your death I *did* see you.[44] (2) If, for heaven's sake, you were to try to rob me of the clothes so familiar to me when my only son wore them, I should say: Come to the rescue of what gives me comfort! All these things are for me living parts of my son: I shall kiss them, embrace them, weep over them." (3) This is not the voice of reason, perhaps; so true is it that feeling is everything that overcomes reason.[45] Nothing is more wicked than common sense in the bereaved.[46]

(4) "These are trifles I am speaking of," she says, "trifles. I used to be able to *see* my son." What luck, what vagary of nature had favored you with him? (5) For you were *not* being blinded by your loss,[47] you had already, mother, reached the point of thinking the young man absent dur-

---

[45] To regard the clothes of a deceased son as "living" may not be rational, but it is dictated by something much more powerful than reason—feeling.

[46] They should cast aside common sense and give way to their feelings.

[47] See again n. 17.

mam perdidit mors acerbitatem, si possis videre quem
6 amiseris. Videre ergo tibi contingebat, o mulier, vultum,
habitum, corpus, incessum? Non crederem, nisi te perdi-
7 disse sentirem.[64] Tempora ergo cum morte diviseras, et
superstite filio fruebaris omnibus tenebris. Quantum per-
dideris, hinc aestima: hoc tibi si non contigisset, non eras
8 tam improba ut optares. Aliquis, o pietas, sepultus et
conditus, veteris[65] corporis cinis et favilla, tamen corpus
sumebat in noctes, et[66] ad solida viventis membra revoca-
tus praebebat se matris oculis qualem non crederes reces-
surum! Nec queri de luce poteramus; quantum licebat,
9 aderat. Videbas ergo, mulier, ac[67] praesentia fruebaris?
"Videbam" inquit "et fruebar, et ad quem pertinebat, rogo,
10 etiamsi decipiebar?" Sed quid ego utor testimonio tuo?
Mago credo et vidisse te filium et nunc non videre.

13. At tu misera nihil crudelius ex marito timebas,
quam ne tibi non crederet. "Nemo" inquit "oculis meis
2 fidem detrahat. Fili,[68] indulgentissime adolescens, vidi te,
nec semel vidi: certum est, fixum est, eripi non potest.
Quatenus impius pater? Et hoc tibi auferre conatur, ut te
3 venisse nunc[69] credam.[70] Nec illud garrula nec vana voce
vulgavi; venire te nulli indicavi, nisi qui deberet optare ut

64 -em *scripsi*: -es *codd.*   65 veteris *Bendz*: ceteri *codd.*
66 -tes et *Bur.*: -te sed *codd.*   67 hac V   68 vidi *Obr.*
69 nunc *scripsi*: non *codd.* (*cf. ad 10.10.3*), *contra sensum*
70 quatenus—credam *dist. Schn.*[2]

48 And then only: cf. 10.8.4.
49 Sc., by the sincerity and intensity of your grief (AS).
50 I.e., complain that Son did not appear during the day too.
51 I.e., to appear.

ing the day.[48] Death has lost its worst sting if you can see the one you lost. (6) So you, woman, were lucky enough to see his face, his manner, his body, the way he moved? I should not believe it, if I didn't *feel*[49] that you have lost all this. (7) You had, then, divided up the time between yourself and death, and you still enjoyed the living presence of your son every time darkness fell. How much you have lost you may reckon thus: if this had not befallen you, you would not have been so presumptuous as to wish for it. (8) To think that a man (O the affection he showed!), buried and laid to rest, the ashes and embers of his past body, nevertheless took on a body for the nights, and, summoned back to the solid limbs of the living person, presented himself to his mother's eyes so clearly that you could not imagine he would go away again! And we could not complain about the *days*:[50] he was present as much as was permissible. (9) So you used to see him, woman, and enjoy his presence? "Yes," she says, "I used to see him, I used to enjoy it—and whose business was it, I ask, even if I was deceived?" (10) But why do I employ *your* testimony? I believe the *sorcerer*, both that you saw your son and that you do not see him now.

13. But you, poor woman, had nothing more cruel to fear from your husband than his disbelieving you. "Let no one," she says, "try to discredit my eyes. (2) Son, kindest of young men, I saw you, I saw you not once only: it is certain, it is assured, it cannot be taken away. How far will your father go in his lack of affection? He tries to take this too away from you: my present belief that you *did* come. (3) I did not noise it abroad out of garrulity or vainglory; I told no one that you had come, except the one who ought to have prayed you could have this power.[51] I revealed it

273

hoc posses. Patri tantum tuo, patri—ignosce deceptae—confessa sum, dum interrogo an te et ille vidisset."

4   Itaque das, mulier infelix, graves ⟨nimium⟩[71] nimiumque poenas. Effecit magus ne filium videres, et solum

5   apud te reliquit ut meminisses quod videras.[72] Totum tamen illud solacium tuum refer, misera, si potes, et primum confitere simpliciter an soporis pondus illud et nesciae quietis vanitas fuerit. Apud me quidem satis misera, satis eras, mater, infelix, etiamsi tale somnium perdidisses.

6   "Miserere," inquit, "melius de affectibus meis sentias. Non ego fatigata planctibus sensi venisse noctem; videre

7   filium pervigiles meruistis, oculi. Sed primum, dum metuo, umbra processit.[73] Subito, dii boni, quod ego gaudium, quam vidi felicitatem: constitit ante me filius dis-

8   cussis tenebris—ita dimittatur aliquando! Prosilui protinus et accessi, vultus, comas, ora perspexi: meus erat. Quam laetum se, quam hilarem offerebat, quomodo persuadebat mihi ne crederem morti! 14. Scelerate, nescis, pater, quam similem viventi filium cluseris. Circuibant totum corpus

2   oculi: non inveniebam quid ignis egisset. Subinde dicebam: hunc ego extuli, hunc rogo imposui? Ex hoc ego cineres et ossa collegi? Si talis est, quid habeo quod lugeam?

3   Perisse filium meum hoc uno intellegebam, quod illum non poteram et patri ostendere.

---

[71] *suppl. Watt*[3] 52   [72] -eras *β*: -ebas *cett.*
[73] *dist. Gr.-Mer. (firm. Håk.): post* subito *vulg.*

---

52 And not a "real" vision.
53 Than to think that I merely *dreamed* of my son.
54 The fear lasts till she recognizes the boy.
55 Freed from the spell and allowed to return to her.

only to your father, your *father*—forgive my deluded heart!—, by asking him whether he had seen you too."

(4) So, unlucky woman, you are paying ‹too› heavy, all too heavy a penalty. The sorcerer stopped you seeing your son, and left behind no more than the memory that you saw him. (5) But tell us, poor thing, if you can, about all the comfort you received, and first confess honestly whether it was heavy sleep and the delusion of unconscious slumber. To my mind at least, mother, you would be wretched enough, unlucky enough, even if you had lost a *dream* like that.[52] (6) "For pity's sake," she says, "please think better of my feelings.[53] Tired out by my laments, I did not realize that night had fallen; by keeping awake you, my eyes, *deserved* the sight of my son. (7) First, then, to my dismay,[54] a shadowy figure came forward. Suddenly (good gods!) what cause for joy, what cause for happiness did I see: the veil of darkness was parted, and there before me stood my son—O may he be released like that one day![55] (8) I darted forward instantly and approached, gazed at the face, the hair, the lips: it was my own boy. How joyful and happy he looked as he offered himself to view, how well he persuaded me not to believe he was dead! 14. Wicked father, you do not know how like a living man your son was when you shut him in. My eyes ranged all over his body: I could find no trace of fire. (2) I kept saying: Is this the boy I bore to his funeral, did I place *him* on the pyre? Was it from *him* that I collected up the ash and bones? If he is like *this*, what have I to mourn? (3) I only realized my son had perished because I could not show him to his father too.

4   "Confitebor: primae tamen nec ego credidi nocti, et tamquam victis irascebar oculis et erubescebam misera, si quies fuisset. Ecce iterum iuvenis, ecce iam cotidie venit!

5   Quid habeo quod[74] interpreter? Verum est utique quod semper est. Novissime, non tamquam umbra veniebat sed assidebat, sed amplexus dabat. Ego sentiebam et re-

6 cipiebam. Quotienscumque domus fuerat grato sopore prostrata, aderat ille, quales humanis se offerunt oculis propitii dii, quale laetissimum numen est, cum se patitur

7 videri. Sicut omnis religio templorum, omnis religio luco-rum, cum tacuere mortalia et profani[75] procul erravere sedibus totis, solitudine frui et de suis dicitur exire simu-lacris, ita iuvenis meus noctibus totis agebat filium et pa-terna domo et penatibus suis fruebatur, placidus et mitis et matri propitius; ut numen et deus delabi sideribus et

8 venire de liquido puroque aere videbatur. Quid imprecer sceleratissimo patri? Umbram probare voluit!"

15. Miseremini, iudices, ut hoc facinus, quibus debetis, accipiatis animis, maius parricidio, maius quam si filii se-pulcrum funditus eruisset et sacratos morte lapides, etiam cineres et ossa religiose quiescentia fracta sparsisset urna.

2 Advocatur homo, cuius ars est ire contra naturam,[76] qui

---

[74] q. <aliter> vel q. <quietem> vel sim. Håk., sed vd. Schn.[2]
[75] -i E: -is cett.
[76] hic levius, post fama est gravius dist. Håk.[2] 91–92

---

[56] I.e., in what I thought I saw then.
[57] She does not need to understand how it is possible for her son to appear to her: it is enough for her to realize that it is not a passing illusion, since it happens regularly.
[58] Cf. Verg. Aen. 6.258–59.

(4) "I will confess it: all the same, even *I* did not believe in the first night;[56] I was angry with my eyes as though they had been overcome by slumber, and (poor thing) I was ashamed to think I might have been asleep. But look, here comes the youth a second time; look, he comes every day! (5) Why need I cast around for an explanation?[57] What always happens must surely be true. By the end, he didn't come like a ghost: rather, he would sit by me, he would hold me close. I felt him and welcomed him. (6) Whenever the house was plunged in grateful sleep, he was there, in the form taken by favoring gods when they offer themselves to human eyes, by a most propitious power when it allows itself to be seen. (7) Just as, when the world of men has fallen silent and the profane have withdrawn far from every part of a sacred enclosure,[58] all divine beings in temples, all divine beings in groves (it is said) delight in the solitude and come forth from their statues, so my boy would play a son's part all night, every night, and take pleasure in his father's house, his hearth and home, untroubled and gentle and propitious to his mother; he seemed to glide down from the stars like a god, a divinity, and to materialize out of thin clear air. (8) What curse can I invoke against so wicked a father? He wanted to test out a *shadow*!"

15. Pity me, judges, and see this crime for what it is: worse than a parricide, worse than if he had uprooted his son's tomb, broken the urn, and scattered the stones sanctified by death, and even the ashes and bones resting there in revered peace. (2) A man is called in, whose art lies in going counter to nature; as soon as he has thundered forth

simul ore squalido barbarum murmur intonuit, pallere[77]
superos, audire inferos, tremere terras vel[78] experimentis
3 loquentium fama est. Constitit iuxta tumulum miserrimi
iuvenis mors certior: "Nunc" opinor, inquit,[79] "arcana mea
tenebrae adiuvate me dignae,[80] nunc omne pervium[81] numen et religio, quam isti inrogo, propius adeste, succur-
4 rite. Magis mihi laborandum est quam cum sidera mundo
revelluntur, cum iubentur hiberni fluviorum stare decur-
sus, cum potentiore carminis veneno victi rumpuntur in
5 mea instrumenta[82] serpentes. Custodiendus est iuvenis,
assignandus est inferis et densioribus transfuga clauden-
dus est tenebris. Quanto facilius opus erat, si revocaretur!"
6 Mox in ipsam dicitur incubuisse pronus urnam et inter
ossa et inter cineres verba clusisse. Hoc tamen subinde
respiciens confitebatur: "Repugnat umbra, itaque[83] carminibus non satis credo; praefigamus omne tumuli latus
7 et multo vinciamus saxa ferro. Iam bene habet: expiravit
aliquando, non videri, non progredi potest. An mentiar,
scies proxima nocte."
8 Omnes mehercules parentes, utique qui liberos perdi-

[77] palle- 5: falle- *codd.*: fave- *Meurs.[1] 8*
[78] vel *scripsi*: ut *codd.*
[79] nunc—inquit *sic dist. Vass. 115*
[80] -ae *Engl. 101–2 (corrob. Håk.[2] 92)*: -a *codd.*
[81] terrenum *Obr., sed vd. Str. ap. Schn.[2]*
[82] inst- 5 *(vd. Schn.[2])*: st- *codd.*
[83] iamque *Wint.[9]*

[59] Three things traditional sorcerers can famously do (see
Schneider [2013, 261–63nn381–84]).

his barbarous formula from filthy lips, it is commonly said—even by people who speak from experience—that the gods above grow pale, the gods below give ear, the earth quakes. (3) He stood by the tomb of the wretched young man, a second and surer death: "Now," he said (I imagine), "assist my arcane arts, darkness worthy of me; now come nearer, come to my aid, every accessible divinity and the supernatural power that I invoke against this man. (4) This task demands more of me than when stars are plucked from the firmament, when winter torrents are ordered to stand still, when serpents, overcome by the potent poison of my spell, burst open to give me the wherewithal I need for my spells.[59] (5) The young man is to be placed under custody, the runaway consigned to the underworld and shut away in thicker darkness than before.[60] How much simpler a task it would be to summon him back!"[61] (6) Then, it is said, he lay flat on the urn, and shut in magic words among the bones and ashes. But this he avowed, all the time looking over his shoulder: "The shade is fighting back, so I have no confidence in my chants. Let us seal off the mound on every side, clamping the stones together with a wealth of iron. (7) *Now* all is well: he has expired at last. He cannot be seen, he cannot walk abroad. Tonight,[62] you[63] will know if I am not telling the truth."

(8) For heaven's sake, all parents, especially those who

---

[60] I.e., in some abode of the netherworld even darker than the one where he was before—and, unlike that (cf. 10.8.4), escape-proof (AS).   [61] Cf. 10.7.1 with n. 28.

[62] I.e., on the coming night.

[63] Father.

derunt, ire in istos oculos, in ista ora debebant! 16. Tu sic
filium tuum clusisti, tamquam nocentes ad inferos revo-
cari soleant animae,[84] quae inter languentium familiam et
tristes penatium morbos vagae errantesque magica sani-
2 tate captantur. Laqueone vitam damnatus eliserat, noxium
per sua viscera exegerat ferrum, an ex conscientia venena
praesumpserat, nec recipiebat se nisi carmine inclusus?
3 Quando domum tuam funereus et squalidus, quando te
terruit? Crudelissime omnium pater, de filio tuo malam
4 umbram fecisti! Quas nunc putas uxoris miserrimae esse
cogitationes, qua materna viscera persuasione torqueri?
5 "Nunc filius meus illic, unde venire consueverat, iacet
strictus, alligatus, impatiens. Queritur subito terram gra-
viorem, utique cum sentit venisse noctem, quando um-
6 brae feliciores dimittuntur ad matres. At vero, si qua inter
manes colloquia sunt (et esse credo), non deest qui iuveni
meo dicat: 'Quam vilis tuis fuisti, quam libenter te perdiderunt. Quid? Illa mater, ad quam ire consueveras, has tibi
7 catenas, haec vincula pro merito reddidit?.'" Ita infelicissima omnium mulier, etsi[85] magus iam[86] recedat, hoc peri-
clitatur, ne filius se putet venisse ad invitam.

[84] tamquam—animae *sane suspectum, sed vd. Str. ap. Schn.*[2]
[85] etsi *B. Asc.*[1] *lxxii v.*: et si *vulg.*
[86] iam *Franc. (firm. Str. ap. Schn.*[2]*): etiam codd.*

---

[64] What Father has done is compared to what exorcists do in
order to lay malevolent ghosts: they send them back to where they
belong, in Hades (DAR).
[65] Cf. Ov. *Fast.* 2.533–70.

have lost children, should have flown at these eyes, this face! 16. You imprisoned my son like one of the guilty souls that are usually sent to their due place in the underworld:[64] vagabond souls that haunt a sick household amid the diseases infecting a home, souls that magic remedies seek to entrap.[65] (2) Had he hung himself after being condemned? Had he driven through his own guts the sword he had used to kill? Had he taken poison out of remorse, to avoid punishment, and would only retreat if a spell shut him in?[66] (3) When did he, in funeral garb and disheveled, terrify your house or yourself? Cruelest of all fathers, you have made a malevolent ghost out of your son! (4) What do you think your so pitiable wife is thinking now, what conviction is tormenting her maternal womb? (5) "Now my son is in the place he used to come from, bound, tied up, impatient. He is complaining that the earth, suddenly, is lying heavier upon him—especially when he feels that night has come, when happier shades are set free to visit their mothers. (6) Yet, if spirits of the dead can converse (and I believe they can), there certainly is someone to say to my young son: 'How little your people valued you, how glad they were to lose you! How can it be? Is it the mother you used to visit who has rewarded you for that service with these fetters, these bonds?'" (7) Thus she is the most unfortunate mother in the world, even if the sorcerer steps back[67] now: she is in danger of her son thinking he came to her against her will.

[66] The souls of suicides were not admitted to find rest in the underworld: so they could haunt the living, unless they were put under a spell.

[67] Sc., from the spell, i.e., undoes it.

8   Agit iam hoc loco nobiscum maritus gravius, altius, sapientius, ut homo sine dolore; negat ullos esse manes, contendit omnia perire cum corpore, nec remanere[87] viventes a cinere sensus, nec tam videri imagines hominum 9 quam cogitari et oculos luctibus credere. Quod si ita est, magum ad[88] quid advocavit? Pessimi[89] parentium, qui liberos suos sepeliunt flere contenti, ut[90] obiter ab rogo 10 siccis oculis revertantur! Negat ad manes, negat ad umbras pervenire[91] quod plangas, adfirmat perire lacrimas, adfirmat perire singultus. O sceleratum hominem, quisquis luget et timet ne hoc perdat! 17. Vana ergo sapientes persuasione frustrati, qui constare homines et perfici corporis 2 elementis[92] animaeque dixerunt: corpus caducum, fragile, terrenum, ut sicca humidis, calida frigidis, resolutis adstricta pugnarent, particulatim[93] doloribus adfici ac[94] novissime[95] annis et[96] senectute dissolvi; animam vero flammei vigoris impetum pernicitatemque[97] non ex nostro igne sumentem, sed quo sidera volant et quo sacri torquentur

---

[87] remanere remeare P (remanere *del. manus alia*): remeare *cett., sed vd. Håk.*[2] *92–93*   [88] *om.* V (*prob. Bur.*)

[89] -mi *Sh. B.*[2] *204*: -me *codd.*

[90] *vi ps.-finali q.d.* (H.-Sz. 642, 837)

[91] -tinere *Franc., sed* pervenire *et* perire (*ideoque non pervenire*) *hic opponuntur*   [92] elem- ς: alim- *codd.*

[93] particulatim *scripsi* (*cf. ThlL X.1.514.59–65*): partim aut *codd.*   [94] ac *Wint.*[9]: aut *codd.*   [95] -me *Bur.*: -mis (-mus D) *codd.*   [96] et *Meurs.*[2] *110*: aut *codd.*

[97] perni`c´it- B: perennit- V Φ

---

[68] Father is credited with arguments that sound Epicurean: cf. Introduction to the present declamation.

(8) At this point the husband proceeds to argue his case against us in a graver, loftier, more philosophical tone,[68] like a man who feels no pain. He says there are no spirits of the dead; he claims that everything perishes with the body, and that no living feeling remains over from the ashes. Ghosts of men—he says—are products of the mind rather than the sight, and eyes believe grief.[69] (9) If that is so, what did he call in the sorcerer to do? Worst of parents are those who are content to weep while they are burying their children, only to go home dry-eyed straight from the pyre! (10) He denies that the spirits of the dead, he denies that the shades, are reached by any lament one may make: he claims that tears are lost, he claims that sighs are lost. Criminal is the man who laments—and is afraid it is time wasted.[70] 17. Foolish then is the delusive conviction of philosophers who have said that men are framed and constructed from the elements that go to make up body and soul.[71] (2) The body—they say—is fleeting, fragile, earthly, with the result that dry battles with wet, hot with cold, dense with loose; it is affected by pain in one part after another, and in the end it is broken up by years and old age. (3) The soul, on the other hand, takes on its drive and speed not from *our* fire, but the kind that makes the stars fly round and turns the sacred poles. It comes from the

---

[69] I.e., believe they see what grief suggests.

[70] Like so many others, Father displays tears in public for "social reasons" (cf. Sen. *Tranq.* 15.6)—only to go on to claim that customary beliefs on mourning and afterlife are really nonsense. Yet he summoned a sorcerer!   [71] The speaker's reply exploits pre-Socratic doctrines, later accepted by the Stoics: see Introduction to the present declamation.

axes, inde venire, unde rerum omnium auctorem paren-
temque spiritum ducimus, nec interire nec solvi nec ullo
mortalitatis adfici fato, sed, quotiens humani pectoris carcerem effregerit et exonerata membris mortalibus levi se
igne lustraverit, petere sedes inter[98] astra; donec in alia
fata saeculo purgante[99] transmigret, diu[100] prioris corporis
4   meminisse. Inde evocatos prodire manes, inde corpus et
vultus et quicquid videmus accipere, occurrere suis imagines caras, aliquando et oracula fieri et nocturnis ad-
monere praeceptis, sentire, quas mittamus, inferias et
honorem percipere tumulorum. Rogo, cum filius perit,
nonne satius est hoc credere?

5   "Tuae tamen" inquit "hoc quieti praestiti, ne attonitis
agitata terroribus sollicitas[101] semper ageres suspensasque
6   duceres noctes." Ita, parricida, commune facinus fecisti
et imputas quod filium videre desiimus? Somnum enim
7   a te[102] petebamus et placidum soporem? Crudelis, nunc
inquieta, nunc attonita mater est, nunc perdidimus
noctes![103] 18. Umbramne tu fili rem formidulosam, rem
plenam putasti esse terroris? Quid illa laetius facie, quid

---

98 inter ς: in *codd.*   99 purga- *Sch.* (*cf.* levi—lustraverit):
pugna- *codd.* (*plura ap. Schn.²*)   100 diu *Håk.²* 93–94: dñi
codd.   101 -ta *Cast. 106, sed cf. 10.18.3*
102 a te V: ante B Φ   103 ita—noctes *verba advocati, plu-
ralibus sociativis q.d.* (*Kr.-Str. 132–33.51*) *usi*

---

72 Cf. 10.2.7, 10.7.2.

73 Again, Mother and her advocate: cf. n. 18.

74 I.e., making Son die again: he implicates Mother in this
crime by claiming he committed it to relieve her fears.

same place from which we derive the spirit that originated and generated everything. It does not perish, is not dissolved, is not subject to any mortal contingency, but, every time it breaks out of the prison of the human breast and, freed of mortal limbs, purifies itself in light fire, it seeks its home among the stars. Until eons purge it, and it transmigrates into another destiny, it for a long time remembers its previous body. (4) That is why spirits of the dead come forth when they are summoned up, why they take on body and countenances and all that we see, and encounter their relatives in the form of welcome phantoms—sometimes even becoming oracles, and advising by means of precepts at night; they are aware of the sacrifices we send them, are conscious of the honors paid to their tombs. I ask: when a son dies, is it not preferable to believe this?

(5) "But," he says, "I did this for the sake of your peace and quiet, to prevent you being disturbed by shocking terrors and having always to spend your nights in anxiety and drag them out suspensefully."[72] (6) So, parricide, you have implicated us[73] in your crime,[74] and you give us too the credit[75] for our ceasing to see our son? Was it then sleep and quiet slumbers we asked of you? (7) Cruel man, it is *now* that the mother is agitated, *now* that she is distressed, *now* that we have lost our nights! 18. Did you[76] think the ghost of your son was something to be frightened of, did you think it something fraught with terror? What is more cheerful than that face, what more winning than

75 I.e., the blame (sarcasm).
76 Father.

illo blandius vultu, quid magis adulatur oculis, quid possunt videre libentius lacrimae? Non magis metuenda est umbra filii quam cadaver: necesse est ut mors horrida fiat
2 aliena.[104] Sed alienae[105] forsitan animum imagines territant, et tunc inferi vocantur, cum ignoti sunt; itaque prudenter, si tantum ad suos veniunt. Sceleratus ille, ille impius, quicumque defunctum filium vidit et meminit
3 quod elatus est! "Terrebaris" inquit "et sollicitis noctibus laborabas." Itane es, marite, crudelis? Tu clusisses filium,
4 etiam si ad te veniret? "Nec magus" inquit "inclusit umbram, sed persuasioni tuae succurrit, ideoque putas non venire illum, quia nec ante veniebat, [quia][106] nec factum
5 est aliquid, nisi[107] quo avocareris." Hoc ipso incipit mater sibi gratulari. "Ita non tenetur" inquit "ille, non premitur, nullo carmine, nullo inclusus est ferro? Removete ergo
6 omnia et interrogabo—[108] Ego autem scelerata tam cito credidi; ita non ille ad me veniret solutus et liber, non ad
7 hos oculos, non ad hos properaret amplexus? Quando enim me iuvenis ipse nisi flentem, quando non lividum

---

104 necesse—aliena *secl. Håk.*[2] *94–95, sed vd. Str. ap. Schn.*[2]
105 alienae *Sch.* (*firm. Wag. 445*): aliae *codd.*
106 *del. Sh. B.*[1] *77*   107 nisi *Håk.*[2] *95*: in *codd.*
108 *aposiopesin significavi*

---

77 I.e., does not think he is still in some sense alive (cf. 10.19.5). This is a generality: it does *not* apply to Father, who has not seen his son, but only to Mother (who is therefore not wicked).

78 Father speaks.   79 I.e., your hallucination.

80 I.e., from your fantasies.

81 I.e., the iron and stone: cf. 10.8.6.

that countenance, what pleases the eyes more, what can tears see more willingly? The shade of a *son* is no more to be dreaded than his corpse: you only have to fear a dead man if he is from outside your circle. (2) Maybe, indeed, the specters of outsiders cause fright, and only the unknown are called creatures from hell: so they do well, if they come only to their relatives; but then wicked and impious is anyone who sees *his* dead son—and remembers that he has been buried![77] (3) "You were frightened," he says, "and were troubled by anxious nights." Are you *that* cruel, husband? Would you have shut your son up, even if he had come to *you*? (4) "It[78] was not that the sorcerer imprisoned the shade: rather, he came to your aid in your belief,[79] and if you think your son does not come, that is because he did not come before either, and all that was done was something to distract you."[80] (5) The mother starts to congratulate herself on this very point: "Is he then really *not* under restraint," she says "*not* under pressure? Is he shut up by no spell, no iron? Take everything away,[81] and I will ask *him* . . . [82] (6) But I was wicked to believe so quickly! If he were unconstrained and free, would he not come to me, would he not hasten to these eyes, to these embraces? (7) For when indeed[83] did the young man see me except when I was in tears, when did he not see my

[82] Sc., if he is really free, or perhaps (Badius Ascensius [1528, lxxiii *v.*]) why he stopped coming to visit me. Here Mother breaks off, as she realizes that her deduction—i.e., that Son's shade might be free—was wrong, and corrects herself.

[83] = *ipse*, which here gives emphasis not to *iuvenis* specifically, but to the entire sentence (see on this idiom Shackleton Bailey [1956, 257]; Stramaglia [2017², 225–26]) (AS).

pectus et sanguinantes vidit lacertos, quando non erubuit
matri fecisse maerorem?[109] Arte cluditur miser, arte reti-

8 netur. Quid vis carmina amplius tibi praestent? Effecerunt
quod repromiserant: desinis erubescere iam quod filium
non vides."[110]

19. At tu, cuius in leges di superi manesque torquentur,
qui nocturno terribilis ululatu profundum specus et ima
terrarum moves, modo servientium revocator[111] anima-
rum, nunc idem crudelis et inexorabilis custos, aliquando

2 preces et matris admitte. Paciscere quantilibet, totos lugentis posce census, non ut labores, nec ut horridum carmen exerceas, sed ut ferrum tuum refigas, ut verba tua

3 resolvas, ut nihil feceris; dimitte tantum, et evocasti. Nihil
ipse crudeliter: patri, scio, paruisti; sed et huius etiam lacrimis, planctibus huius indulge. Consule famae tuae:
execrabilem te, mage, facies et invisum, si facilius de filio

4 exoraris ut includas. Nec tu, marite, nec tu timueris ne
ultricis umbrae vanis exagitere terroribus, falsis[112] imagi-

---

109 maer- *Håk.²* 95: terr- *codd.*

110 effecerunt—vides *sic dist. Håk.²* 95 (*praeeunt. Gr.-Mer.*);
verba personata hucusque agn. Wint.⁹

111 saev- ev- *Reitz.²* 23, *sed vd. Str.¹* 282–83

112 falsis *Russ.³* (*cf. Verg. Aen. 1.406–7*): ullis *codd.*

---

84 She had always been in a pathetic state when he came to
visit, and he would not be reluctant to see her like that again;
hence he has no reason not to visit her as before—but he is not
free to do so.

85 Sarcastic. Father should be satisfied with what the incantations have achieved: he no longer needs to feel ashamed of not
having visions of his son, because his wife now does not have them
either (DAR).

breast livid and my arms covered in blood, when did he not blush to have made his mother grieve?[84] The wretched boy is shut in by *art*, and by *art* held back. (8) What more do you want spells to do for you? They have done all they had promised to do: now you can stop blushing because you do not see your son."[85]

19. But you,[86] in obedience to whose laws the gods above and the spirits of the dead are put to the torture, who spread horror at night with your shrieks and move the deep abyss and the lowest regions of the earth, once caller back of souls enslaved to you, now, equally, their cruel and pitiless guard, find room at last for the prayers of the mother too. (2) Make a bargain, name your own price, demand all the mourner's wealth: not that you should toil,[87] not that you should work your fearful spells, but that you should unfasten your iron bars, unsay your words, make it as though you did nothing; release him—and you have[88] called him up. (3) You yourself did nothing cruel: you obeyed the father, I know; but now think of this woman too, indulge her tears, her laments. Take thought for your own reputation: you will make yourself, sorcerer, accursed and loathed if when a son is concerned you are more easily won over to shut him in.[89] (4) But as for you, husband, do not fear you may be harried by the empty terrors of an avenging shade, by vain phantoms: from

---

[86] Sorcerer.

[87] Cf. 10.15.4.

[88] By that same act: Son will appear promptly, as soon as he is released.

[89] Than to let him go. See also n. 28.

nibus: hinc[113] secura dabitur quies; scit ad quam debeat venire dimissus.

5   "Iuvenis piissime, iuvenis indulgentissime, numquam matri tuae umbra nec manes, si modo veneficum pondus et terris[114] omnibus verba graviora mago patiente discusseris, ad me," inquit mater infelix, "ad tuas noctes, ad meas lacrimas, ad illos viventes mihi semper amplexus, miserere, propera. Scio quid mihi nocuerit, scio quid me torserit. Fruar et tacebo."

[113] hinc *scripsi* (*vd. ad Angl. vers.*): huic *codd.*
[114] -ris *Håk.*[2] 96: -roribus *codd.*

here[90] you will be granted undisturbed repose; he[91] knows the *woman* he must come to once he is set free.[92]

(5) "Young man so dutiful, so indulgent, never shade or spirit in your mother's eyes: if now, with the sorcerer's leave, you shake off the burden of magic, and words heavier than any earth, to me," says the unlucky mother, "to your nights, to my tears, to those embraces that will always be living for me, if you pity me, hurry! I know what[93] has caused me such harm, what has brought me such agonies. I shall enjoy your presence—and not speak a word."[94]

[90] Surely with a gesture pointing to the ground, i.e., to the underworld (AS).

[91] Son.

[92] He will not come to trouble Father.

[93] I.e., that she had told her husband.

[94] Cf. 10.6.3.

DECLAMATION 11

INTRODUCTION

At the outbreak of a war, Rich Man is put in charge of the army of his city and goes to the front. In his absence, word spreads that he is in league with the opposing side; Poor Man, who is—as expected[1]—his enemy, accuses him publicly of treason; this results in a popular uprising in which Rich Man's three sons are stoned to death. Rich Man leads the army to victory, thus proving that the allegations were false. On his return to the city, he requests that Poor Man's three sons be killed; Poor Man counters that he himself should be killed instead. The declamation gives us Rich Man's speech.

In this case the Poor Man's responsibility for slander is not in doubt; the dispute concerns what his punishment for that should be.[2] The legal background is provided by the combination of two laws, specified in the theme: a law

[1] Cf. Introduction to *DM* 7. Yet this speech exploits a rather unusual characterization of Rich and Poor Man, the former being an innocent victim of the ruthless scheming of the latter: cf. Santorelli (2014b, 16–26).

[2] This is in effect a "demonstrative" case (cf. Quint. 7.4.3), which elicits a reflection on the wordings of the law (*scriptum*) as opposed to the real intentions of the lawgiver (*voluntas*): see below.

against false accusations states that the slanderer shall be subjected to the same punishment he tried to inflict on his victim;[3] and who betrays the state is to be sentenced to death.[4] Relying on a literal interpretation of these laws, Poor Man maintains that he himself should be executed: he has leveled a charge leading to the death penalty, therefore this is the punishment he should suffer for his slander (4.4). Rich Man objects that the judges should not consider what the false accusation *intended* to achieve (allegedly, Rich Man's death), but what it lead to *in fact* (the death of Rich Man's sons); since the spirit of the law is to inflict on the slanderer the same pain he caused to his victim, the judges should have Poor Man experience the same bereavement he inflicted on Rich Man. Additionally, the circumstances in which the treason charge was brought by Poor Man prove that he never intended to hurt his enemy directly: he had planned his slander to achieve exactly what happened (7.1–3).

The speaker needs to avoid appearing too cruel: he is requesting the execution of three innocent youths, and he will need to prove that their father, not he, is responsible for their deaths (2.1). This leads to a eulogy of the law of retaliation: if a criminal suffers exactly the same pain he

[3] A principle that was actually enforced in Roman practice, from the Severan epoch up to Constantine: cf. *Cod. Theod.* 9.1.19; *Cod. Iust.* 9.46.10; Giomaro (2003, 55–56).

[4] As was stated in the earliest Roman laws (Liv. 1.26.5–6), and then enforced by the Twelve Tables (*XII tab.* 9.5); in the imperial age, treason became part of the *crimen maiestatis*, and as such it was still punished by death. See Querzoli (2013, 187–91).

has inflicted on others, nothing but his actions may be blamed for the punishment that follows (5.1–4). However, the victim of a crime has reasons not to be satisfied with the revenge provided by the law of talion: both the victim and the criminal eventually receive the same damage, but the latter is only atoning for his actions, while the former is suffering without any fault (4.4–7).

Similar caution must be observed toward the city assembly, which cannot be attacked directly by the speaker, despite its responsibilities in the murder of Rich Man's children. In this regard, the speaker shows an ambivalent attitude, sometimes revealing his resentment (1.1, 4.1–3), but eventually acknowledging that his fellow citizens were themselves victims of Poor Man's scheme (7.3–7).

Moving to the specifics of his case, the speaker clarifies why Poor Man's offer to be killed instead of his sons cannot be accepted. On a general level, allowing one convicted to choose his own punishment would deprive the sentence of its effectiveness: even the most terrible pain becomes acceptable if the victim is prepared to bear it; a punishment is effective only if it is imposed against the will of the man convicted (8.2–7). Additionally, in this specific case, Poor Man had planned to inflict bereavement on his enemy and then to die, so that this victory would be a legacy to his sons (1.2, 8.8); what he cannot stand is the prospect of going on living—like Rich Man—after the loss of his own children, and this is what would make retaliation particularly effective against him (9.1–4).

The speech can be analyzed as follows:[5]

5 Santorelli (2014b, 33–38).

DECLAMATION 11

The language of this piece, as well as its treatment of the *crimen calumniae*,[6] suggest a dating to the early third century AD; a relative closeness to *DM* 4–5 and 18–19 may be suggested.[7] A modern reply to the speech is included in Patarol's *Antilogies*.[8]

[6] See n. 3.
[7] See General Introduction, §4.
[8] (1743, 310–25).

11

Dives accusatus proditionis

Pauper et dives inimici. Utrique terni liberi. Bellum inci-
dit civitati. Dives dux creatus profectus est in castra. Rumor ortus est ab eo prodi rem publicam. Processit pauper
in contionem[1] et accusavit divitem proditionis. Absente eo
populus lapidibus liberos eius occidit. Reversus dives est
victor a bello, petît ad supplicium filios pauperis. Pater se
offert. Contradicit dives. Erant enim leges ut proditor
morte puniretur, et calumniator idem pateretur quod reus
si convictus esset.

1. Expectaveram quidem ut de inimici mei supplicio non
quaereretur, nec me decipi posse credideram in ultione,
quam mihi debebat civitas tam liberi doloris; sed quatenus
eo malorum novitate perveni, ut in vindicta primum mei

[1] -tentio- B D (*vd. ad* 11.3.3)

11

The rich man accused of treason

A poor man and a rich man were enemies. Each had three sons. The city became involved in a war. The rich man was made general and went to join the camp. A rumor arose that he was betraying the state. The poor man addressed the public assembly and accused the rich man of treason. In his absence, the people stoned his children to death. The rich man returned victorious from the war, and requested execution for the poor man's sons. Their father offers himself.[1] The rich man speaks against. For there were laws providing that a traitor should be punished with death, and that a false accuser should suffer the same as the accused in the event of his conviction.

(Speech of the rich man)

1. I had expected that no question would be raised as to my enemy's punishment: I had not thought that I could be disappointed of the requital owed me by a city so ready to act on its resentment. But since my strange misfortunes have reached a point where you[2] thought it best, in the

[1] As a substitute.
[2] People in general. The judges are not mentioned till 11.1.2.

consulere leges ac iura velletis, quaeso, ne quis prodesse
pauperi velit quod nec defendi potest nisi[2] genere poenae.
Plus meretur pati homo qui, si ipsi creditis, debet occidi.
2 Hoc est quin immo, iudices, quod super omnes calamitates meas ferre non possum: videtur sibi satis vixisse pauper, postquam occidit liberos meos. Operae pretium putat
coram impatientia mea felicem consummare patrem, et
gaudiorum suorum satietati hoc quoque adicit, ut orbita-
3 tem meam liberis suis relinquat. Fidem vestram, iudices,
ne pereat quod ultioni meae contigit bonus pater! Actum
erat de solaciis meis, si liberos suos pauper mallet occidi.
4   Illud plane, iudices, etiam in hac pauperis impudentia
miror: liberos meos pudore[3] deceptae civitatis occidit, deinde me crudelem vocat, parvulos suos ostendit, allegat,
tamquam non ego potius querar hoc de quoquam patre
fieri, nec intellegit quantum debeat ad impatientiam nostri doloris accedere, si passus sum quod et in ultione miserum est. 2. Facinus est, iudices, quemquam calamitatum
suarum invidiam pati. Sic ultionem meam debetis aspicere, tamquam et liberos suos pauper occiderit.

---

2 nisi (*vel* si non) *Reitz.*[2] 62–63: sine *codd.* (*frustra def. Helm*[1]
380–81)
3 furore *Gron., sed vd. Sant.*

---

3 The case is open-and-shut, and all that can be argued about
is the type of penalty: death of Poor Man or of his sons.
4 Than mere death.   5 Rather than himself: see Introduction to the present declamation.
6 I.e., the danger of losing sons.
7 Cf. 11.11.3–4.
8 As well as mine. The speaker knows that his request that

matter of my vindication, to turn first to the laws and their procedures, I do ask that no one should wish the poor man to profit from the fact that he cannot even be defended except by dispute over the type of punishment he merits.[3] A man who, on his own admission, must be killed, deserves to suffer more.[4] (2) In fact, judges, what, over and above all my calamities, I find quite unbearable is this: the poor man thinks he has lived long enough now that he has killed my sons. He thinks it worth his while to finish his days as a fortunate father while *I* suffer beyond endurance, and adds to his overflowing cup of joy by being able to give my bereavement as an heirloom to his own sons. (3) I appeal to you, judges: let it not go to waste that my vengeance has chanced on a good father! All would be over with my hopes of recompense, if the poor man preferred his sons to be killed.[5]

(4) What absolutely astonishes me, judges, even considering the poor man's shameless behavior, is this: having, to the shame of the city he deceived, killed my sons, he proceeds to call *me* cruel, puts his own little boys on display in court as though it were not rather for *me* to complain of this[6] happening to any father at all, and does not realize how much it must add to my insupportable pain if I have suffered something that it is distressing[7] even to avenge. 2. It is shocking, judges, for anyone to become unpopular because of his own calamities. You should look at my revenge in this light: it is as if the poor man killed his own sons too.[8]

Poor Man's sons be killed will make him seem cruel, but the judges need to consider that Poor Man was responsible for all this, not Rich Man.

2   Nec me fallit, iudices, plerosque credere callidissimum pauperem nec mori velle, et hoc quod nudat iugulum,[4] pectus opponit, artes esse pro vita. Sed ego illum non

3 credo mentiri, ego qui scio quid maluissem. Numquam hoc adversus nos excogitasset nisi impatientissimus pater, et hanc poenae meae suppliciorumque novitatem de sua pietate commentus est. Nihil magis de inimico efficere velis, quam quod ipse ferre non possis.

4   Habet hoc mali, iudices, principum[5] innocentia, quod inimicos esse nobis, nisi postquam nocuerint, nescimus, et tunc omnibus patemus insidiis, quotiens nos odit inferior.

5 Homo, qui omnem adversus superiora rabiem de sui vilitate sumebat, qui genus libertatis putabat odisse maiores, nulli caritati, nullis implicitus adfectibus, quod humilis, quod esset abiectus, in furorem se magnae conluctationis

6 exeruit:[6] primus se meum dixit inimicum. O dii deaeque, cuius ego monstri artes pertuli, in cuius feritatis conluctatione duravi![7] Inimicum habui neque occidere contentum et mori paratum.

    3. Gratias ago civitati quod in illis necessitatibus, in quibus nihil adulationi, nihil praestabatis obsequiis, laudatus sum testimonio periculorum: bellum mihi fatumque publicae sollicitudinis credidistis. Sed neque ego rem melioris ducis facere potui quam quod sine liberis meis profectus sum: non reliquisset illos dux proditurus.

---

[4] nudatum iugulo B, *unde* -to -lo *Reitz.*[2] 24.2

[5] -pum M[pc] H: -pium *cett.*   [6] -ru- *Hdk.*[3] *132 (firm. Sant.)*: -rcu- *codd.*   [7] *exclam. dist. Obr.*

---

[9] I.e., to die, rather than to go on living as a bereaved father. Contrast 11.11.6–7 (with n. 59).

(2) Nor am I unaware, judges, that the general belief is that the poor man is very cunning, that he does not really want to die, that his baring of his throat, his proffering of his breast, are devices to save his life. But *I* don't think he is lying: I know what *I* should have preferred.[9] (3) Only a father incapable of bearing up to distress would ever have contrived this against us: it is out of his love for his sons that he has devised this novel way of punishing and torturing me. You would wish nothing better to do to an enemy than what you would yourself find impossible to tolerate.

(4) Great men who are innocent, judges, have a disadvantage: we know people are our enemies only when they have already harmed us, and we are open to all kinds of plot whenever an inferior hates us. (5) A man who derived from his own worthlessness his unhinged resentment against all that is superior to him, who thought it a kind of freedom to hate those greater than himself, restrained as he was by no ties of affection or sentiment, because he was lowly, because he was mean in status—this man was mad enough to take on a great rivalry: *he* began it, by calling himself my enemy. (6) Gods and goddesses, what a monster this is whose plots I have endured, what barbarity have I long had to struggle against! I had an enemy who was not content to kill—he was ready to die.

3. I am grateful to the city that in such a crisis, at a time when you were in no way influenced by flattery or partiality, the danger spoke in my favor: you entrusted to me the war and the destiny of a people full of anxiety. Well, I could have done nothing more appropriate to a good general than to go to the front without my children: a general who had it in mind to turn traitor would not have left them behind.

2   Non puto, iudices, adhuc quaeri unde illae falsarum
sollicitudinum fabulae repente proruperint, quis primus
trepidae civitatis aures rumore compleverit,[8] cum videatis
quis sic egerit, ut crederetis. Vidit hanc inter metus vestros
occasionem et, quia semper apud sollicitos in deterius
prona persuasio est, abusus est hoc, quod poterat videri
3 timere vobiscum. Igitur homo, qui nullum conscium
meum, nullum mihi crimen obiecit, de mendacii magni-
tudine fidem veritatis aptavit.[9] Civitas deinde, cui accu-
sator proditam se esse persuaserat, fecit quicquid hic de
me facere potuit: liberos meos, quos inimicus tota sua
contione[10] monstraverat, occidit genere quo pereunt in-
4 nocentes. Feretis me, iudices, liberius aliqua dicentem?
Rem pessimi exempli passus eram etiam si prodidissem.
5   Scio vos, iudices, hoc loco mirari innocentiam meam.
Ut primum enim mihi calamitates meas nuntius in castra
pertulit, non arma proieci, non stationes vallumque dese-
rui: totam orbitatem meam in bella converti, tamquam
liberos meos ibi perdidissem. Si umquam, iudices, in me
habuissent profanae cogitationes locum, si patriam odisse
vel pro liberis meis possem, proditorem me feceratis.

    4. Necesse est, iudices, hoc primum reversus excla-
mem: "Ita pauper etiam nunc liberos habet? Adhuc ini-

8 -leverit *Reitz.*[2] 43: -levit *codd.*: -lerit *Bur.* (*sed vd. Sant.*)

9 cap- Φ (*clausula in hac decl. inaudita: Håk.*)

10 -tenti- B AD, *sed cf. 11.6.9 et ad arg.*

---

10 I.e., in the city (while the alleged traitor was on the battle-
field).

11 I had every reason to turn traitor after what happened to
my children, but it was not in my nature to do so.

(2) I don't think, judges, that any doubt remains as to the source of the tales of imaginary worries that suddenly surfaced, as to who was the first to fill the ears of an anxious city with rumors: for you see who it was who made you believe them. He saw the opportunity your fears presented, and, because the worried are always prone to fear the worst, he exploited his ability to appear as frightened as you were. (3) So, without identifying anyone as my accomplice, without preferring any charge against me, he made the size of the lie a proof of its truth. Then the city, which took the accuser's word that it had been betrayed, did all it could to me *here*:[10] it killed my sons, whom my enemy had openly pointed to throughout his speech to the people—they died the death of innocents. (4) Will you bear with me, judges, if I say something rather outspoken? I would have been the victim of an act that set the worst possible precedent even if I *had* been a traitor.

(5) I know, judges, that you are at this point amazed at the innocence shown by my behavior. When the messenger first came to the camp and brought me news of the disaster that had befallen me, I did not throw away my weapons, I did not desert the sentry posts and the rampart: I threw myself, with all my loss upon me, into the task of war, just as though I had lost my sons *there*. If, judges, there had ever been a place in my mind for wicked thoughts, if I were capable of hating my country even on account of my children, you would have made a traitor of me.[11]

4. Judges, on my return I cannot help exclaiming first of all: "Does the poor man then still have children? Is my

mici mei plena domus est?" O miserae cogitationes, o de-
2 cepta solacia! Sic ego revertebar quasi vindicatus. Quas
ego legionum vestrarum indignationes, quem fortissimi
exercitus compescui dolorem, dum omnibus promitto liberos suos,[11] dum minus pro vindicta mea puto quicquid
ipse fecissem! Congerantur iam licet adversus omnium
mortalium nocentissimum cuncta supplicia, ego tamen
maximum ultionis meae solacium perdidi, quod pauperi
vos potius debueratis irasci.

3   Quoniam igitur adhuc cum paupere legibus ac iure
consisto, liberos eius in supplicium patris peto. Quid satius[12] imprecer homini, qui fecit ut quisquam deberet sic
vindicari?

4   "CALUMNIATOR" inquit "IDEM PATIATUR." Permittunt
mihi, iudices, calamitates meae queri de hac lege, tamquam parum nobis in ultione prospexerit. Contra nos
inventus est vindictae modus, quo non debeamus esse
5 contenti. Quisquamne mortalium idem vocat facinus et
poenam, tantumne[13] doloris venire de suppliciis quantum
de calamitatibus putat? Nescit profecto, nescit quantam

11 suos B AD δ β (def. Sant.): tuos V: meos E
12 -tius Wint.[7] 152: -tis codd.   13 -tundem Gron.

12 I.e., that Poor Man had already been brought to account
(with *talio*) for the death of Rich Man's sons. Echoed in last words
of the piece (11.11.7).

13 He promised they would find their sons—unlike his—safe
and sound on their return.

14 I calmed my legions, while I could still anticipate my *own*
baleful revenge; but now you have to a great extent deprived me
of that revenge.

enemy's house still fully stocked?" O pitiable thoughts, o disappointed hopes of requital!—I came back thinking I had been avenged.[12] (2) What indignation among your legions, what resentment in the brave army did I quell, while promising them all their sons,[13] while thinking that whatever I might have done would be too little for my revenge![14] All possible punishments may *now* be heaped upon on the guiltiest of all mortals: but I have lost the greatest consolation in my revenge, for *you* rather[15] should have been angry with the poor man.

(3) So then, since after all this I am at law with the poor man,[16] I request his sons,[17] in order that their father may be punished. What better curse am I to invoke against a man who has brought it about that someone[18] had to be avenged like this?

(4) "THE FALSE ACCUSER IS TO SUFFER THE SAME," he says. My calamities, judges, allow me to complain of this law, for not having made me enough provision in my quest for revenge. A method of requital has been contrived that works against me, a method with which I ought not be satisfied. (5) Does any living man give a crime and its punishment the same name, or think that penalties cause the same pain as calamities? He surely does not

---

15 Sc., than me: Rich Man has had to bring a case, which the people should have dealt with themselves before he returned.

16 I am still having to get my revenge, though earlier I thought I had already got it.

17 For execution.

18 Cf. n. 8. By his actions, Poor Man has forced Rich Man to exact a hateful form of revenge, and this is part and parcel of the crime he should be punished for.

patientiam paret mereri,[14] quantum animo membrisque
6 rigoris induat,[15] quod patiaris agnoscere. Innocentia opus
est, ut miserum faciat dolor. Constet licet utrimque mortium numerus, totidem nobis ultio cadavera adsignet, plus
tamen est de innocentibus, et quicquid patiuntur de-
7 prehensi, licet solacio idem sit, aequitate minus est. Ut
idem sit supplicium nocentis et facinus, una ratione ef-
ficias: ut illud ferre non possit. Frustra aestimatis quam
crudele, quam saevum sit quod petimus, in quantum ex-
cesserit usitata genera poenarum: 5. explicata est, iudices,
explicata legis invidia cum quis, quod patitur, et fecit.

2   Quid, quod hoc solum est poenae genus, in quo non
debeat nocens nisi de se queri, et tanto minus debeat esse
miserabilis, in quantum maiore[16] est quod patitur invidia?
3 Quid aequius excogitari, quid iustius potest? Grassatus
aliquis[17] est ferro: praebeat et ipse cervices; miscuit
noxium virus: refundatur in suum facinus auctorem; oculos rapuit, effodit: reddat de sua caecitate solacium.
4 In nullo mortalium perferre possum sceleris sui impatientiam. Rectissima[18] est iustitia vindictae cum facinus men-

---

14 -rori Φ   15 -ducat (-dic- A) Φ
16 -tum *Håk.,* -ore *Sh. B.*[2] *204:* -to -or *codd.*
17 aliquis πM AE: qui V: aliqui *cett.* (*longe peiore clausula*)
18 rectis- *scripsi* (= *talionis* δίκη ἰθεῖα: *Arist.* Eth. Nic.
5.1132b.27, *Sen.* Apocol. *14.2, etc.; cf. 9.19.8*): brevis- *codd.*:
veris- *Håk.*[2] *96–97:* certis- *Sant.*

---

19 Only the innocent will feel the pain, for they (unlike the
guilty) will see no justification for their suffering.
20 Poor Man's sons, now imprisoned and waiting to know
whether they will be killed on account of their father's actions, as

know, he does not know how much the feeling that punishment is merited helps a man to put up with it, how much mind and body are strengthened if you acknowledge that what you are suffering is your due. (6) You have to be innocent if the pain is to make you wretched.[19] Though the number of deaths is equal on each side, though vengeance assigns the same number of corpses to me, yet it is on innocents that more suffering has fallen: whatever those others,[20] once in the clutch of law, may undergo is less by the standard of equity, even if the same in strict requital. (7) There is only one way to ensure that the penalty for a guilty man is equal to his crime: that he should not be able to bear it. It is vain for you to weigh up the cruelty, the savagery of the penalty I am asking, or how far it exceeds the usual types of punishment: 5. the law is freed, yes, judges, it is freed of odium if someone suffers exactly what he did.

(2) What then of the fact that this is the sole kind of punishment in which a guilty man has only himself to complain of, and where the greater the odium attaching to the punishment he suffers, the less pity he must deserve?[21] What can be devised more fair, more just? (3) Someone has struck with a sword: let him offer his own neck in return; he has mixed a fatal poison: let the crime be poured back upon its author; he has removed eyes, dug them out: let him give satisfaction by being blinded himself. (4) In no mortal can I tolerate inability to endure what he himself inflicted. It is the most straightforwardly just

opposed to Rich Man's sons, who were killed despite their father's innocence.　　　[21] The severity of the punishment shows the seriousness of the crime.

sura poenae est, et, si naturam ultionis aspicias, optime
vindicatur quisque quo modo miser est.

5   Fidem vestram, iudices, ne ideo tantum putetis iustum
quod exigit reus, quia ego recuso: non ferretis me pauperis mortem petentem, si liberos suos optulisset. Ex omnibus tamen, quicumque incognita, inaudita passi sunt, nullos hac lege magis vindicandos puto, quam quorum liberos

6 aliquis occidit. Quid mihi pro hoc redditis, leges? Ubi
respiro, ubi claudo gemitus, unde sumo solacium? Bene,
bene admones, dolor: illos, illos liceat invadere, qui nunc

7 magis amantur, quos orbitas nostra commendat. Sic quoque circumscribimur, nisi totidem sunt, nisi illis par est ac
similis aetas—et ante omnia optimus pater. Deceperas
me, fortuna, deceperas, si mihi tam grande fecisset facinus
homo, qui liberos non haberet.

6. Quid, quod ex omnium scelerum comparatione nihil
est detestabilius hominibus, qui leges ipsas faciunt nocentes? Vestro mehercules nomine calumniantibus debetis irasci, quorum nefas non potest nisi per iudicum

2 facinus imponere. Actum est de rebus humanis, si de
criminibus nostris tantundem mendaciis licet, nec ullus

---

22 Rich Man is not rejecting Poor Man's offer (his own life
rather than his sons') just for the sake of contradicting his opponent, but because this offer is against the spirit of the law; con-
versely, had Poor Man offered what retribution requires (his sons'
life—not his own), a refusal by Rich Man would have been unac-
ceptable.

23 Poor Man's sons are the more loved by their father now that
Rich Man has lost his: a point made in the next clause too.

24 Cf. 11.1.3.

25 Judges.

retribution when the crime dictates the degree of the punishment: if you consider the nature of revenge, a man is best requited in the same way as he became wretched.

(5) I appeal to you, judges, not to think that what the defendant demands is just only because I reject it: you would not tolerate me seeking the poor man's death if he had offered his sons instead.[22] But of all those who have undergone unknown, unheard of sufferings, none, I think, more deserve requital under this law than those whose children someone has killed. (6) What do you give me to make up for this, judges? Where can I recover breath, where can I cease my groans, from what can I take comfort? Distress, you give good, yes, good advice: let me be allowed to attack those, those, who are more loved now,[23] whose value is enhanced by my bereavement. (7) Even so, I am being cheated of my full revenge unless they are the same in number, unless they are much the same age—and have a good father, above all.[24] You would have let me down, fortune, you would have let me down, if it had been a man with no children who did something so monstrous to me!

6. What then of the fact that, if we compare all crimes, nothing is more detestable than men who make the laws themselves guilty? You,[25] I swear, ought to be angry with false accusers on your own account, because their wickedness can do its work of deception only when judges are at fault. (2) All is over with humanity[26] if lies have as much weight[27] in dealing with charges against us, for no inno-

26 Cf. 16.7.8.
27 Sc., as truth.

innocens hucusque felix est ut diligentiae fingentium par
sit. Quemquamne mortalium in re quam finxerit, quam
composuerit, ⟨non⟩[19] invenire aliquid quod potest probationem vocare, et facinus explicare facilitate verborum?

3 Magis oderis mendacium cum simile vero est. Quotiens
manifestum est aliquem perisse sine causa, calumniantibus irasci debeas, ut possis illis ignoscere qui crediderunt.

4   Adicite huic execrationi quod calumniatus est in bello,
quod de proditione, quod de duce, quod haec omnia fecit
inimicus. Non est quod se publico tueatur errore, nec in
excusationem adferat tamquam crediderit et ipse fingentibus. Nemo sic decipitur, ut de inimico suo mentiatur.

5   "Rumor" inquit "fuit te prodidisse." Bene admones.

6 Hunc primum calumniae tuae obicio rumorem. Quis
enim, iudices, nesciat hanc famae esse naturam, ut sit
primo unius hominis audacia? De nulla re locutus est continuo populus, nec quicquam adeo subito statimque no-
tum[20] est ut in illud[21] pariter omnium sermo consentiat.

7 Quam non possis[22] movere civitatem, quem non replere
populum, si quid omnibus obviis[23] narres, in nullo non
coetu loquaris et, de re quam cum maxime fingas, iam

8 dicas esse rumorem? Quanta tibi deinde mentiendi materia de periculorum nostrorum occasione succurrit![24] Nihil

---

19 *suppl. Bur.*   20 no- ς: to- *codd.*
21 -lud *Håk.*: -lum B V: -lo Φ   22 -is *Wint. ap. Sant.*: -it
codd.   23 obviis *Gron. (firm. Håk.²* 97): nobis *codd.*
24 *sic dist. Str. ap. Sant.*

---

28 = needs to be.   29 I.e., a *whole* people.
30 With the rumor. Cf. Verg. *Aen.* 4.189.
31 I.e., the dangers of the city arising from the war.

cent man's luck extends so far as to make him equal to facing down the assiduity of tale-tellers. Is it possible for any mortal, in something he has himself made up and shaped, ⟨not⟩ to find something that he can call a proof, and elaborate on a crime by his readiness of speech? (3) One should hate a lie the more when it resembles the truth. Whenever it is obvious that someone has been wrongfully killed, one ought to be angry with false accusers—in order to be able to forgive those who believed them.

(4) Add to these grounds for loathing him that he brought his false accusation in wartime, concerning treason, concerning the general, and that he did all this as a personal enemy. He cannot defend himself by saying that the mistake was made by the whole community, or offer the excuse that he himself believed those who invented the story: no one is[28] tricked by others into telling lies about an enemy of his.

(5) "It was rumored that you were a traitor," he says. You do well to remind me: this "rumor" is the first point I make in charging you with false accusation. (6) For who, judges, could be unaware that it is in the very nature of report that it is, in origin, the result of *one* man's shamelessness? A *people*[29] has never talked of anything straightaway: nothing is so suddenly and immediately known that everyone's conversation agrees on it simultaneously. (7) What city could you not influence, what people could you not fill,[30] if you tell a story to all you meet, relay it in every circle of friends, and say "there is a rumor going around" concerning something you are that very moment making up? (8) Then again, what a great opportunity for lying was given you by our dangers![31] Nothing is more susceptible

313

est tam capax malignitatium sermonumque quam bellum.

9   Quid interest unde sumpserit rumor ortum? Quod negari non potest, tu contionaris, accusas, tu crimen de fabula facis. In rumore, cuius probationes, cuius argumenta non habes, calumniae genus est primum credere.

7. "Sed" inquit "mori debeo, quia lex, qua te accusavi, hoc proditorem pati iubet." Poteram quidem breviter respondere legem, quae calumniatorem idem pati iubet, eius poenam exigere quod fecisset, non quod facere voluisset; fingamus tamen non hoc pauperem captasse, quod accidit: cui debet imputari exitus, qui de calumniae tuae

2   fluxit errore? Vultis scire, iudices, aliud quaesitum quam quod lex [quae mori]²⁵ iubeat? Accusavit me eo tempore, quo non poteram damnatus occidi.

3   Dic nunc: "Non ego effeci ut occiderentur liberi tui," et aude civitatis illud vocare facinus; non tamen ullis efficies artibus ut non potius miserear rei publicae meae. Non minus et illa facinus est passa quam pater: coacta est

4   liberos imperatoris vincentis occidere. Fallitur, iudices, quisquis ullum facinus in rebus humanis publicum putat. Persuadentium vires sunt quicquid civitas facit, et quodcumque facit populus, secundum quod exasperatur, irascitur. Sic corpora nostra motum nisi de mente non sumunt,

---

²⁵ *secl. Wint. ap. Sant. (q.v.)*: quae <me> mori *Russ.*³

---

³² Cf. 18.6.7.

³³ For the argument see Introduction to the present declamation.

³⁴ Sc., if not to you, Poor Man? He is culpable whether he intended the killing of the sons or not.

to malevolent gossip than war. (9) What difference does it make where the rumor started? What is beyond denial is that it's *you* who spoke in the assembly and preferred a charge, *you* who made a crime out of a story. In rumor, where you have no proof and no evidence,[32] the first type of false accusation is to believe.

7. "But," he says, "I ought to die, because the law under which I accused you orders a traitor to suffer this penalty." I might well have replied briefly, that the law ordering the false accuser to suffer the same penalty enjoins punishment for what he did, not what he meant to do; but let us imagine[33] that the poor man did not intend what actually took place. To whom[34] should be ascribed the result of the mistake arising from your false accusation? (2) Do you want to be convinced, judges, that something else was intended than what the law orders?[35] He accused me at a time when I could not be found guilty and killed.

(3) Say now: "It wasn't I who caused the killing of your sons," and have the effrontery to call it a crime on the part of the *city*; yet you will by no device be able to stop me *pitying* my country instead. It too suffered no less from that evil act than did the father: it was forced to kill the children of a general who was in the process of winning a victory. (4) It is a mistake, judges, to think that in human affairs any crime is collective. Whatever a city does, it does because it has been overborne by those who persuade it to act: in anything it does, the people feels anger only in so far as it is provoked. In the same way, our bodies only move at the behest of the intellect: limbs stay at leisure till

[35] Poor Man had a different aim—getting the sons killed— from that envisaged by the law, viz., the death of the traitor.

5   et otiosa sunt membra, donec illis animus utatur. Nihil est
facilius quam in quemlibet adfectum movere populum;
nulli, cum coimus, sua cogitatio, sua mens, sua[26] ratio
praesto est, nec habet ulla turba prudentiam singulorum,
sive quod minus[27] publicos capimus affectus, sive negle-
gentior est qui se non putat solum debere rationem, et
6   multi fiducia facimus omnium. Quam non possit rem publicam turbare, confundere, si quis repente proclamet:
"Prodidit vos imperator vester, addixit, et nunc ille liberos
habet"? Si mehercules post hanc, inimice, vocem templa
monstrasses, sacrilegum continuo flagrasset incendium; si
convelli simulacra voluisses, fecisset omne de numinibus
7   suis facinus audacia. Vis scire tuum esse, quicquid civitas
fecit? Gloriareris illo, si prodidissem.

    8. Non est, iudices, quod vos a gravitate iustitiae dolor
ultionis abducat; quod mortem suam inimicus offert,[28]
2   non petit illud nisi quisquis ipse non debet occidi. Seposita
igitur paulisper lege mei doloris, hoc tantum ab adfectibus
vestris omnium mortalium nomine peto, ne cui nocenti
poenae praestetur arbitrium. Infinitam, iudices, sceleri-

---

26 sua W: ulla *codd.*   27 minus *codd.* (*def. Håk. et Sant.*):
nimis *Sh. B.*[2] *204*: quisque *Russ.*[3]
28 abducat—offert *dist. Sh. B.*[2] *204*

---

36 I.e., we are unable to control emotion we derive from public sentiment.
37 Had Rich Man been found guilty, Poor Man would have
claimed credit for denouncing him; this hypothetical scenario is
here used as evidence that Poor Man was responsible for the
rumor.

the mind makes use of them. (5) Nothing is easier than to move the people to any emotion; no one, when we are assembled together, is in control of his own thought, his own mind, his own reason, and no group is as wise as the individuals making it up, either because we have no control over collective emotions,[36] or a man takes less care if he does not think that he is solely accountable, and we act as one among many because we count on the complicity of all. (6) What state could not be disconcerted and thrown into confusion by someone suddenly announcing: "Your leader has betrayed you, sold you out: and he still has sons?" If—by heaven!—after this cry, my enemy, you had pointed at temples, a sacrilegious fire would have broken out at once; if you had wanted statues to be overthrown, audacious men would have gone to any lengths in insulting their own deities. (7) Do you wish to be convinced that yours is the responsibility for all the city did? You would be claiming the credit if I *had* been a traitor.[37]

8. The suffering involved in giving me my revenge[38] should not distract you, judges, from the stern requirements of justice. It is true that he is offering his own death; but no one requests that, except one who ought not to be killed himself.[39] (2) So putting to one side for the moment the law concerning my grievance, I only ask this of your feelings, in the name of all mortals: no guilty person should be given the choice of his penalty.[40] You are, judges,

[38] Giving Rich Man the due revenge implies the killing of three youths; however painful (cf. 11.2.1), this is the duty that the judges must fulfill.

[39] Because someone else, viz., his sons, ought to be killed.

[40] Cf. 12.12.2.

bus aperitis audaciam, si poenam licet eligere condem-
nato, nec iam ulla[29] mortalium innocentiam trepidatione
contineas, si patitur deprehensus quisque quod maluit.
3 Levat omnes cruciatus, omnem dolorem praeparata men-
tem composuisse patientia. Fallitur, quisquis humana tormenta sola nominum atrocitate metitur: nulla poena est
nisi invito. Non habemus ullum nisi ab impatientia dolorem, et, ut aliquid crudele, saevum sit, metus faciunt.
4 Supplicium quisquam vocat ad quod prosilitur, quod ex-
poscitur, quod circa se non habet moras? Illo, per fidem,
5 illo trahite damnatos, quo non sequantur. Tunc est poena,
cum periturus trepidat, haeret, cum restringit supremo
vincla conatu. Volo perituri prius videre pallorem, audire
6 gemitus, volo circumspiciat, volo queratur. Fidem vestram, iudices, ne nocentibus supplicii sui contingat elec-
tio! Minus iniquum est ut evadat nocens poenam, quam ut
contemnat.
7 Mortem vero damnatis quisquis praestat, indulget [nec
sunt ulla beneficia poenarum].[30] Fallitur, quisquis illam
velut omnium suppliciorum summam putat: occidi non est
poena sed exitus. Neque enim habet impatientiam aut
8 dolorem, quod possis aspicere quasi fatum. Quid, si liberos relinquas, immo si serves? Quam felix exitus est

29 -a *Hål.*[3] *132:* -am *codd.*
30 *secl. Wint.*[3] (*et vd. Sant.*)

---

41 Cf. n. 12.

42 Punishment is far worse for one unwilling to undergo it.

43 I.e., to break loose.

44 Anxiously wondering what else is awaiting him; or, perhaps
(AS), desperately looking for someone to help him.

318

giving unlimited scope to audacious crime if you allow a condemned man to choose his punishment: enforcing innocence on mortals by any feeling of fear would become impossible, if every one in the clutch of the law[41] suffers what he chose to suffer. (3) It is a relief to all agonies, to all pain, if the mind is prepared in advance for what one is to suffer. It is wrong to gauge a man's torments only by the frightful appellations they go by: nothing counts as punishment unless the recipient is unwilling.[42] We have no pain except from inability to endure it, and it is fear that makes a thing cruel and savage. (4) Does anyone give the name of punishment to something which is jumped at, which is demanded, which involves no delay? Drag the condemned there, and only there, where they would be unwilling to follow. (5) Punishment is truly punishment when the man condemned to die is frightened, is at a loss, when he strains against his chains in a last effort.[43] I want first to see the pallor of the man about to die, to hear his groans; I want him to look all round him,[44] to lament. (6) I beg you, judges: do not allow the guilty the choice of their punishment! It is less wrong for a guilty man to escape punishment than to make mock of it.

(7) On the other hand, to grant death to condemned men is to be indulgent [—so there are no benefits in punishments]. It is mistaken to think of this as the greatest of all punishments: to be killed is not a penalty, but an escape route. What could be regarded as a stroke of fate does not involve intolerable pain. (8) What if you leave children behind you, or rather if you save them?[45] How happy an

---

[45] As Poor Man would be doing.

plenusque laetitiae! Lucri facit mortis atrocitatem, quisquis laudatus occiditur.

9. "Me" inquit "occidite." Non habet liberos, inimice,
2 non habet, quisquis hoc te velle miratur. Saeve, crudelis,
ego tibi permittam mori? Et[31] quid iam mihi melius op-
3 tem? Vides quantum feceris nefas: idem pro liberis meis
offerre non potui. Tu vero parvulos tuos tene, ut[32] in isto
4 potius moriantur amplexu. Tu nunc quoque non evades,
non effugies: quacumque te duxerit orbitas, sequar; ef-
fundam, si quod paraveris venenum, subtraham omne
ferrum, incidam quoscumque strinxeris nexus, ab omni
revocabo praecipitio. Etiam occisis liberis tuis non idem
patieris, inimice, nisi vixeris.

5 Nec vereor, iudices, ne putetis utriusque nostrum orbitatem simili esse ratione tractandam. Admoventur en[33]
ecce contra lacrimas meas liberi, quos nemo nosset; patris
innocentis occisi sunt parvuli, quos nunc circa templa fer-
6 retis, circa quos se celebraret vestra laetitia. Facinus est,
iudices, minorem esse transactarum mortium miserationem. Non invenio quemadmodum liberis prodesse debeat
odium patris: perierunt etiam illi, quorum nec pater debebat occidi.

---

31 et *Håk.* (*cf. H.-Sz. 460, 480*): ut *codd.* (*del. Wint.*[3]): at ς
32 *om.* V, *fort. recte*   33 *om.* Φ

---

46 In this case, for saving his children.   47 Unlike my
own children.   48 I.e., now that you are picturing your children dying in your arms, and the unbearable pain that will push
you to seek suicide.   49 = as I have suffered.

50 Had it not been for this trial. Poor Man, unlike Rich Man,
is an unknown.

51 The people.   52 Cf. 4.5.3.

outcome, how full of joy! Anyone who is killed after being praised[46] is turning the hideousness of death to profit.

9. "Kill *me*," he says. Anyone, o my enemy, who is surprised that you make this choice has no children himself, none. (2) Savage, cruel man, am I to allow you to die? And what could I ask better for myself now? (3) You see how wickedly you have acted: *I* was not able to make the same offer for my sons. But as for you, hold your little sons, so that *they*[47] may die in their father's embrace. (4) You will not get away, you will not escape—not even now:[48] wherever the agony of your loss takes you, I shall follow; I shall pour away any poison you get ready, I shall remove every sword, I shall cut every noose you tie for yourself, I shall call you back from every cliff top. Even when your sons have been killed you will not suffer the same as me,[49] o my enemy—unless you live.

(5) Nor am I afraid, judges, that you should think our losses are to be treated in the same way. Look: to counter my own tears, children whom no one would know[50] are brought into court here; whereas an innocent father's little sons have been killed, whom you[51] should now be carrying round the temples,[52] who should be at the center of your happy celebrations. (6) It is outrageous, judges, that the pity felt for past deaths is less. I cannot see why children should be helped by the hatred felt for their father:[53] other sons[54] have died before them, whose father did not deserve to be killed either.

---

[53] I.e., by allowing the unpopular Poor Man to get his request granted.   [54] = my sons. That is, Poor Man's children should not be spared because their *father* is hated—whereas *they* are innocent. *I* was not worthy of death (as Poor Man is), yet *my* sons were killed.

7 Me miserum, quod sic quoque multa habiturus es quibus ego, qui vindicabor, invideam: osculaberis ante perituros, alloqueris, accipies suprema mandata et moriturum
te continuo promittes; exonerabis gemitus tuos cum meorum sepulcra numerabis, siccabit oculos quod meam nunc
quoque respicies vacuam domum. 10. Me miserum! Pauperis tantum solacium futurum est, quod pares sumus.
2 Quid, quod in ipsa comparatione mortis non idem patien-
tur liberi tui? Occidentur uno fortassis ictu, et erit ultio
3 manibus contenta carnificis. Parvulos meos occidit quicquid fuit tota civitate telorum, omnis sexus, omnis aetas,
omnis infirmitas. Nihil est crudelius morte hominum,
quos populus occidit, et solus hic exitus est a quo non
4 est nec cadaveribus salva reverentia. Hoc me nunc com-
plorare tantum putatis, quod non sum liberis meis ante
satiatus? Miser ego nec ad cadavera accessi, non in sepulcra maiorum meis manibus intuli, nec licuit super ipsa
corpora proclamare: "Non feci!"
5 Qualem ego illum, patria, perdidi diem, cum duces ab
explicito bello revertuntur! Non me laetae cinxere le-
giones, non effusi obviam cives triumphali circa currus
meos exultavere laetitia; sequebar captivos meos tristior
victor, maestus undique claudebat exercitus, occurren-
tium lacrimae propinquorum et erubescentis circa me
6 populi timida solacia. O successuum quoque nostrorum
misera condicio! Ergo ego victoriam meam non narrabo

---

55 Cf. 11.4.4–7.

56 You will no doubt suffer in your bereavement; but it will
console you that I am suffering the same because of you.

57 I.e., *I* am not responsible for this (while Poor Man will be
responsible for the death of his sons: cf. 11.2.1).

(7) Ah me! Even as it is, you will have much for me to envy, though it is I who will have my revenge: you will kiss them before they die, you will receive their last requests and promise you will die very soon yourself; your groans will be less burdensome[55] when you count up my sons' tombs, and seeing my home empty as ever will dry your tears. 10. Ah me! Only the poor man will be consoled that we are on a level.[56] (2) What then of the fact that, even if one compares the manner of their deaths, your children will not suffer the same? They will be killed, perhaps, at a single blow, and revenge will be content with the hands of an executioner. (3) *My* children were killed by everything the entire city could hurl at them, by both men and women, people of every age, every disability. Nothing is crueler than the death of those whom the people kills, and this is the only end where even dead bodies win no respect. (4) Do you imagine I am complaining only that previously I had not had my fill of my children? I, to my sorrow, had no access even to their corpses, I did not personally bear them to our ancestral graves, and I was not allowed to proclaim over their bodies: "It wasn't *my* fault!"[57]

(5) My country, what a day it was that I lost, the day when generals return from a successful war! I was not surrounded by happy legions, the citizens did not pour out to meet me, exulting around my chariot with the joy of a triumph; I followed behind my own prisoners, a victor more melancholy than they. Sorrowful the army that hemmed me in on every side, tearful the relations who came to meet me, timid the consolation offered by a city that blushed for what it had done to me. (6) To what an unhappy plight are even my successes reduced! Am I not

323

sine fletu, nemo amicorum propinquorumque coram me de bello meo loquetur? 11. Nihil est crudelius calamitate,
2 quam gaudia reducunt. Quotiens redierit ille laetus vobis in supplicia mea dies, lugubres mihi ferte vestes, renovate, servuli, planctus, parate solacia, propinqui. Nulli liberi impatientius desiderantur, quam qui propter patrem videntur occisi.
3 Sed verum, iudices, fatendum est: timeo mehercules ne par solaciis meis non sim, ne me iste, quo pro liberis
4 irascor, affectus in media ultione destituat. Sed adiuvate, miseremini, propinqui, adiuvate, amici, et, si forte defecero, tu ultionem meam, popule, consumma. Timeo mehercules ne, cum carnifex propius accesserit, subito
5 proclamem: "Iam malo patrem!" Sed si quis est pudor, oculi, differte lacrimas, abite, gemitus; horridum, trucem
6 debeo me parare[34] et[35] miserum. Deprehendam, omnium mortalium callidissime, hunc quem simulas, quem nunc imitaris adfectum. Tunc sciemus, quo animo rogaveris ut
7 potius ipse morereris. Sed si bene novi capax omnium malorum scelerumque pectus, inimice, vives et libenter et fortiter et quasi vindicatus.[36]

---

[34] me parare *Bur.*: praeparare *codd.*: praebere *Håk.*[2] 97–98 (-re ‹me› *Håk.*): praestare *Watt*[2] 28 (*cf. ThlL X.2.922.77ss.*)

[35] et (= etiam *Håk.*) B Φ: ut V: nec *Wint.*[9]

[36] -turus *Sch., sed vd. Sant.*

then to tell the story of my own victory without weeping? Are none of my friends and relatives to talk in front of me about *my* war? 11. Nothing is more cruel than a calamity which is brought back to the mind by joys. (2) Whenever that happy day comes round again to torture me, look out my mourning clothes; renew your wails, slaves; get ready to console me, relatives. No children are more intolerably missed than those evidently killed because of their father.

(3) Still, judges, I must confess the truth: I am afraid that I may not be equal to the requital I am seeking, that the anger I feel on my sons' behalf may fail me in mid-revenge. (4) But, help and pity me, relations, help me, friends, and if I am by any chance found wanting, do you, the people, crown my revenge. I am—ye gods!—afraid that as the executioner comes nearer, I may suddenly shout: "Now I prefer the father!" (5) Yet if you have any shame, eyes, delay your tears; groans be gone: I must present myself as horrid and brutal—wretched as I may be.[58] (6) Most cunning of all mortals, I shall see through this emotion that you feign, that you now counterfeit. Then we shall know what lay behind your request to die instead.[59] (7) But if I know your heart, O enemy, which finds room for all evildoing and all crime, you will live on, blithely and in good heart—and as if you had been avenged.

[58] Because of his sympathy for the children of his enemy.

[59] Of your sons. The speaker implies here that Poor Man has been just pretending so far to be a good father: he does *not* actually want to die (in contrast with 11.2.2). The whole speech, thus, would be a *controversia figurata* (cf. Introduction to *DM* 4).